IMAGES
of America

ROCKINGHAM COUNTY

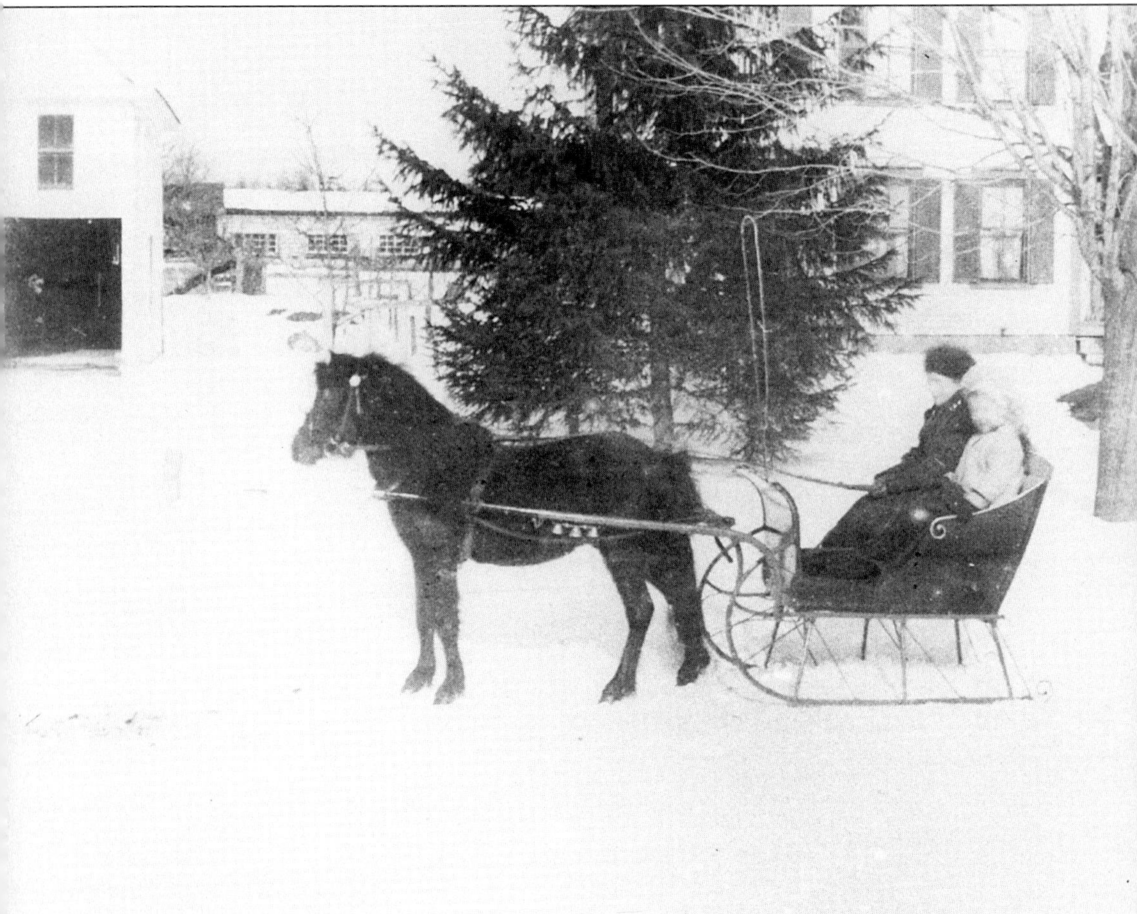

RAYMOND Youngsters out for a sleigh ride on Main Street opposite the Raymond post office, c. 1903.

Cover picture: Hampton Beach Casino during a 1930 New Hampshire State Grange Convention. See pages 34-35 for more of this photograph.

IMAGES *of America*
ROCKINGHAM COUNTY

Compiled by
Matthew E. Thomas

ARCADIA
PUBLISHING

ISBN 978-0-7385-8831-8

Published by Arcadia Publishing
Charleston, South Carolina

Printed in the United States of America

For all general information contact Arcadia Publishing at:
Telephone 843-853-2070
Fax 843-853-0044
E-mail sales@arcadiapublishing.com
For customer service and orders:
Toll-Free 1-888-313-2665

Visit us on the Internet at www.arcadiapublishing.com

Dedicated to my beloved wife, Sharon; and daughter, Rebecca.

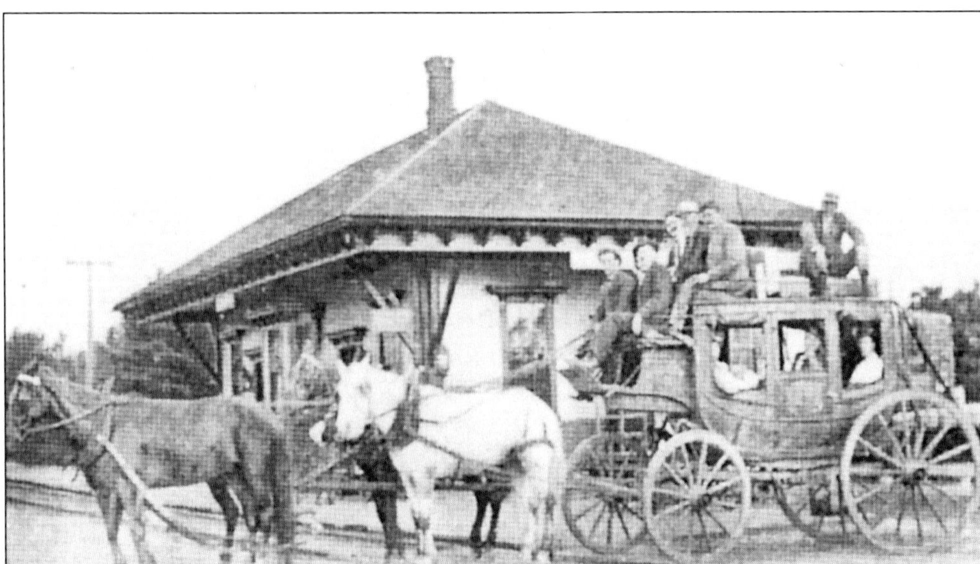

CANDIA In 1852 the Portsmouth and Concord railroad extended its tracks through Candia and two depots were built at that time. Candia depot above was built in 1884 and stagecoaches ran from here to Deerfield before the turn of the century.

Contents

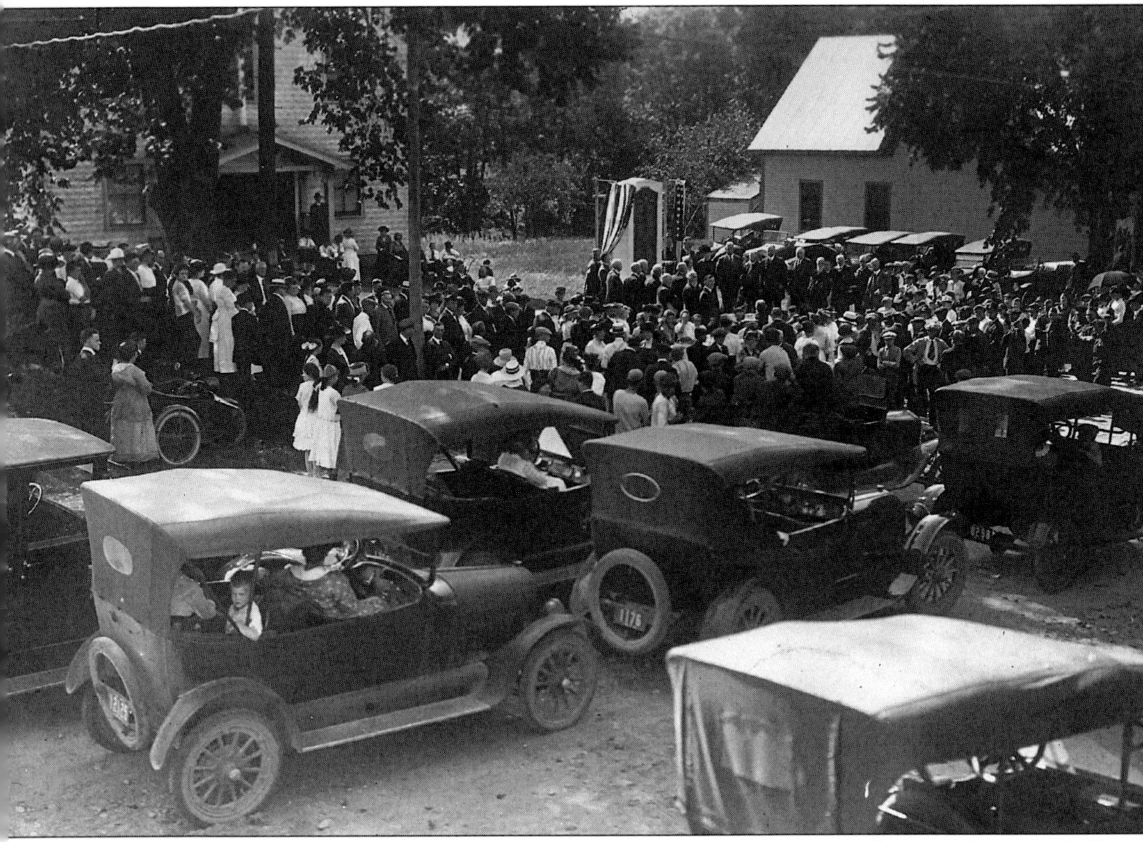

FREMONT Dedicating the War monument on 25 September 1920 in front of the town hall on Main Street.

Introduction

Rockingham County, New Hampshire is a region which brims with history and scenic beauty. It is among the oldest settled regions in the United States. During the spring of 1623, David Thomson and a group of British colonists established the first European settlement in New Hampshire at Pannaway, along the coast of present-day Rye.

Within its 699 square miles, the county encompasses 36 towns and one city. It is situated in the southeastern portion of the state, between Massachusetts and Maine. It is the only New Hampshire county to border on the Atlantic Ocean.

Incorporated on 19 March 1771, Rockingham County was named by royal governor John Wentworth in honor of Charles Watson Wentworth, Marquess of Rockingham. The marquess served as British prime minister in the mid-1760s and again in 1782. Unlike so many of his contemporaries, Rockingham was highly regarded by the colonists of New England. Under his ministry the Parliament had repealed the stamp tax.

Rockingham County was one of five original counties in New Hampshire. In addition to the current municipalities it formerly embraced Allenstown, Bow, Canterbury, Chichester, Concord, Epsom, Loudon, Northfield, Pembroke, and Pittsfield. These towns were severed from Rockingham and annexed to Merrimack County on 1 July 1823. One year later on December 10, 1824 the town of Pelham was annexed to Hillsborough County.

The ancient town of Gosport, incorporated in 1715, was a thriving fishing community until the outbreak of the American Revolution. Its charter was revoked in 1876 due to its steady decline in population. It was annexed to Rye. Gosport was comprised of four out of the nine islands of the Isles of Shoals, the other five being a part of Maine. The Isles of Shoals lie nine miles off the American coast.

Rockingham County's highest elevation is Mt. Pawtuckaway in Nottingham, rising 1,011 feet above sea level. Its principal rivers are the Piscataqua, Lamprey, and Exeter. Pawtuckaway and Massabesic are the largest lakes. Deerfield is the largest town in area, consisting of 51.9 miles. New Castle with just two square miles is the smallest and the only island town in New Hampshire. Based on the 1992 census Derry, with 30,193 residents, is the most populous town in the county. Newington, with 668 residents (and the largest number of retail malls) is the least populated. The entire county has a population of 243,793 inhabitants, roughly one-fourth of New Hampshire's population.

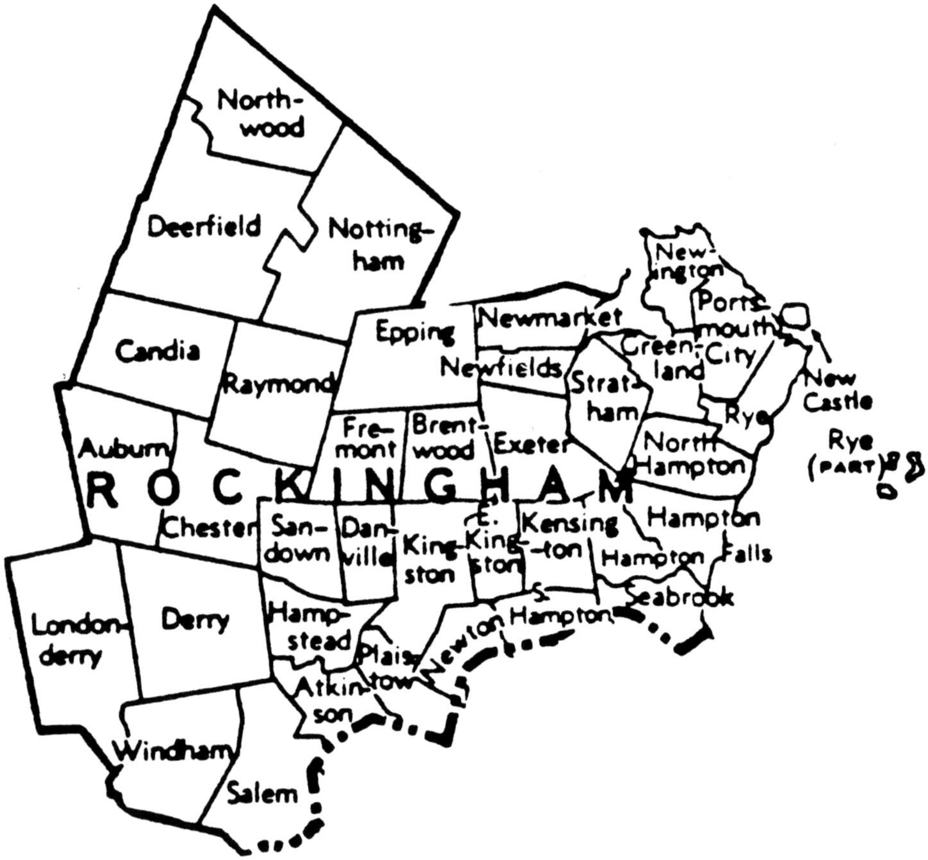
North-
wood
Deerfield
Notting-
ham
Candia
Raymond
Epping
Newmarket
Newfields
New-
ington
Ports-
mouth
City
Green-
land
Strat-
ham
Rye
New
Castle
Rye
(PART)
Auburn
Fre-
mont
Brent-
wood
Exeter
North
Hampton
ROCKINGHAM
Chester
San-
down
Dan-
ville
King-
ston
E.
King-
ston
Kensing
-ton
Hampton
Hampton Falls
Seabrook
S.
Hampton
London-
derry
Derry
Hamp-
stead
Plais-
tow
Newton
Atkin-
son
Windham
Salem

One

The Seacoast

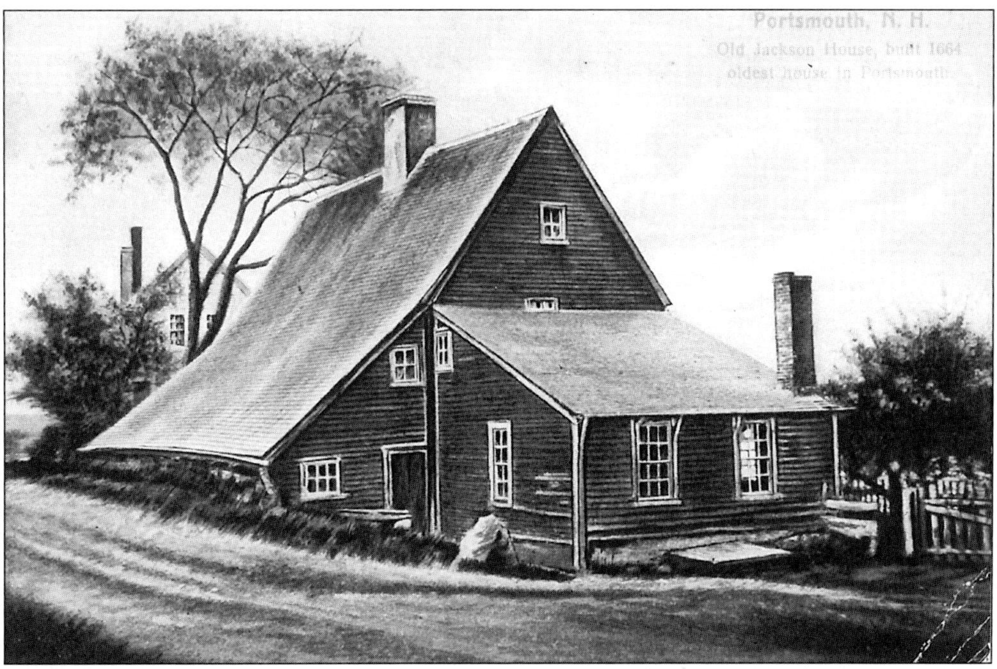

PORTSMOUTH The 1667 Richard Jackson house on Northwest Street, about 1907. This is the oldest house still standing in New Hampshire.

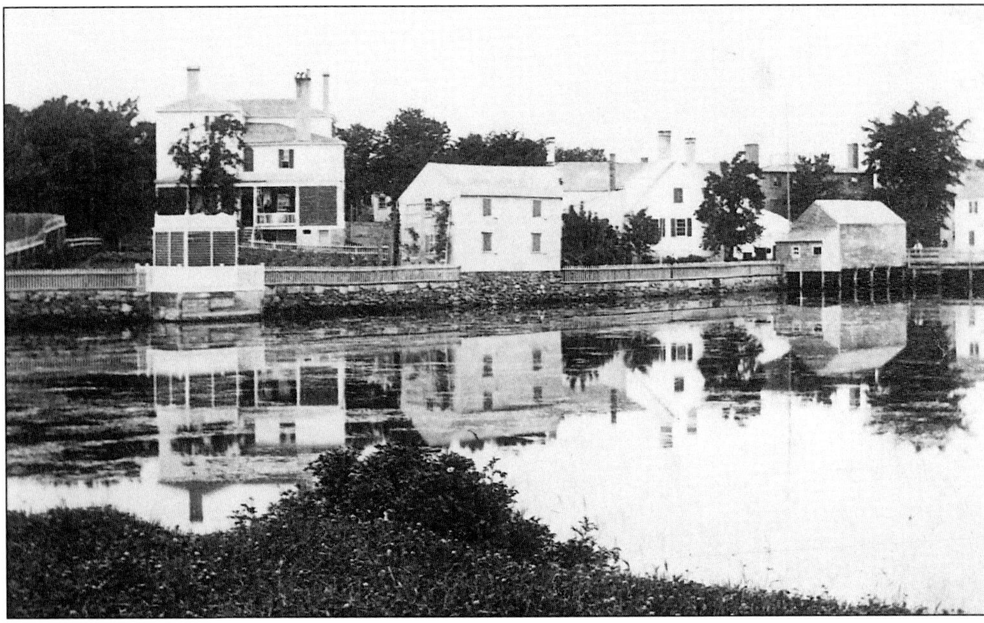

PORTSMOUTH South end Mill Pond about 1865-80. By this time Portsmouth had begun to feel the effects of reduced shipping trade.

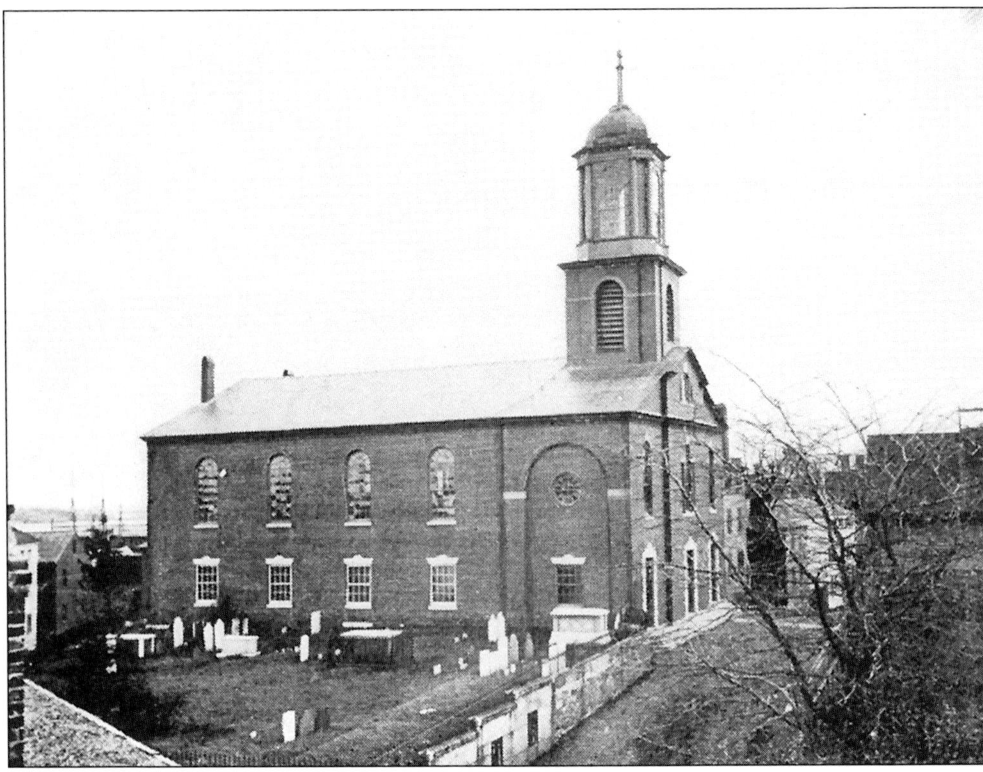

PORTSMOUTH St. John's Episcopal Church about 1905. The church was built in 1807 on the site of Queen's Chapel which burned in 1806. This church contains a rare 1717 "Vinegar Bible".

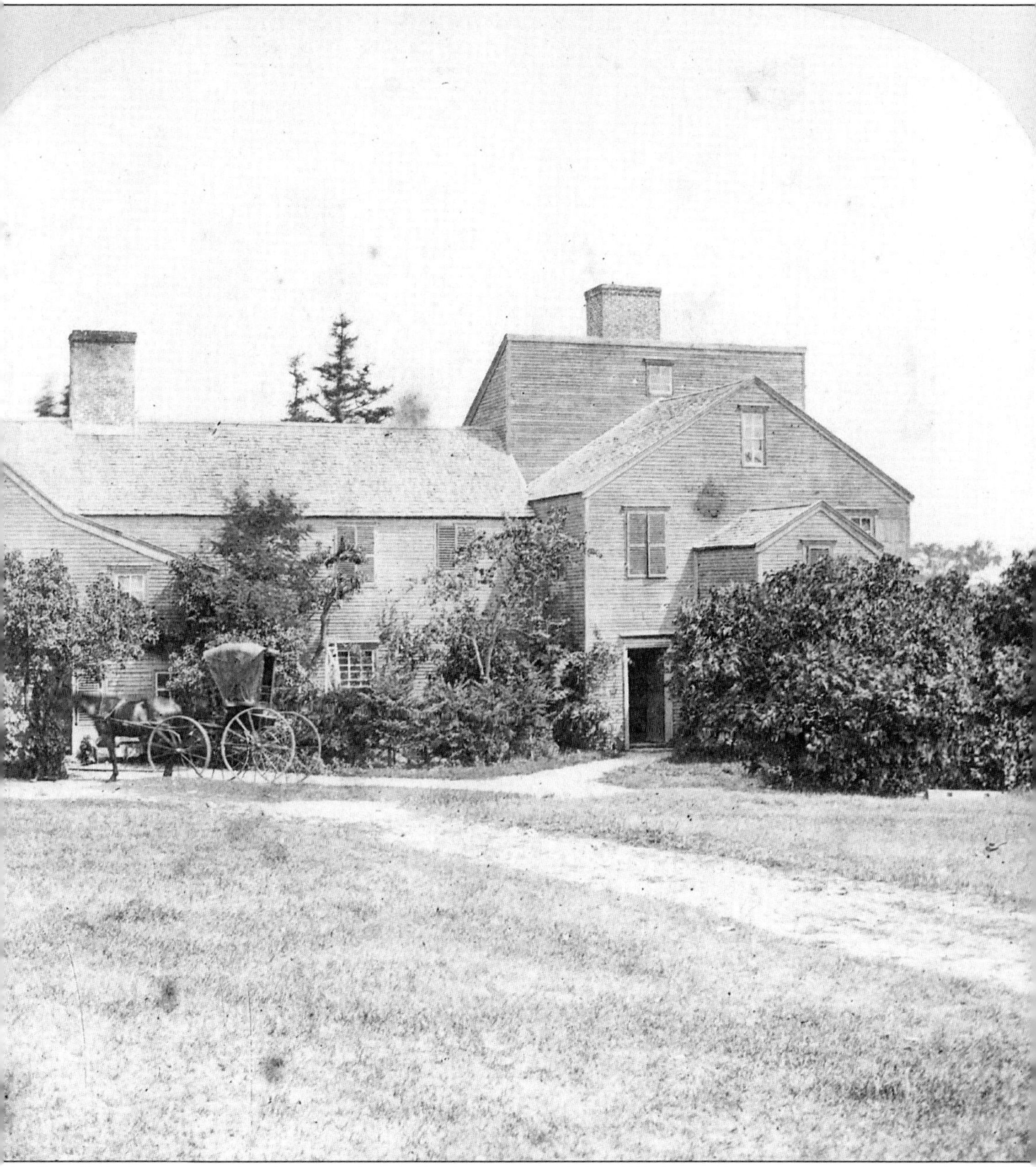

PORTSMOUTH The Wentworth-Coolidge mansion about 1885. Home to Royal Governor Benning Wentworth, the mansion was built about 1750.

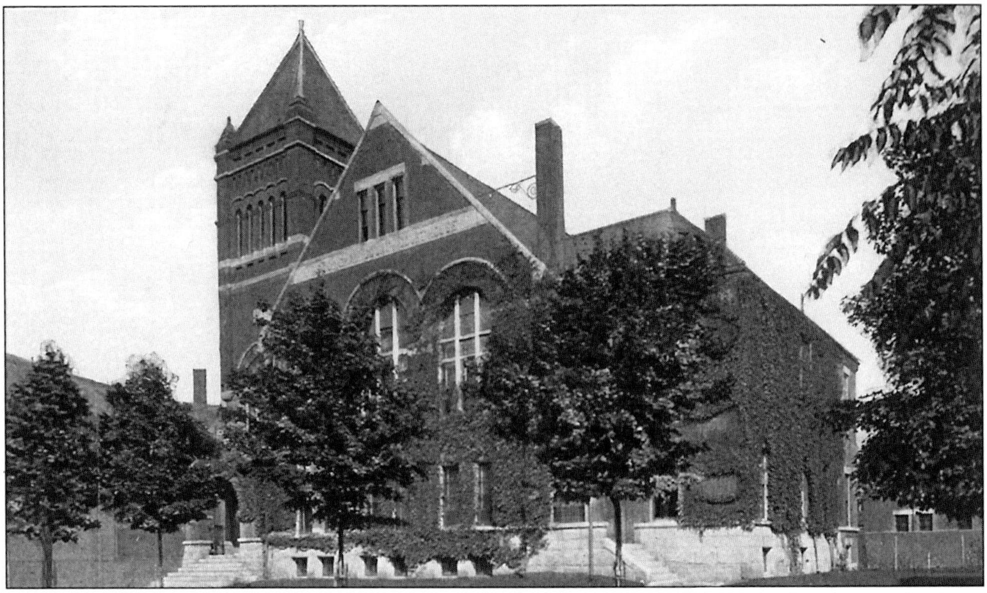

PORTSMOUTH Rockingham County courthouse about 1913. The courthouse was built in 1891 on State Street.

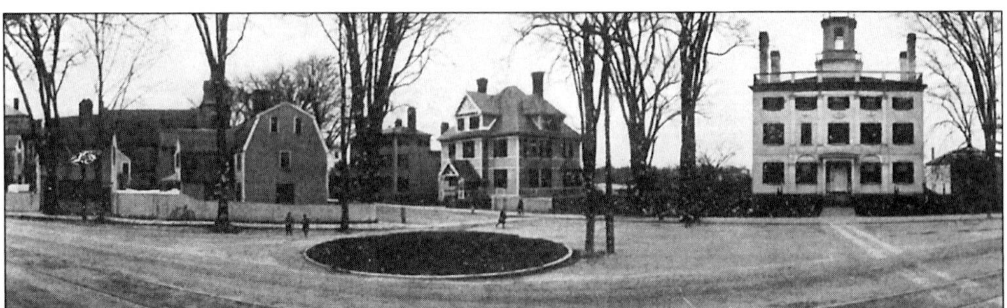

PORTSMOUTH Haymarket Square about 1905. This postcard, sent to Epping, New Hampshire in 1905 reads, "C, B, and I are going to Hampton Beach today for an Electric ride." As today, the seacoast of NH was a popular vacation spot at the turn of the century.

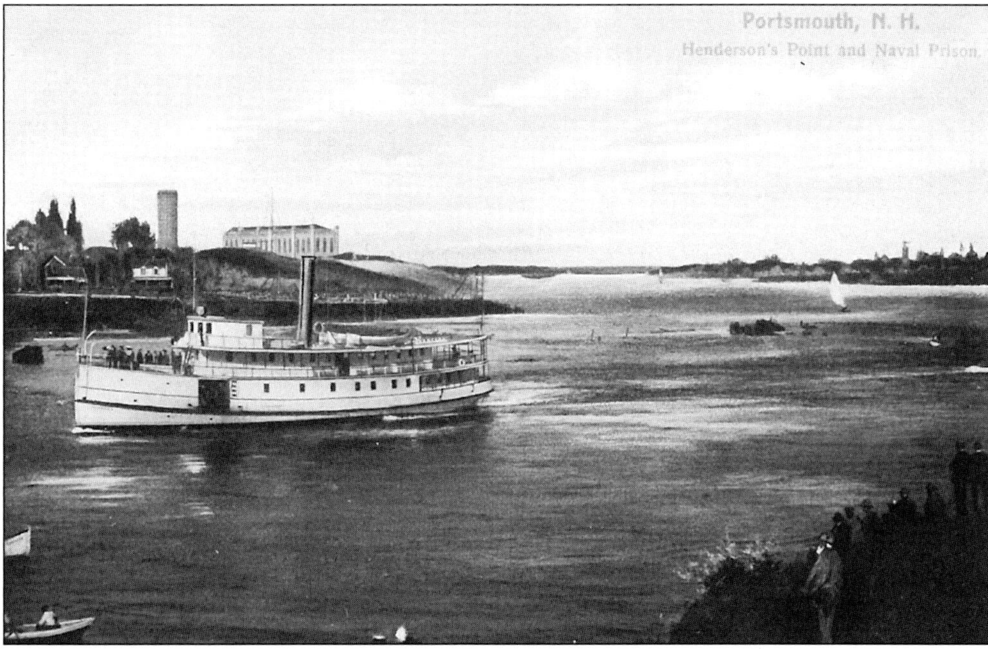

PORTSMOUTH Henderson's Point and federal naval prison shortly after the world's largest explosion on 22 July 1905. The blast was set to remove a mass of rock on the point, allowing for easier movement of boat traffic.

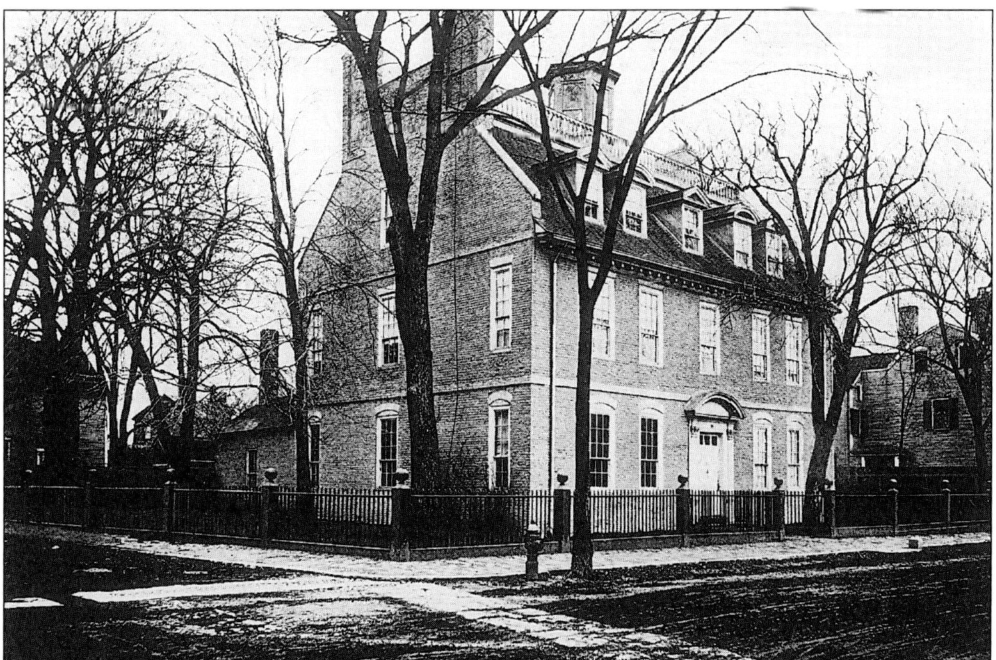

PORTSMOUTH The MacPheadris-Warner house on Daniel Street about 1907. This is a prime example of eighteenth century brick architecture.

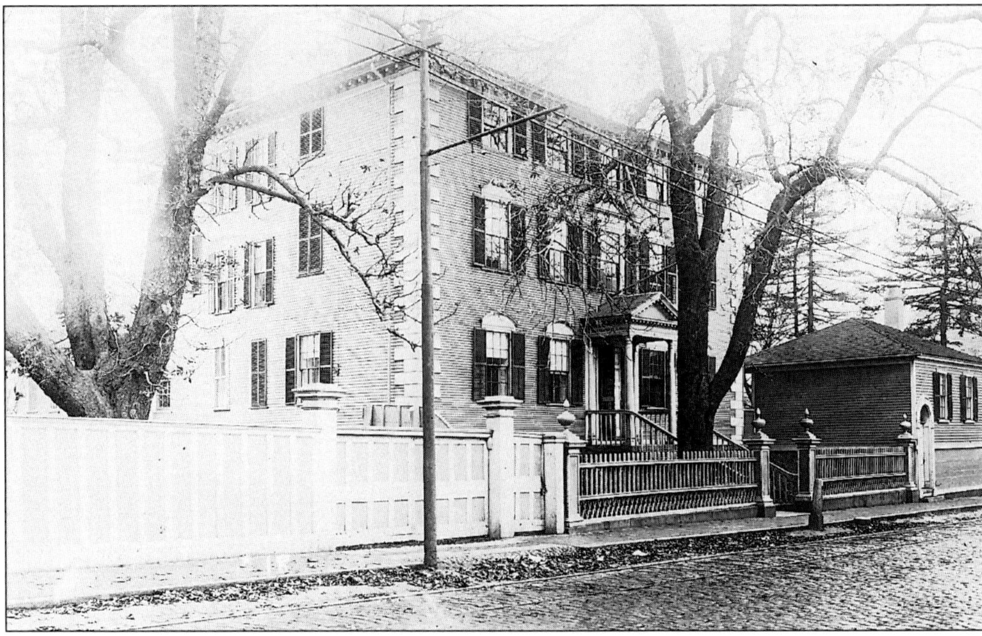

PORTSMOUTH The Moffatt-Ladd house on Market Street, built in 1763. Built by John Moffatt for his son Samuel, the house was also occupied by Gen. William Whipple a signer of the Declaration of Independence. It is one of the finest examples of Georgian architecture in New Hampshire.

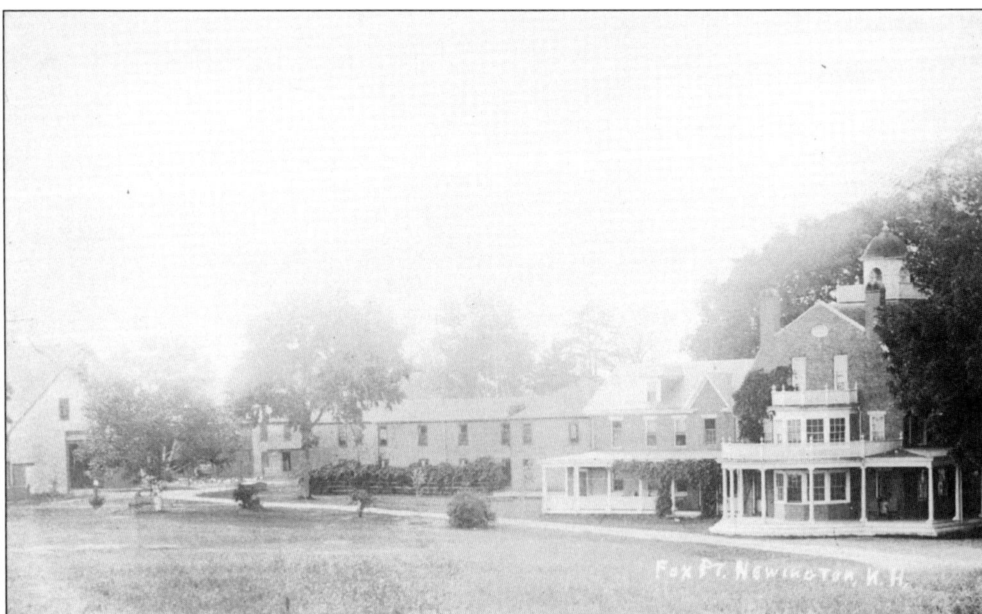

NEWINGTON Fox Point about 1910. This is one of many historic landmarks in this small southeastern New Hampshire community. (Courtesy Barbara Myers & Newington Historical Society)

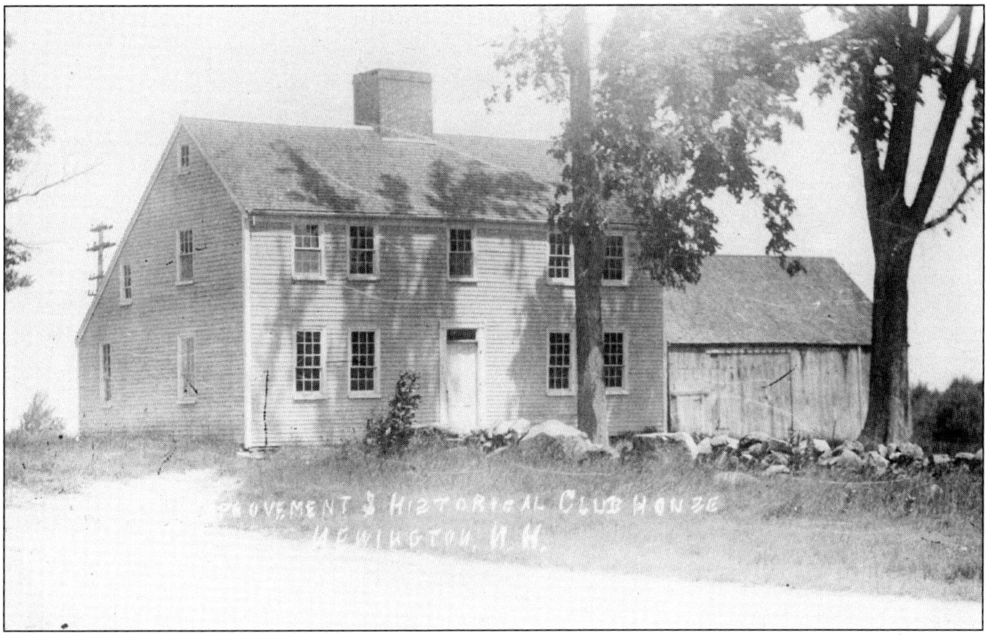

NEWINGTON Congregational parsonage built about 1725 on Nimble Hill Road. Photographed here about 1910, this building has served as parsonage, tavern, poor farm, school, and tea room. (Courtesy Barbara Myers and Newington Historical Society)

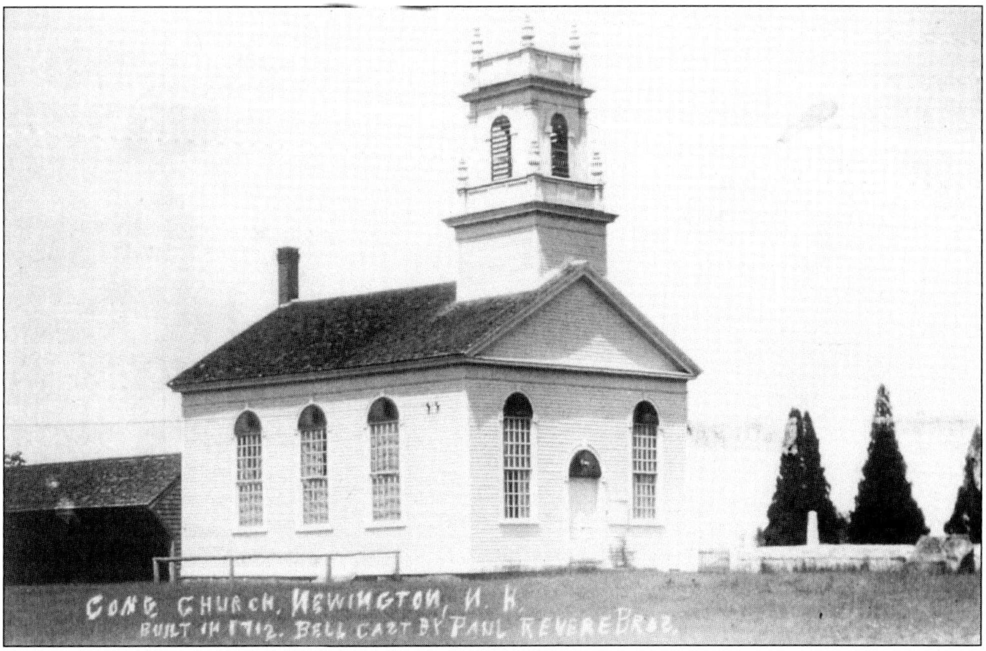

NEWINGTON It is the oldest Congregational meeting house, built in 1712 on Nimble Hill Road. It is one of the oldest Congregational meeting houses in continuous use in the United States. Its bell was cast by Paul Revere and sons in 1804. (Courtesy Barbara Myers and Newington Historical Society)

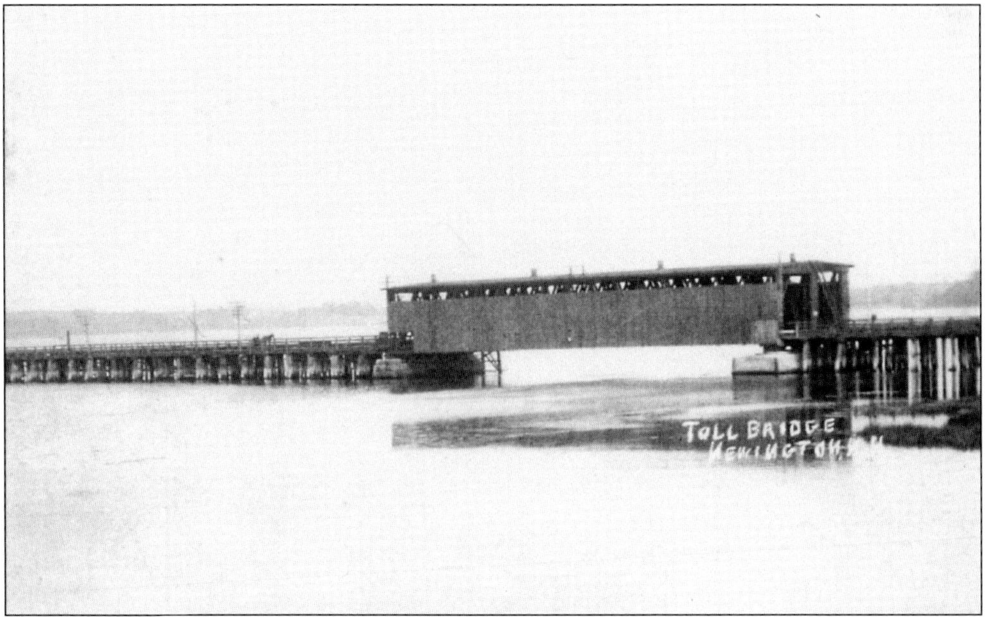

NEWINGTON The Portsmouth and Dover, Boston and Maine railroad bridge was in use between 1873 and 1933 as both a railroad and toll highway bridge. (Courtesy Barbara Myers and Newington Historical Society)

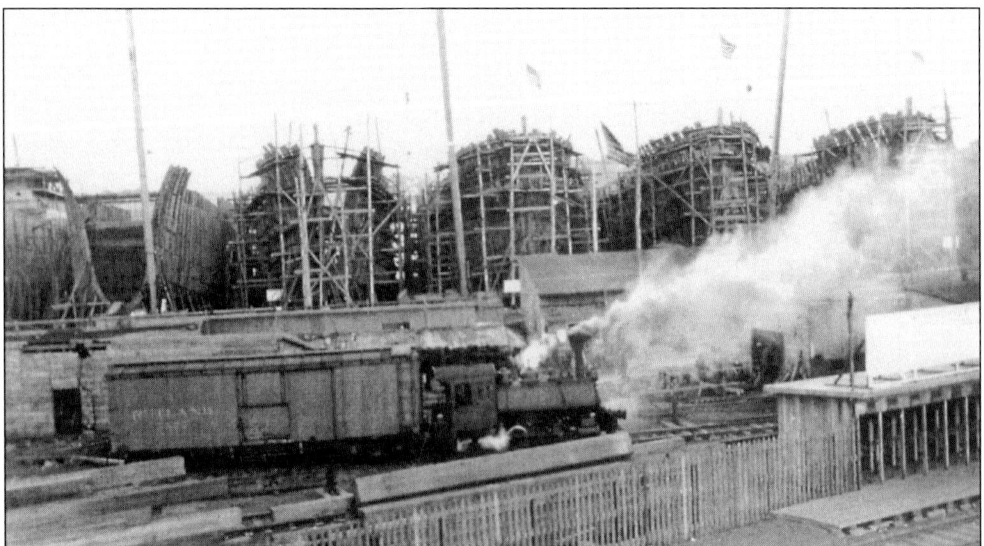

NEWINGTON Shattuck Shipyard during the First World War. Fifteen 3,500-ton wooden steamships were launched from here in less than two years from 1917-19. (Courtesy Barbara Myers and Newington Historical Society)

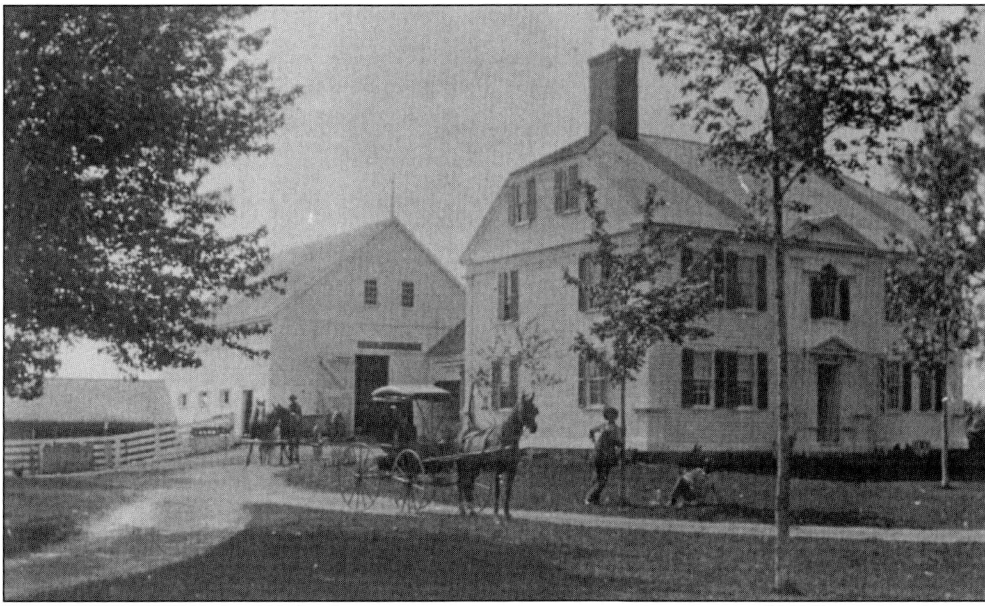

NEWINGTON The Cyrus Frink house which burned in 1902. (Courtesy Barbara Myers and Newington Historical Society)

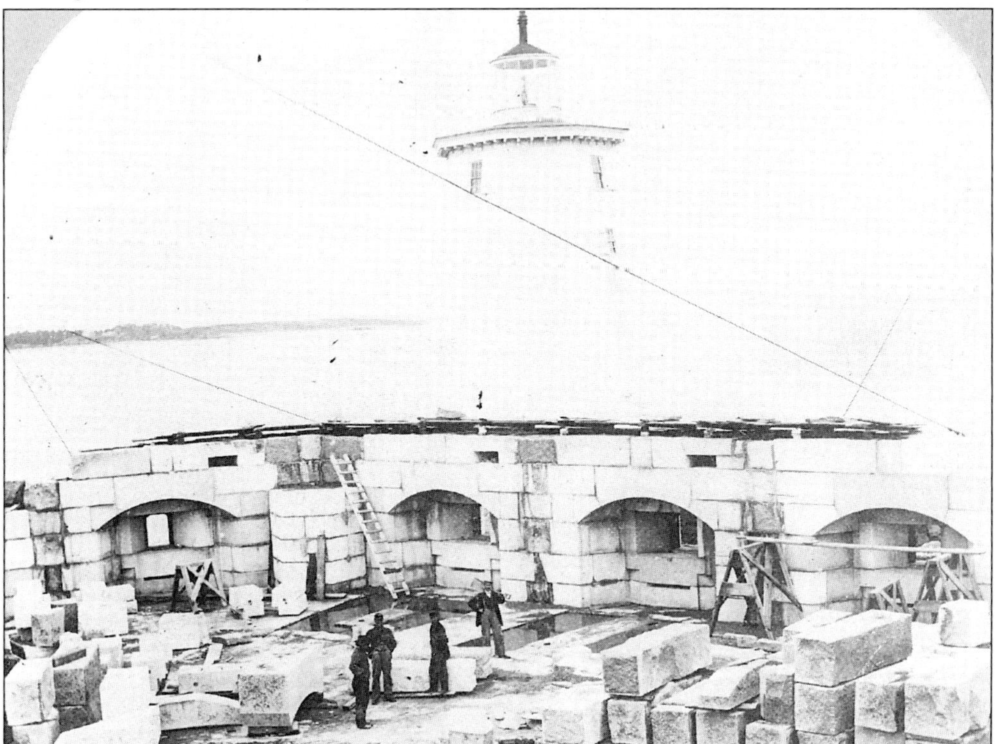

NEW CASTLE Fort Constitution and Fort Point lighthouse as they appeared during the middle of the Civil War. The octagonal lighthouse was built about 1804, replacing a lighthouse built in 1771.

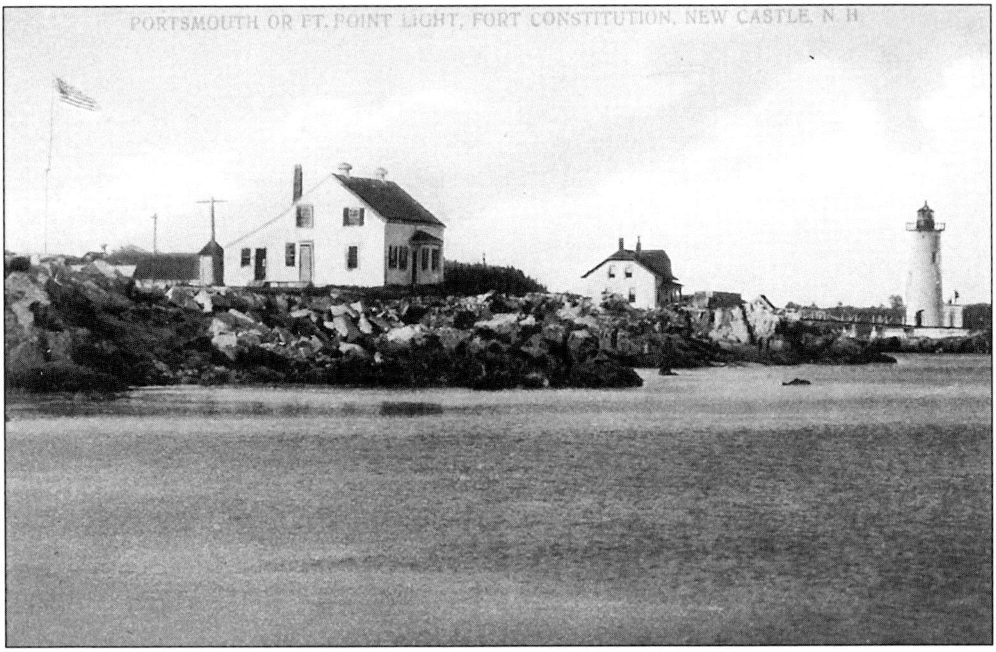

NEW CASTLE Fort Point lighthouse, c. 1913. This structure was built in 1877.

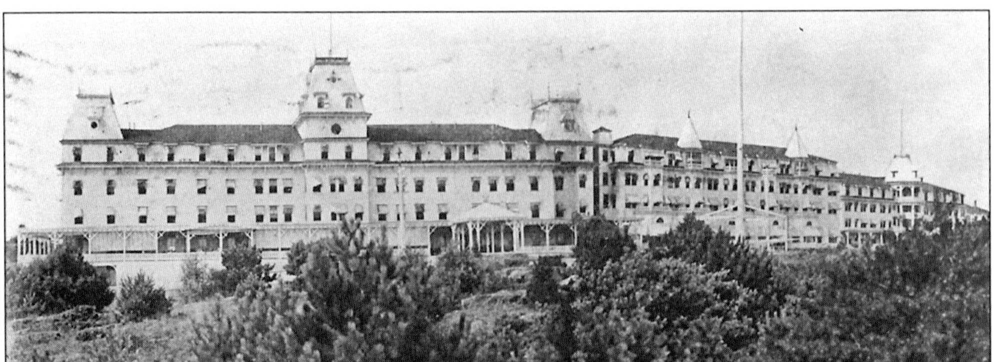

NEW CASTLE Wentworth-by-the-Sea hotel as it appeared in 1905. Currently closed, the building is one of the few remaining examples of hotel architecture from the gilded age. It was also the setting for the opening scenes in Steven King and Peter Straub's novel The Talisman.

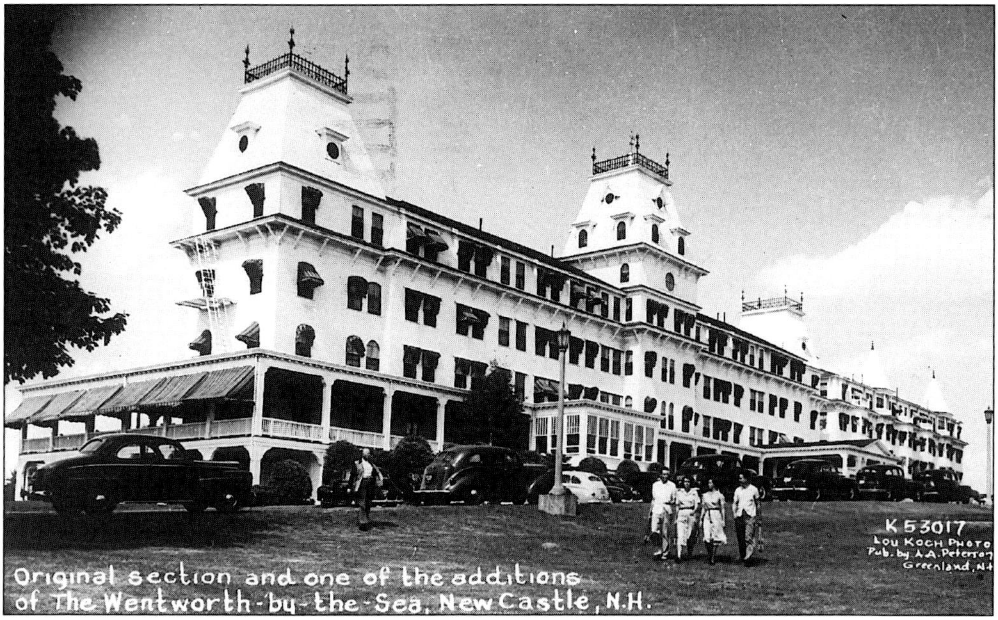

NEW CASTLE Wentworth-by-the-Sea hotel as it appeared in the 1950s. In many instances three and four generations of the same family continued to come to the hotel throughout the twentieth century.

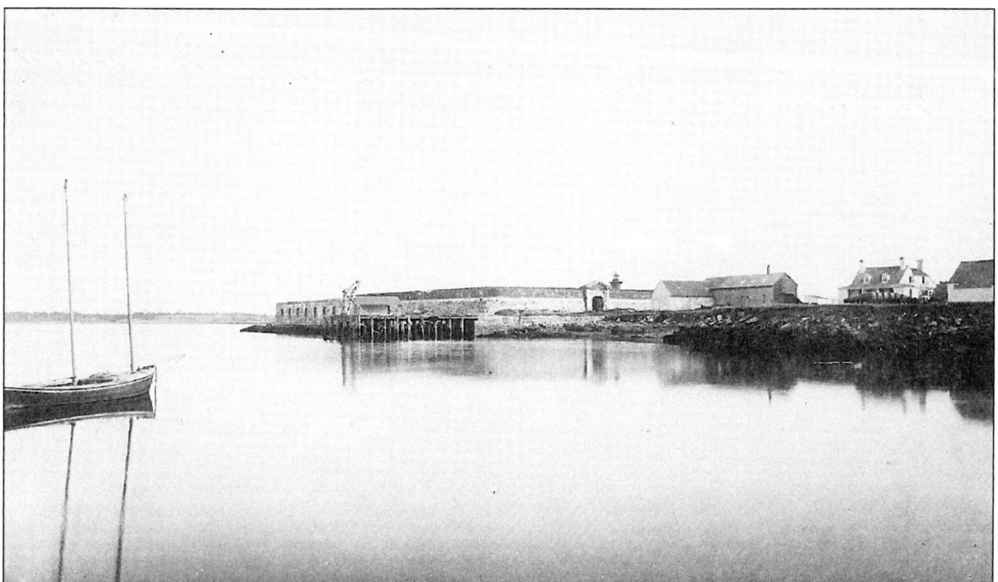

NEW CASTLE Fort Constitution in 1886. Despite the defense emplacements Portsmouth and the New Hampshire seacoast have not been attacked since the United States became a nation. (Courtesy Joseph P. Copley)

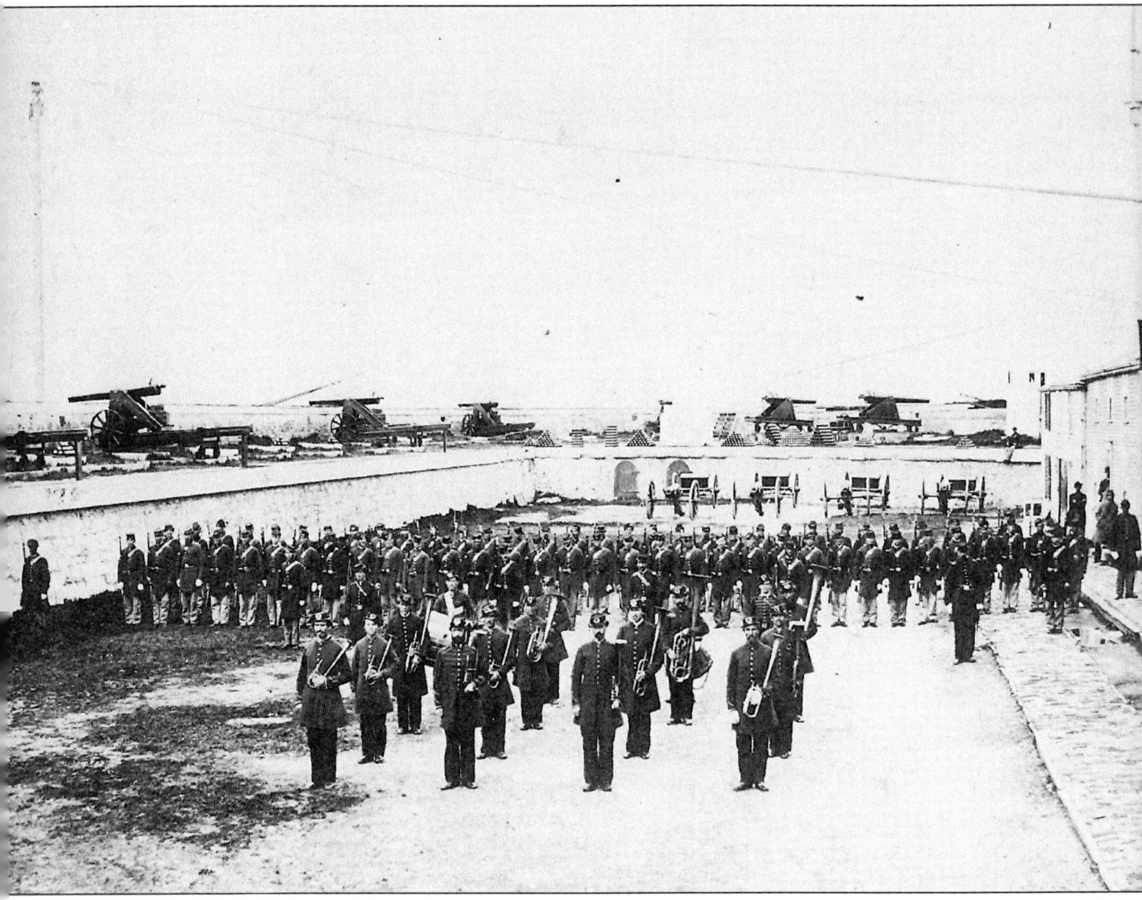

NEW CASTLE A Civil War era view of the interior of Fort Constitution. To the left are several 32-pound seacoast guns. Behind the artillery men and military band are four light artillery pieces. (Courtesy Joseph P. Copley)

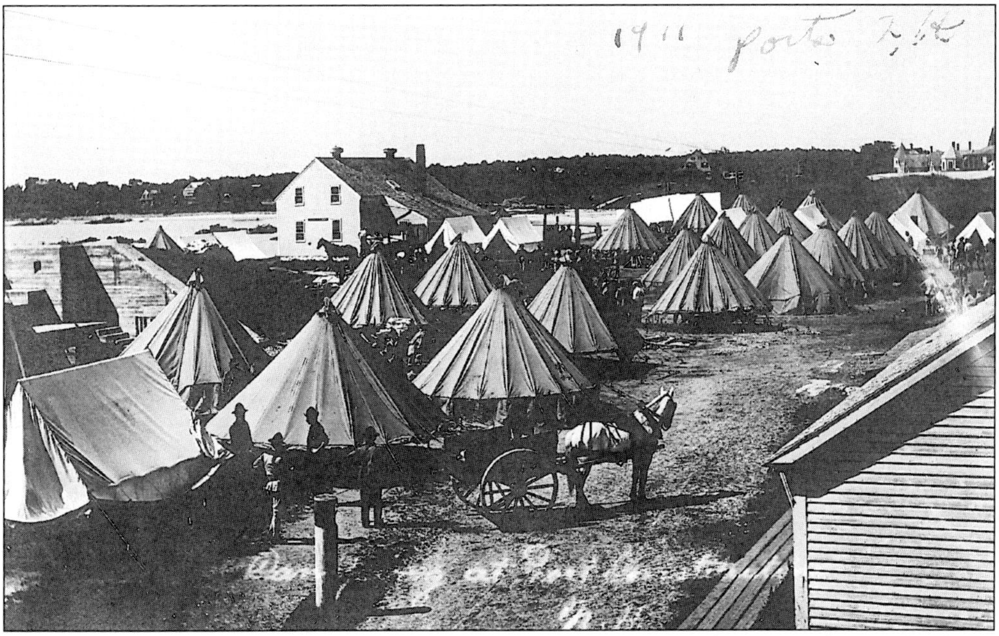
NEW CASTLE Encampment at Fort Constitution in 1911. It was three years before the death of Archduke Ferdinand; three years before modern warfare was to begin.

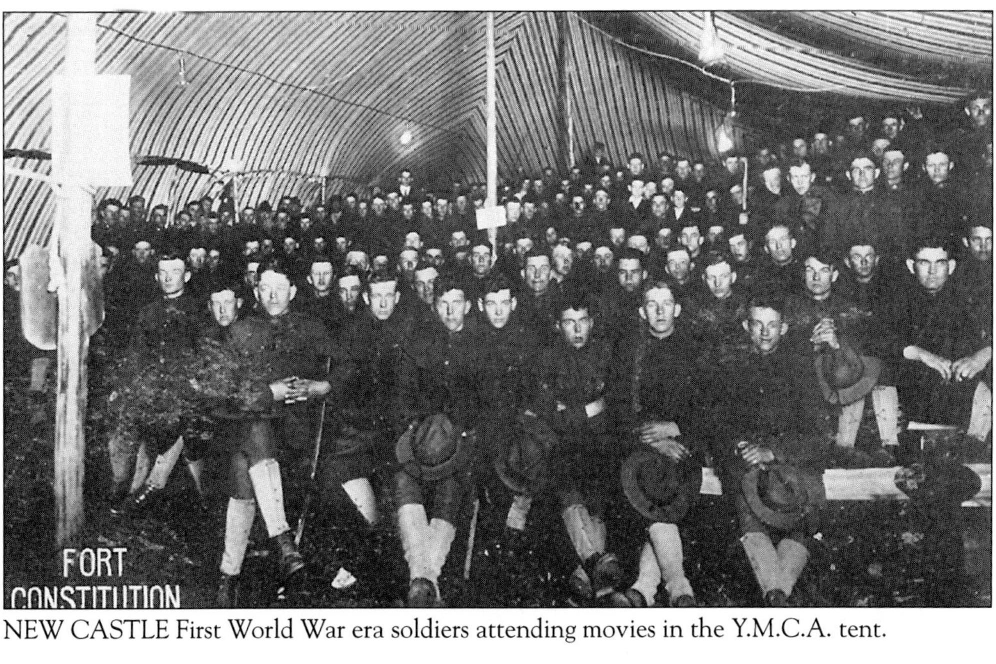

NEW CASTLE First World War era soldiers attending movies in the Y.M.C.A. tent.

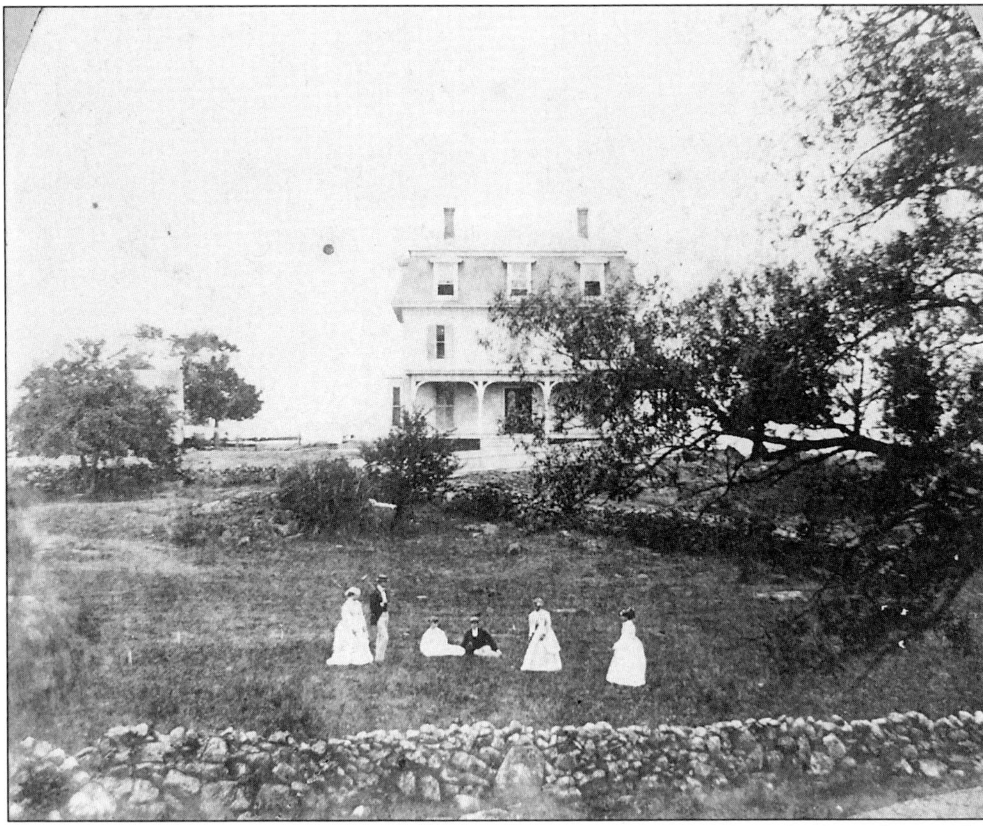

RYE A social occasion at Rye Beach about 1866-75. Despite the formal white dresses this may have been nothing more than afternoon tea. This was the era when to show a glimpse of stocking was considered quite forward.

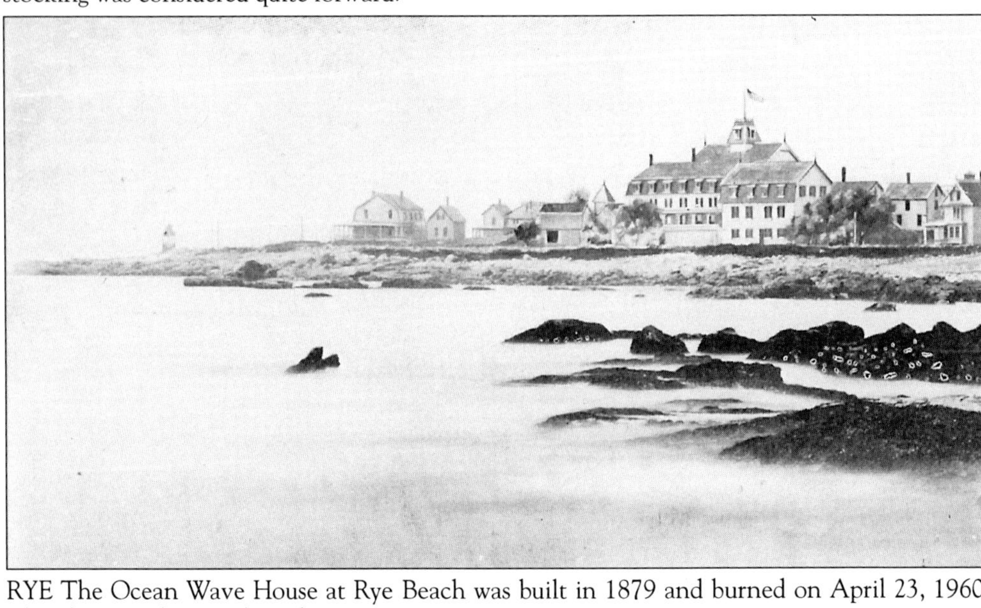

RYE The Ocean Wave House at Rye Beach was built in 1879 and burned on April 23, 1960. The photograph was taken about 1904.

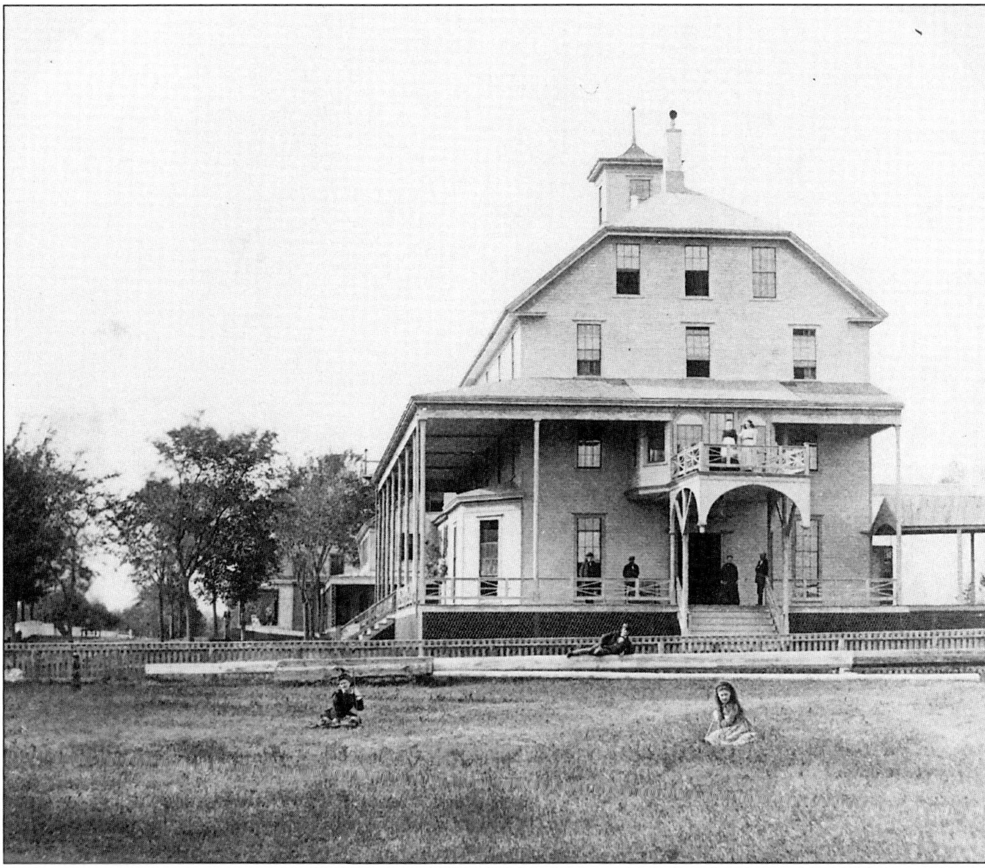

RYE The First Farragut House at Rye Beach was built in 1865 and burned on April 18, 1882.

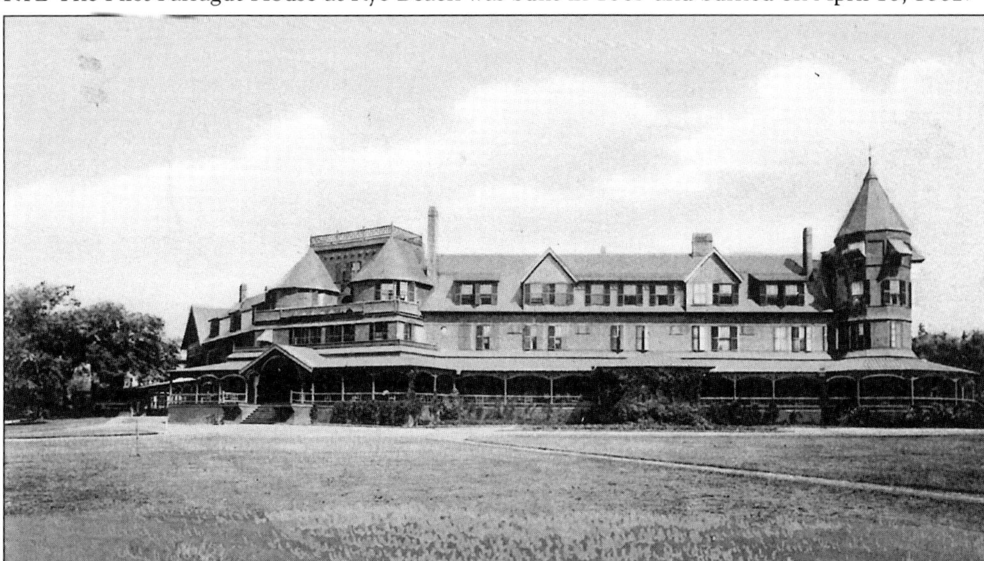

RYE The Second Farragut House was built in 1882 and pictured here about 1906. The turrets were typical of the hotel architecture of this era.

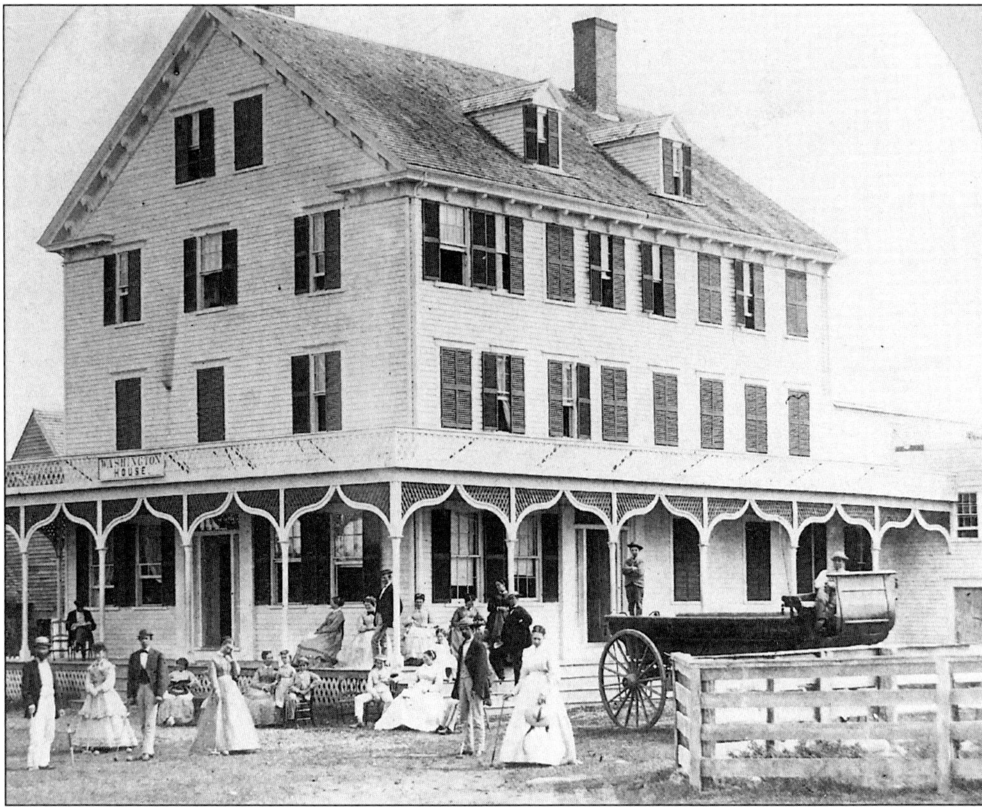

RYE Washington House at Rye Beach was built in the mid-1850s. The photograph was taken in 1875. This lovely old house burned in 1927. Individuals such as these shown were by and large summer visitors from Boston, New York, and Philadelphia.

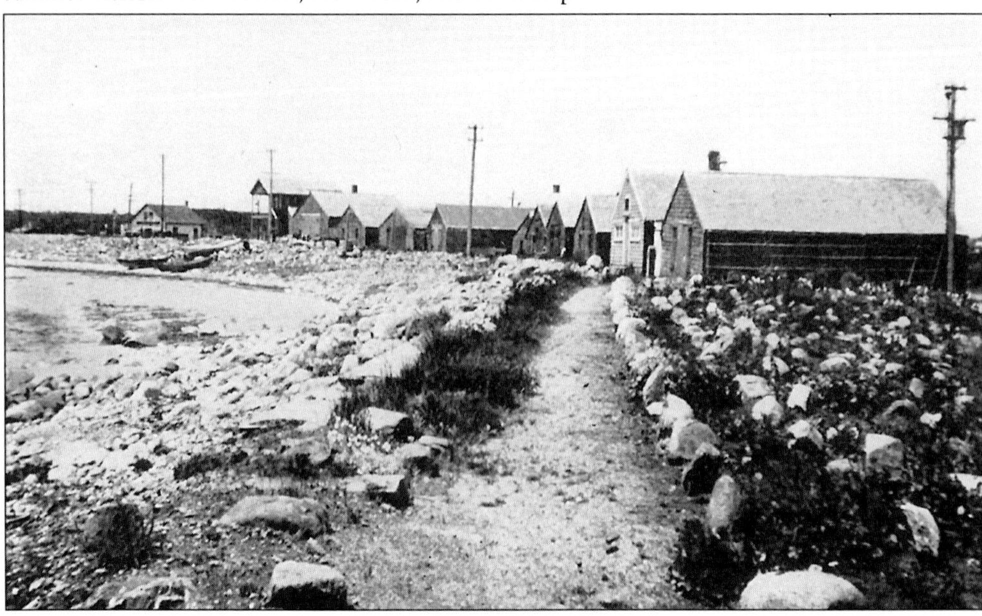

RYE The Rock Garden House and Fish Houses at Little Boar's Head about 1910.

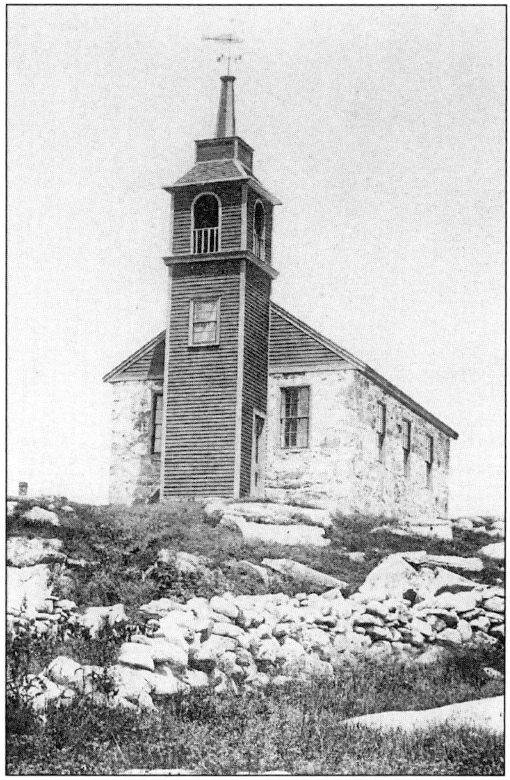

ISLES OF SHOALS Gosport Church on Star Island with original steeple about 1859-75. The original steeple blew down in 1892 and a new stone steeple was erected the same year. The church is still used by worshipers attending conferences on Star Island.

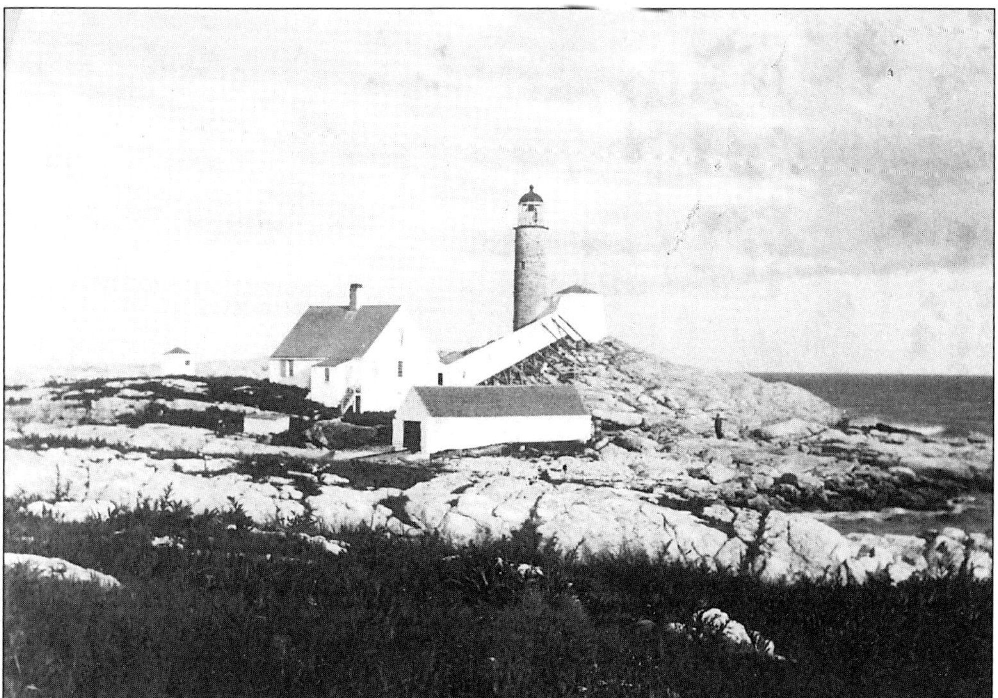

ISLES OF SHOALS White Island lighthouse, built in 1865 and pictured here in the late 1800s.

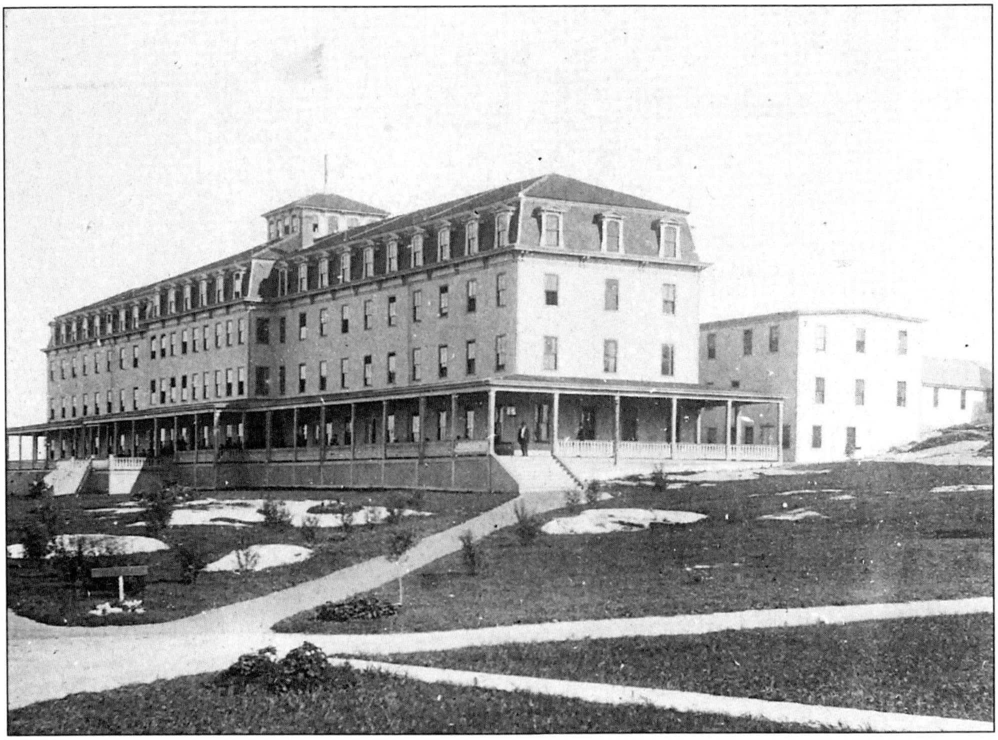

ISLES OF SHOALS The First Oceanic House on Star Island was built in 1873 and burned in 1875.

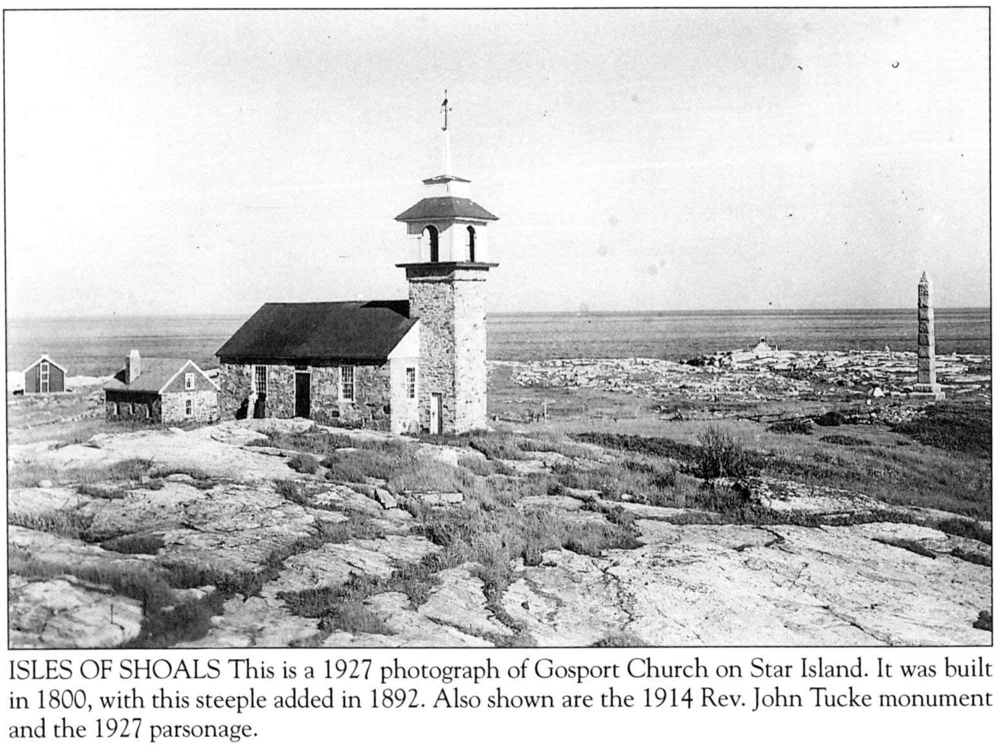

ISLES OF SHOALS This is a 1927 photograph of Gosport Church on Star Island. It was built in 1800, with this steeple added in 1892. Also shown are the 1914 Rev. John Tucke monument and the 1927 parsonage.

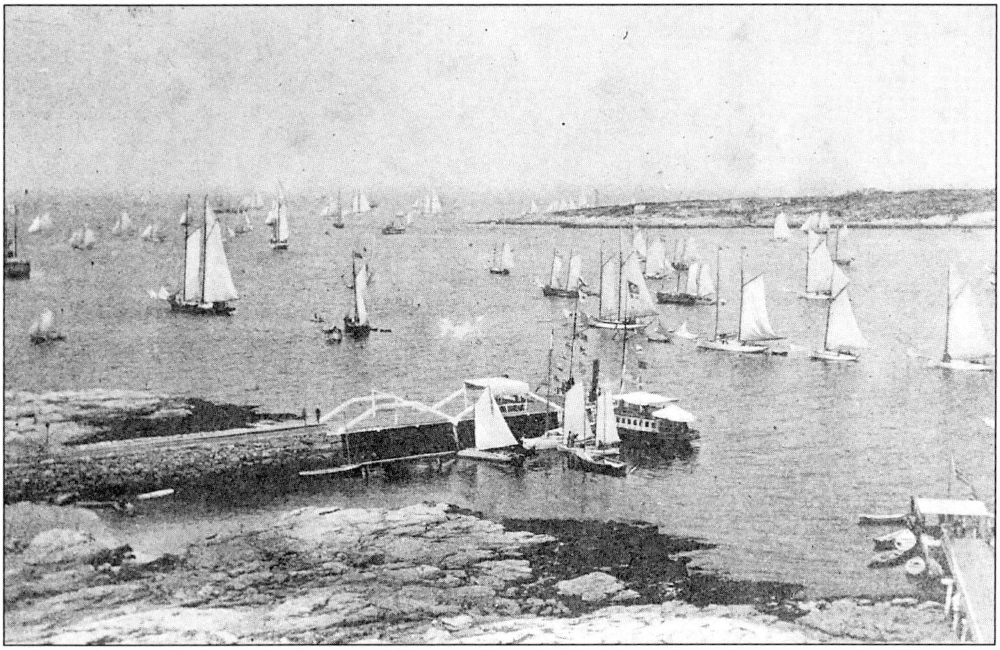
ISLES OF SHOALS Gosport Harbor Regatta about 1880.

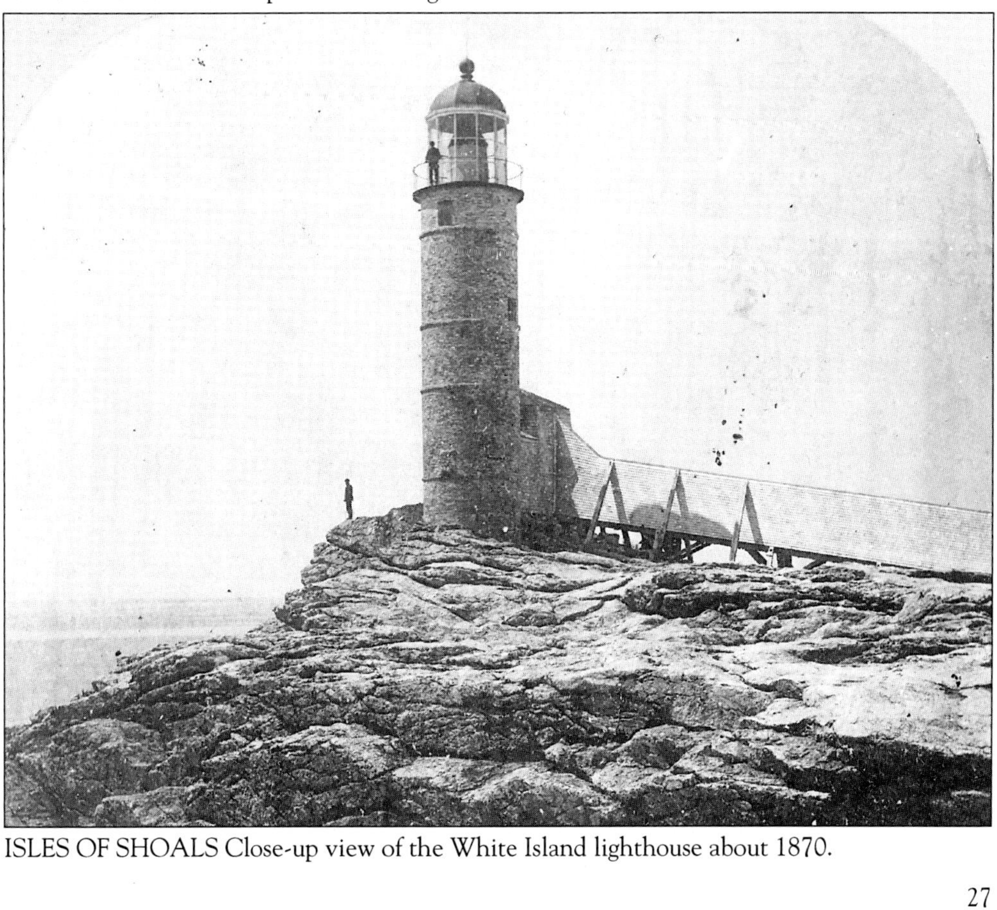
ISLES OF SHOALS Close-up view of the White Island lighthouse about 1870.

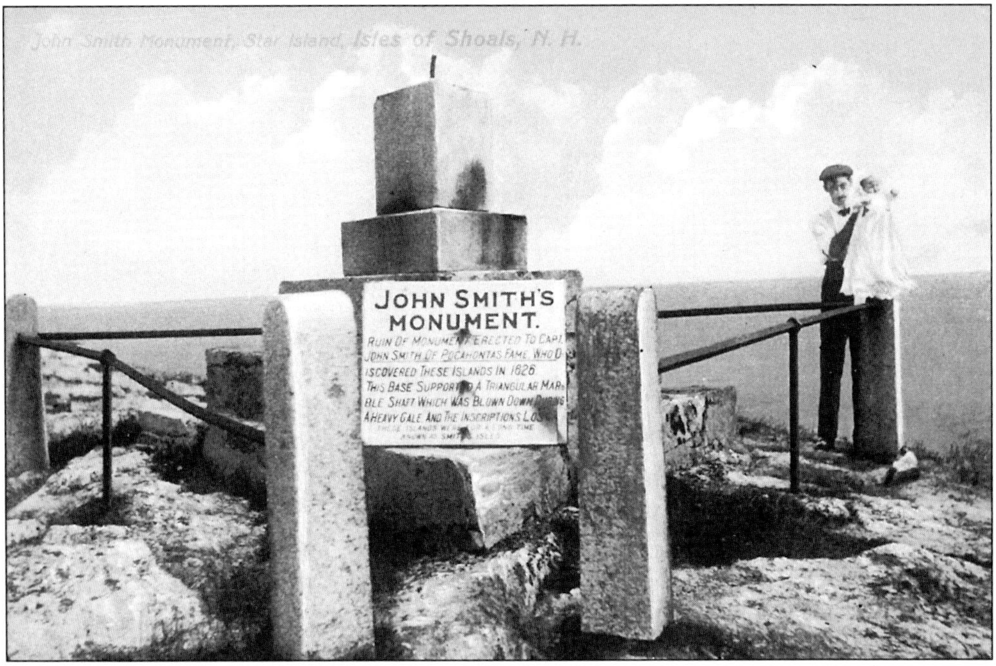

ISLES OF SHOALS In 1914 a new monument replaced the 1864 monument erected in memory of Captain John Smith who sailed by the islands in 1614.

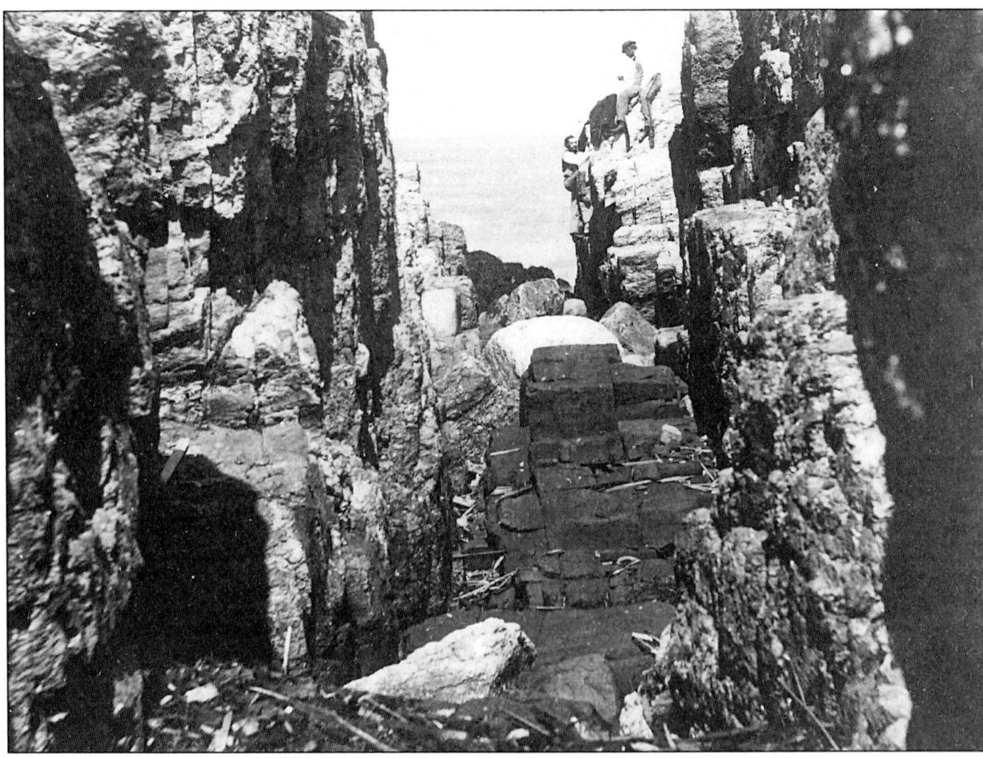

ISLES OF SHOALS Rocky cavern on Star Island about 1870.

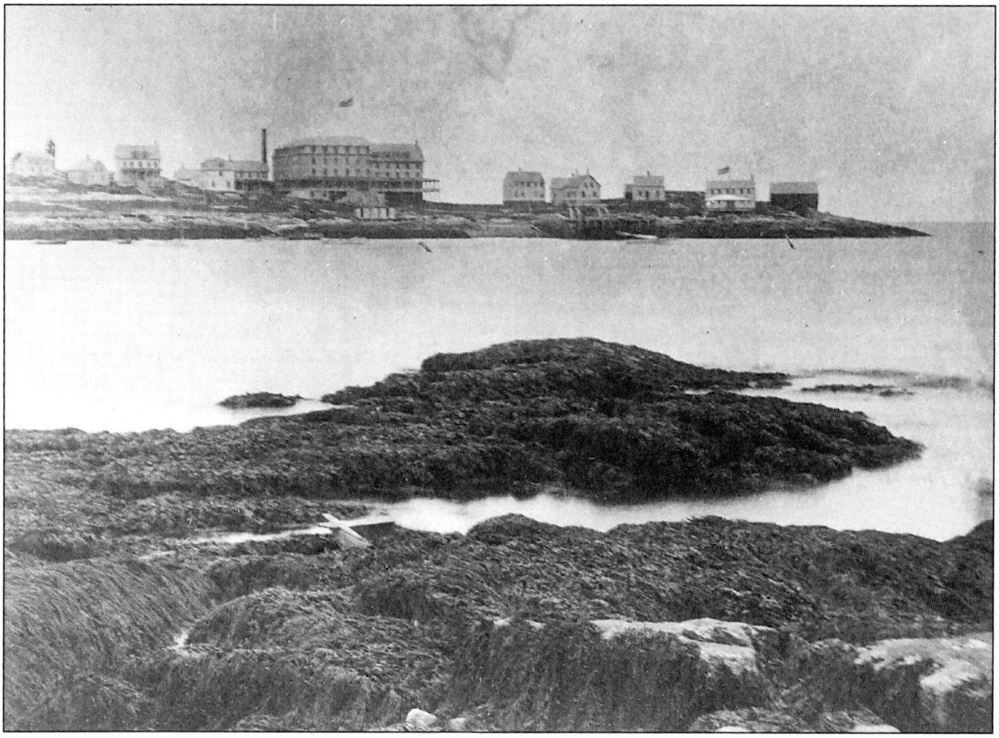

ISLES OF SHOALS A view of Gosport on Star Island taken from Smuttynose Island in August 1876. Gosport was incorporated as a New Hampshire town in 1715 and annexed in 1876 to the town of Rye.

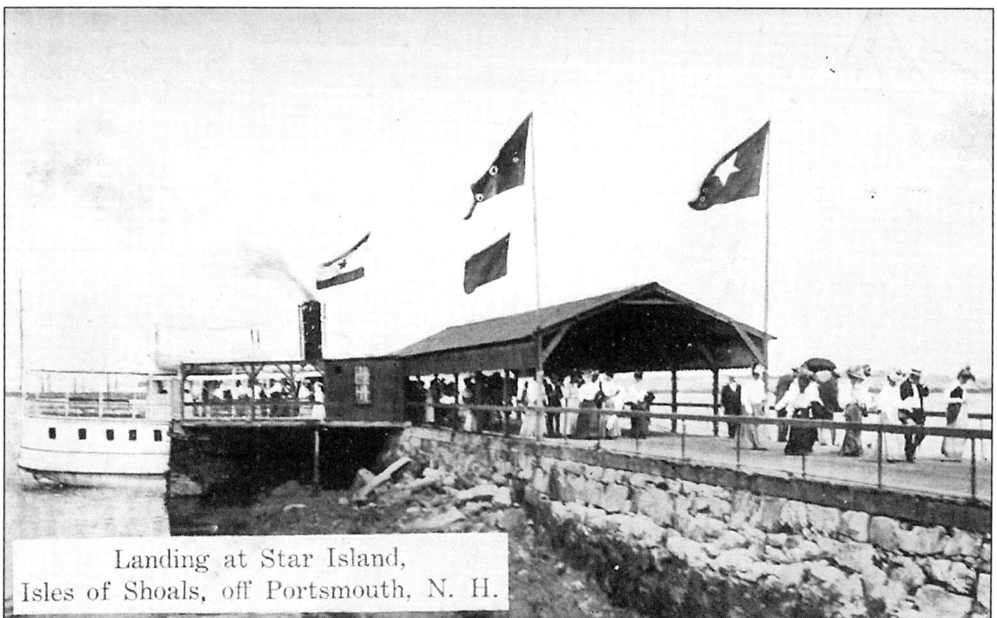

ISLES OF SHOALS The landing at Star Island about 1923. Thousands of tourists visited the islands each summer dating back into the 1850s.

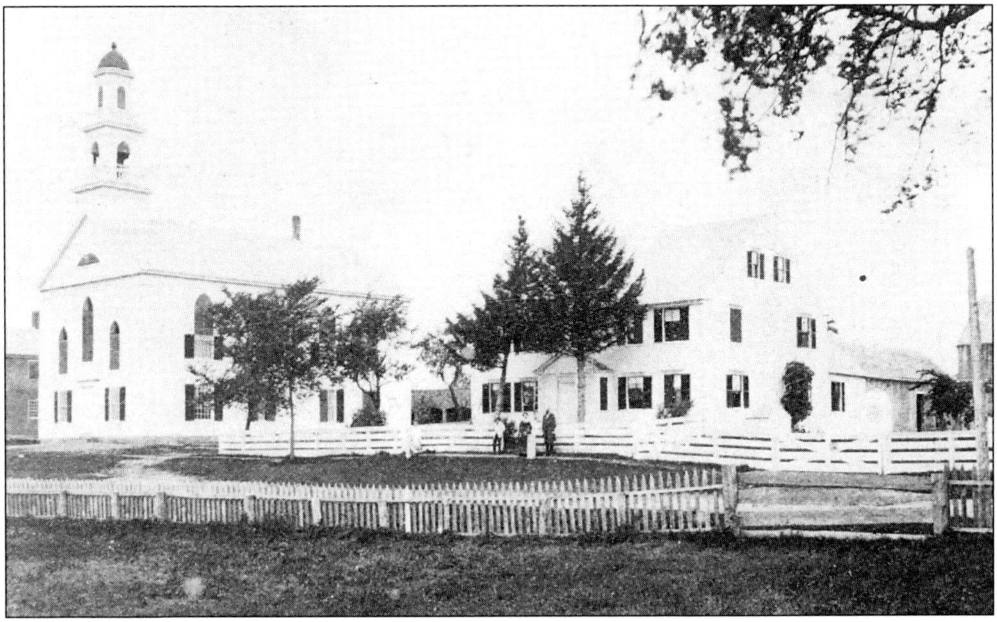

NORTH HAMPTON The 1838 Congregational Church and the 1803 Parsonage about 1880. The parsonage was razed in 1898.

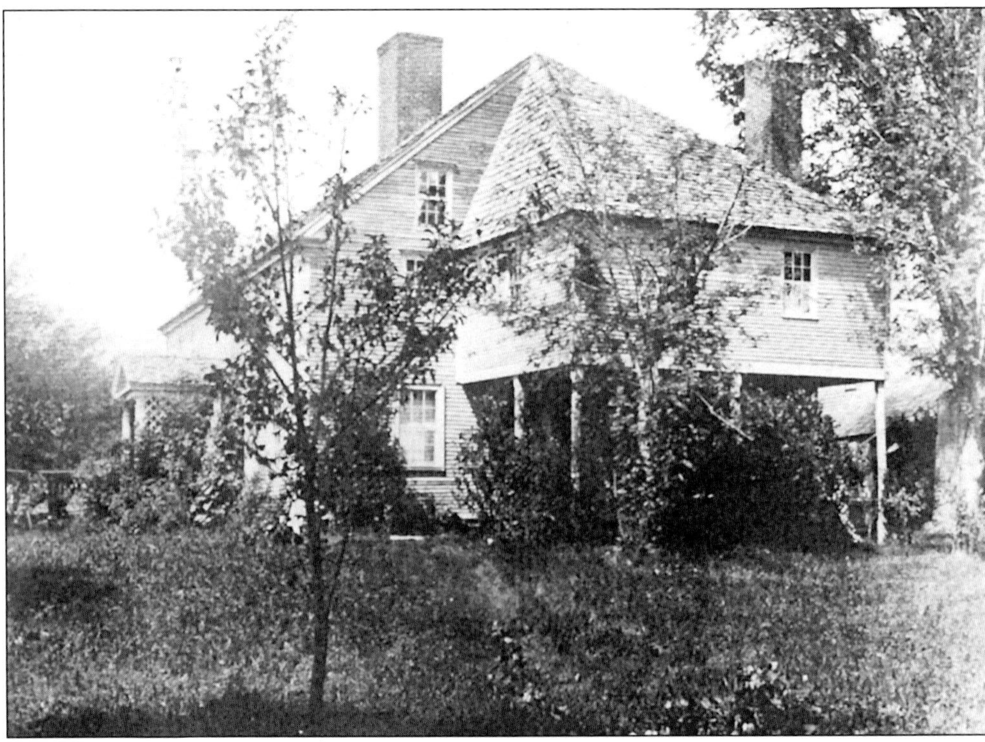

NORTH HAMPTON Leavitt's Half-Way Tavern at the corner of Exeter and Stage Roads in 1938. This landmark served as a stopping point to change horses for John Stavers' Flying Stagecoach route during the 1760s.

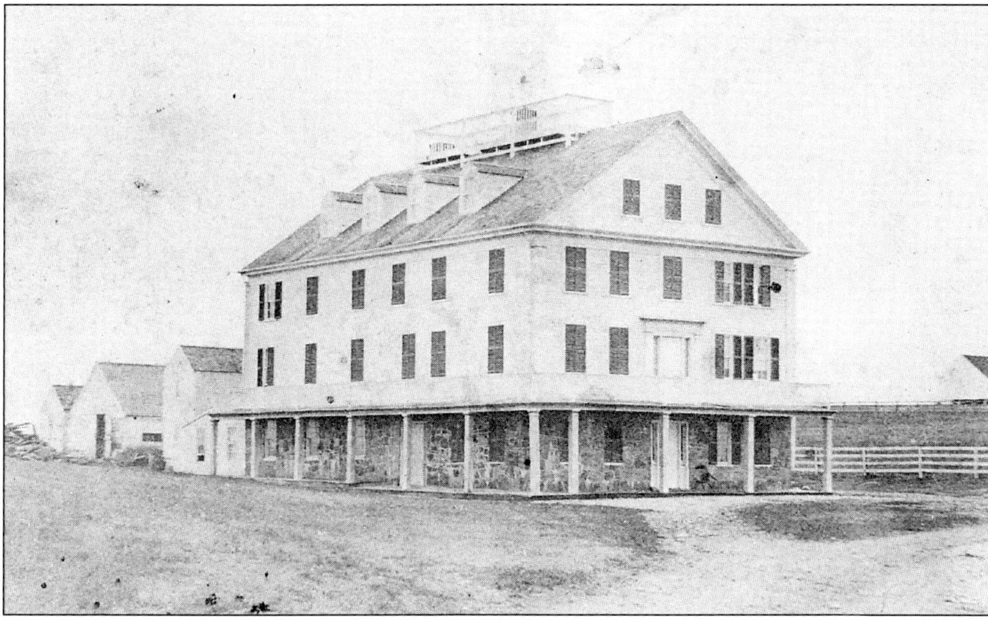

HAMPTON The Granite House at Hampton Beach, also known as the New Boar's Head Hotel. It was built in 1826, enlarged in 1866 and burnt in 1893.

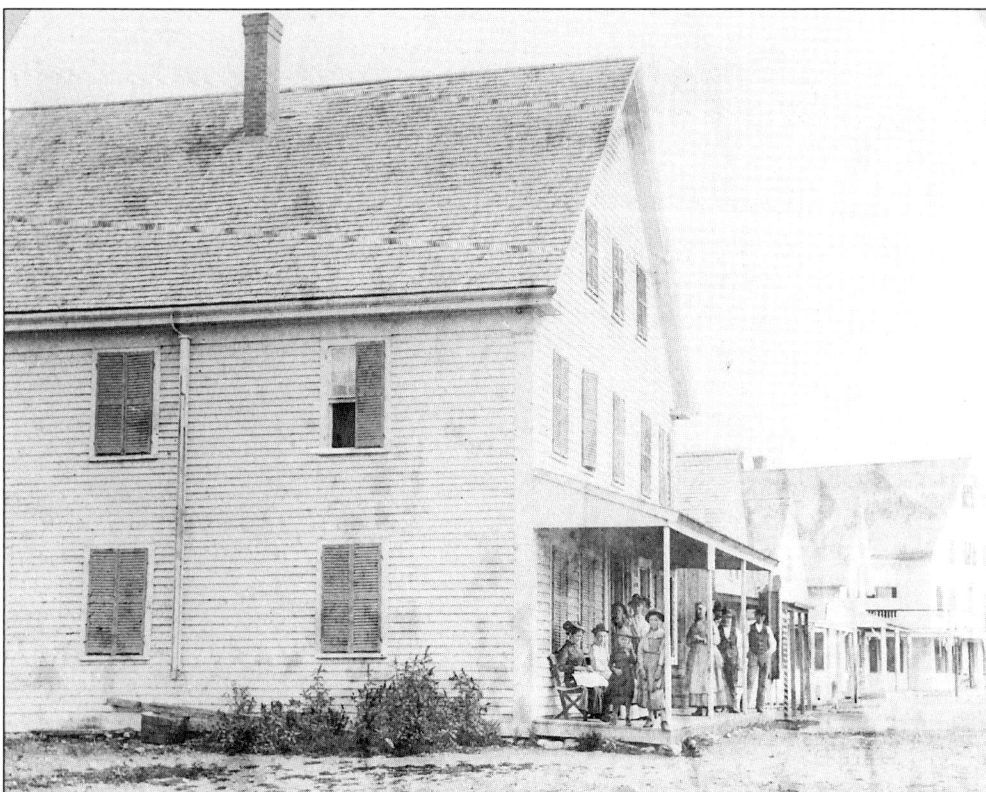

HAMPTON Business buildings on Hampton Beach about 1872.

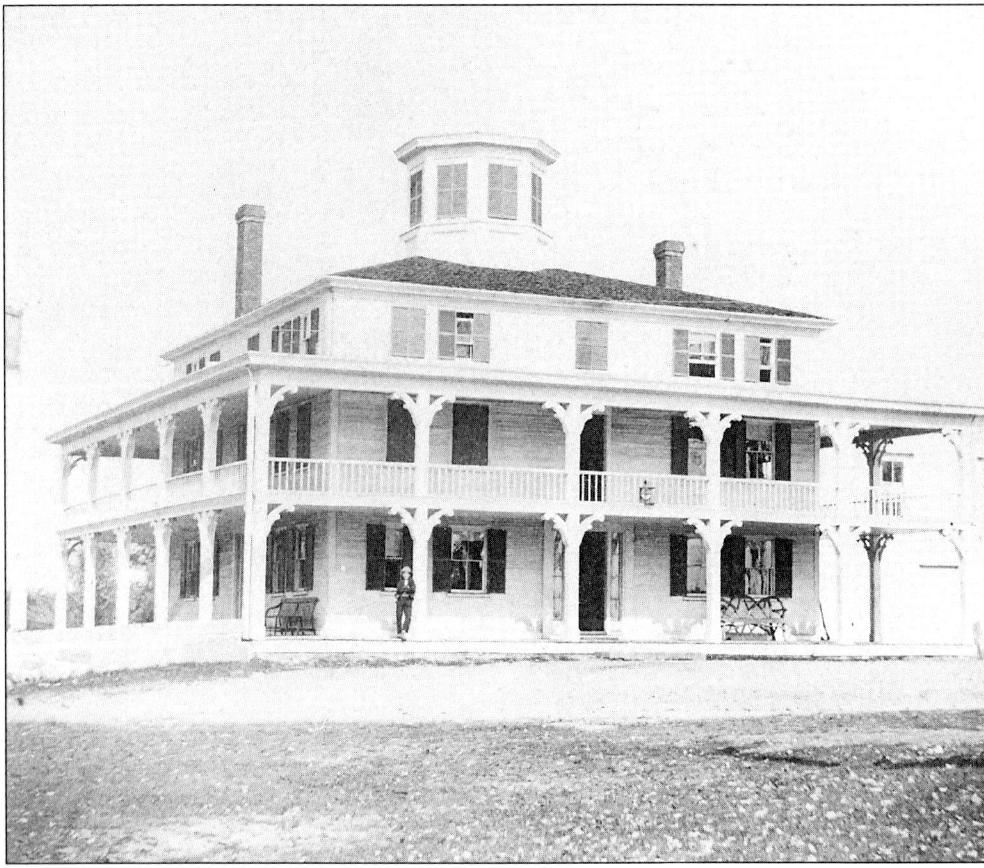

HAMPTON The Hotel Whittier in Hampton Village, built about 1817, burned 1916.

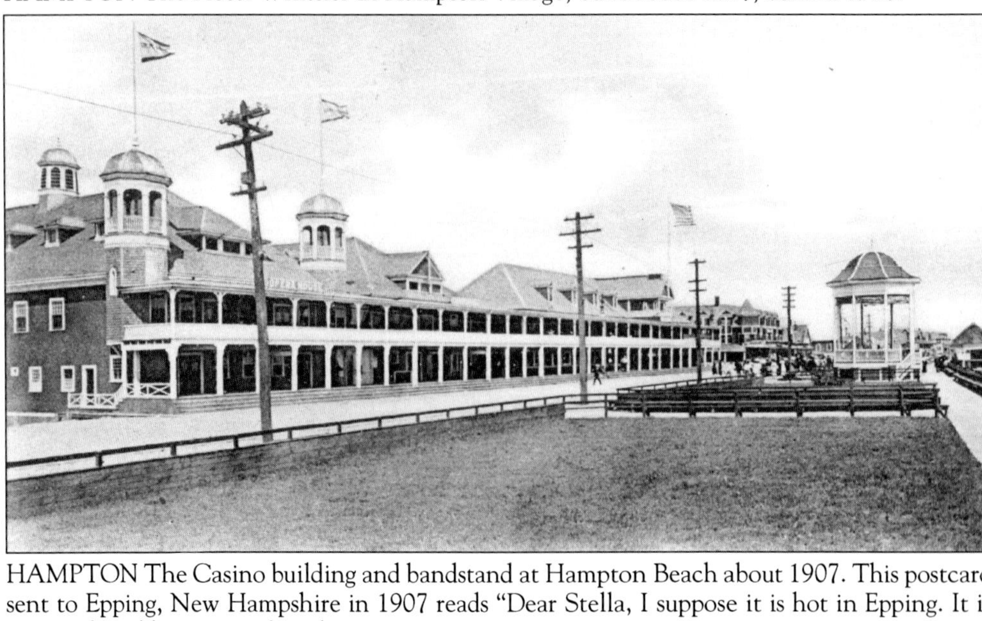

HAMPTON The Casino building and bandstand at Hampton Beach about 1907. This postcard sent to Epping, New Hampshire in 1907 reads "Dear Stella, I suppose it is hot in Epping. It is nice and cool here. Your friend, M.G.S."

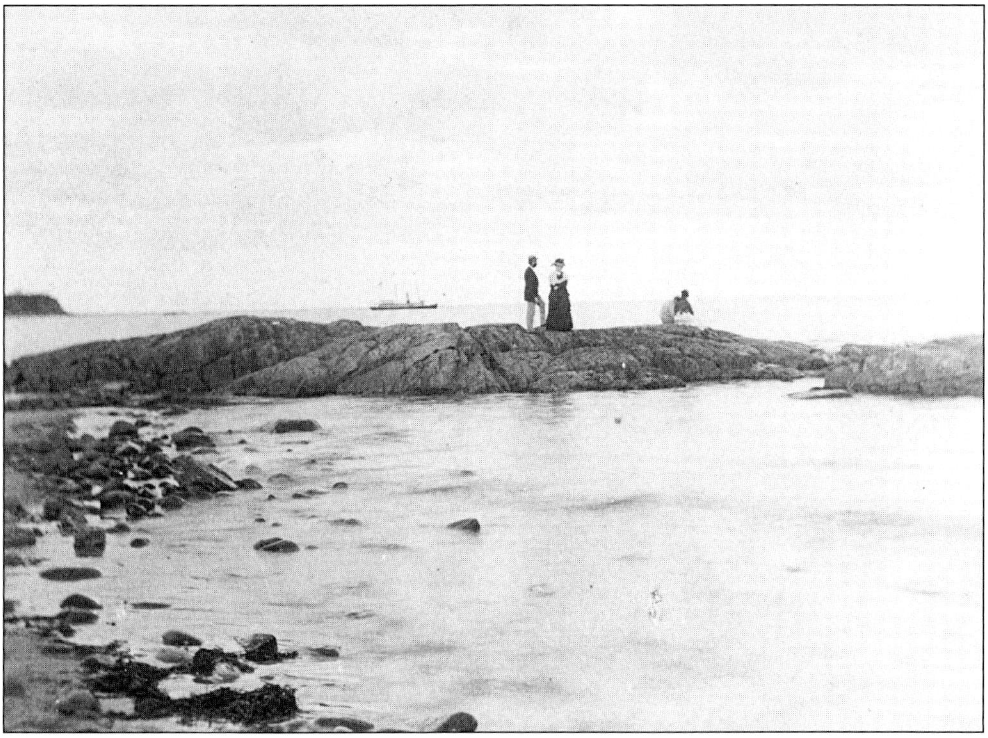

HAMPTON View off Hampton Beach in the 1870s.

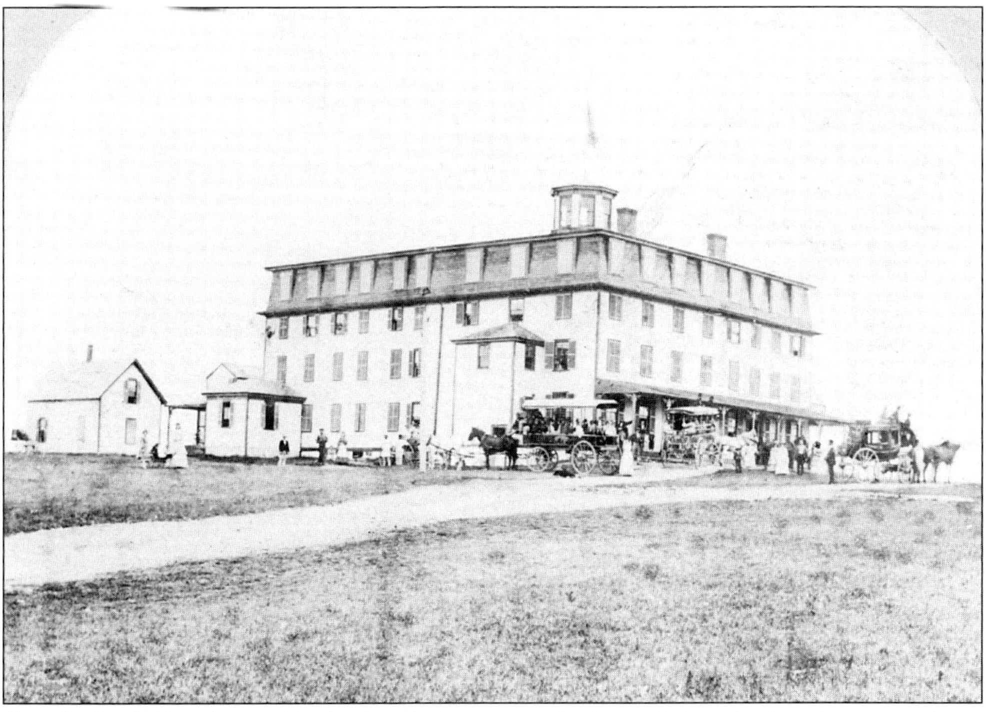

HAMPTON Hotel on Boar's Head between North and South Beaches owned by S. H. Dumas about 1890.

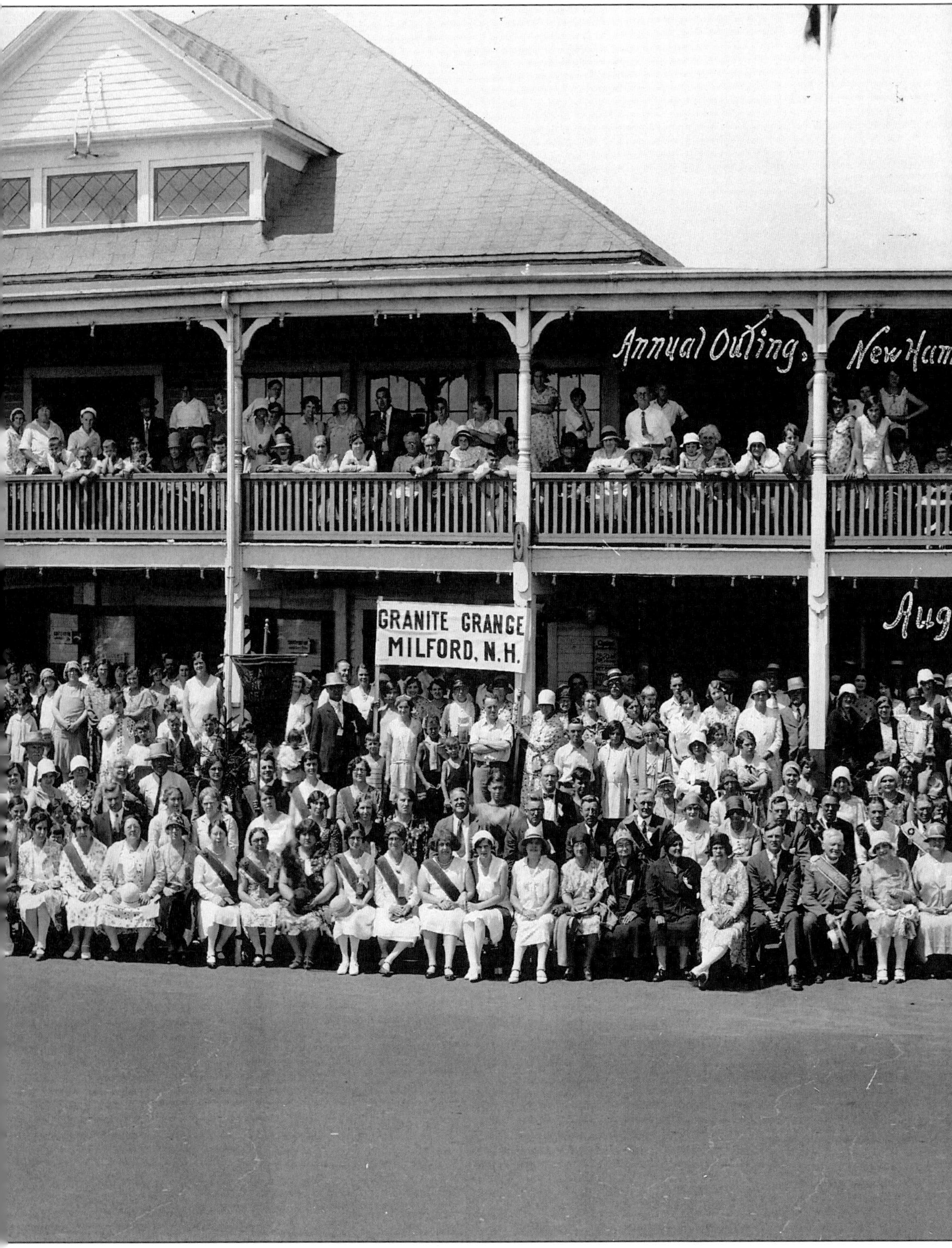

HAMPTON Hampton Beach Casino during a 1930 New Hampshire State Grange Convention.

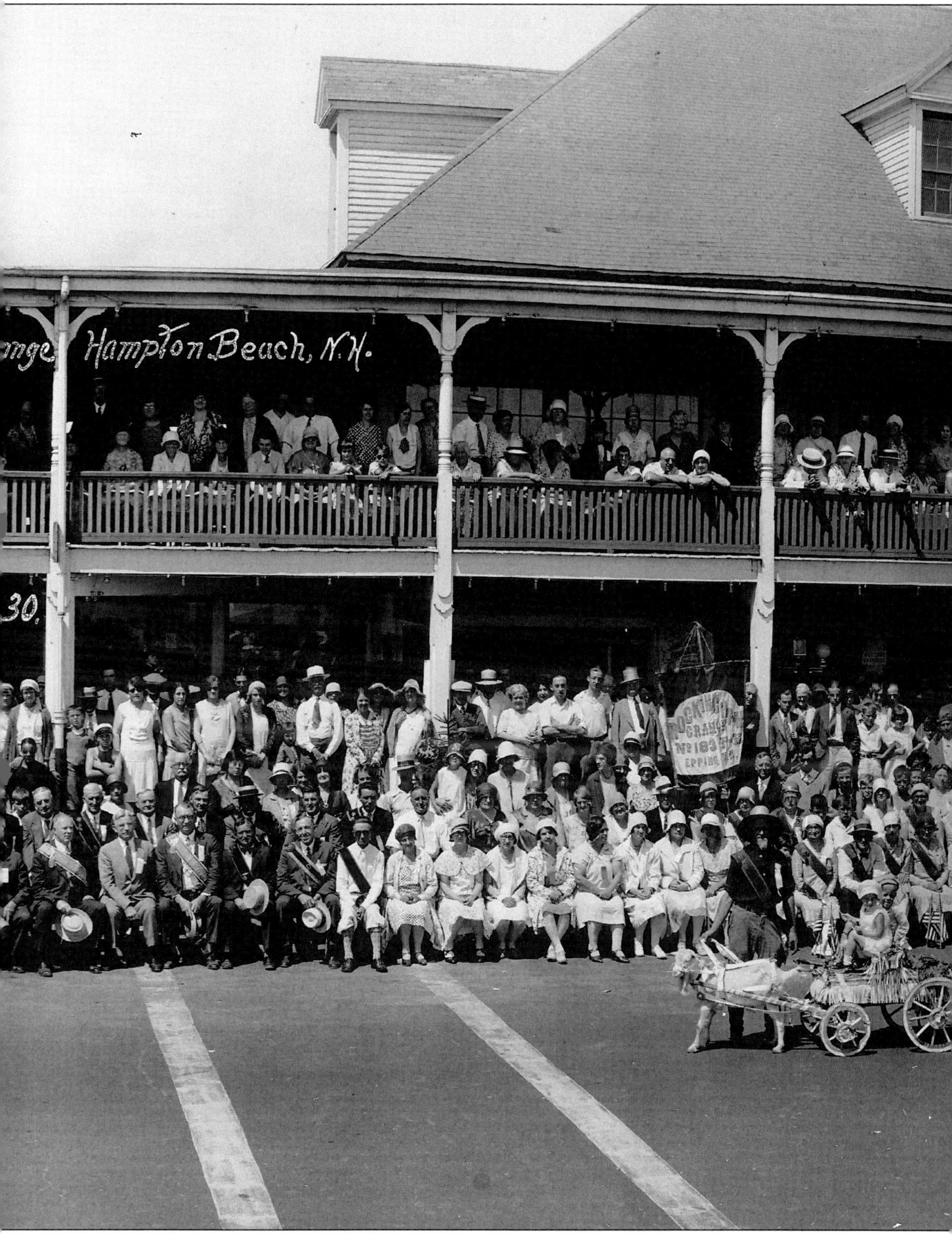

(Courtesy Fremont Historical Society)

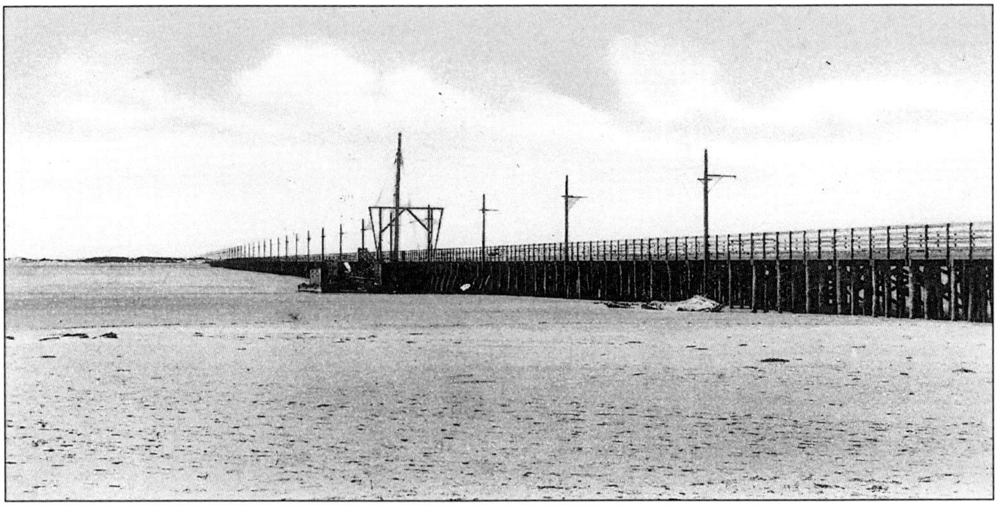

HAMPTON The Mile Long Wooden Bridge about 1906. Built in 1902 and torn down in 1949, this was once the longest wooden bridge in the world measuring 4,621 feet long and 30 feet wide.

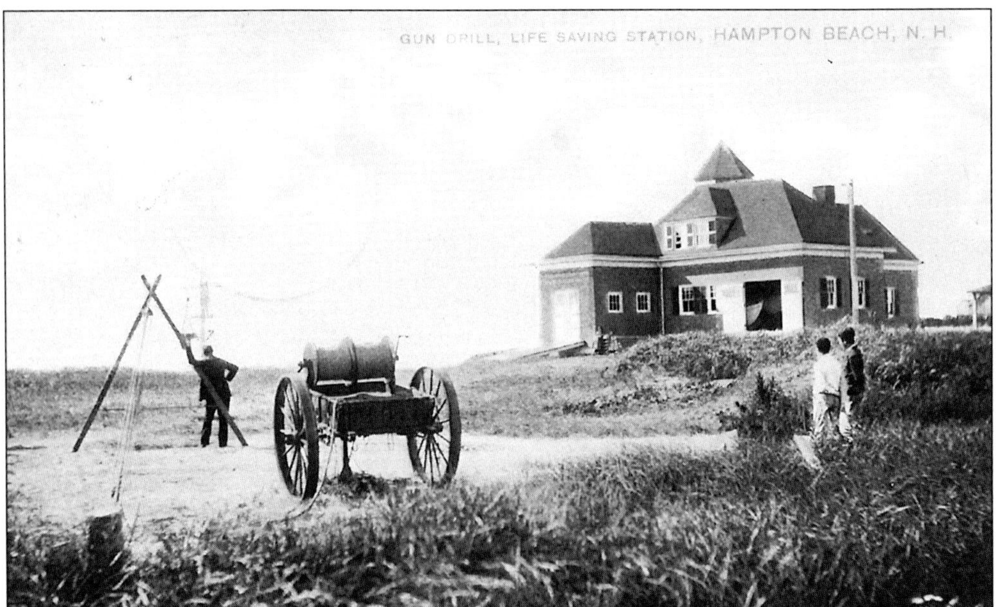

HAMPTON The life saving station at Hampton Beach about 1906.

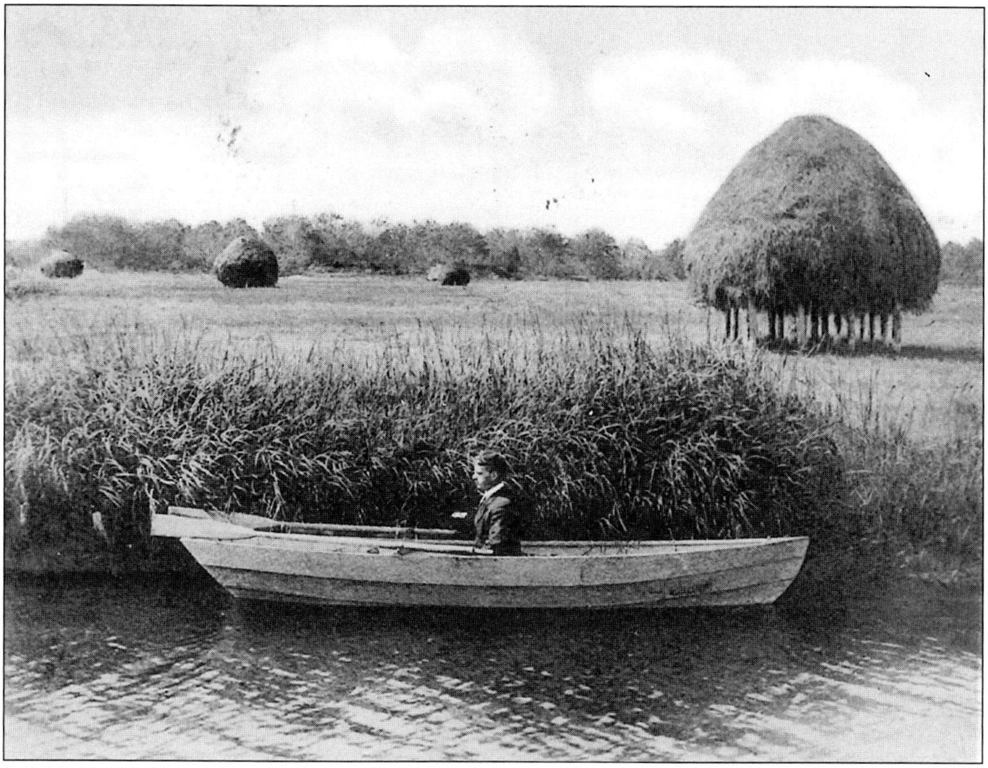

HAMPTON Hampton Beach marshes about 1907. Salt marsh hay was a valuable commodity for seacoast farmers dating back to the colonial period.

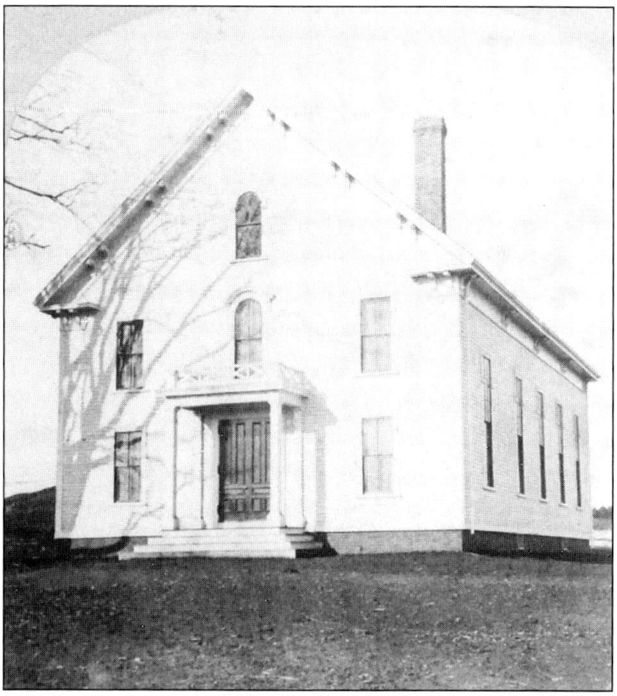

HAMPTON FALLS Hampton town hall built in 1877 on Route 88 and pictured here shortly after its erection. In 1892 a twenty-stall horse shed was built near the town hall and all were blown over in an 1896 windstorm.

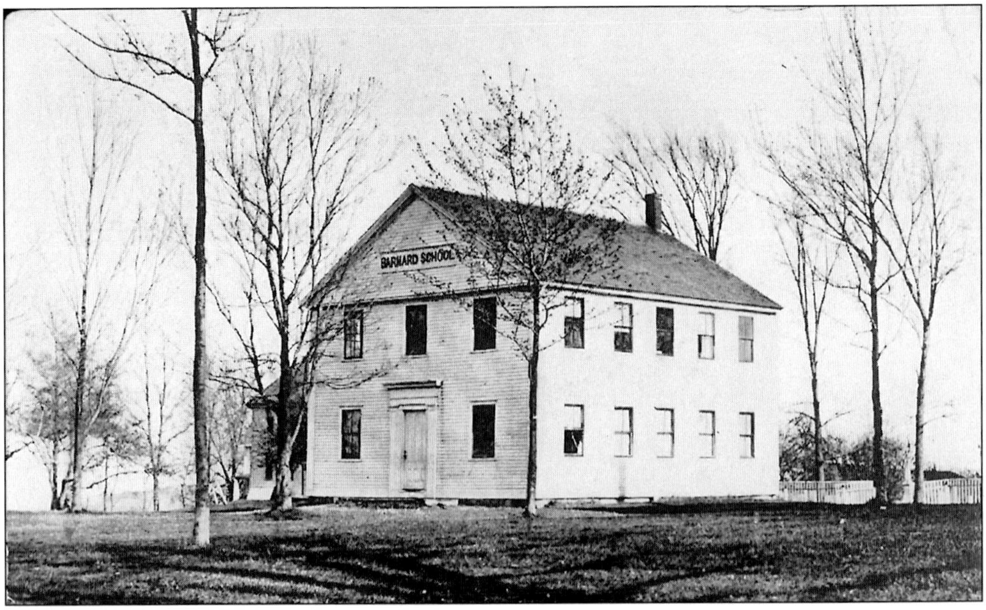

SOUTH HAMPTON Barnard School about 1905. This was built in 1833 overlooking the town common on what is now Route 107A.

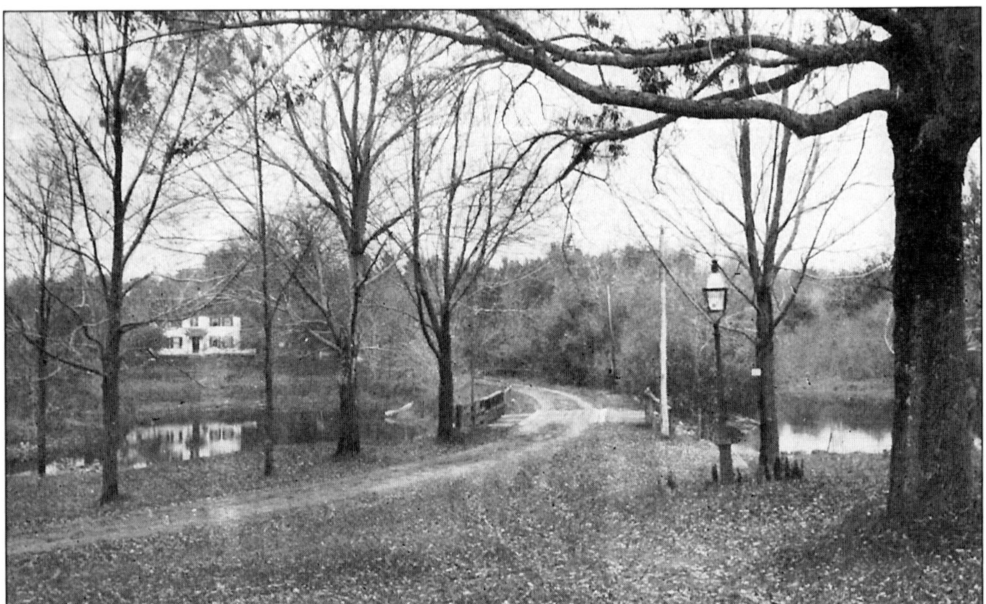

SOUTH HAMPTON Scenic view of rustic countryside about 1905.

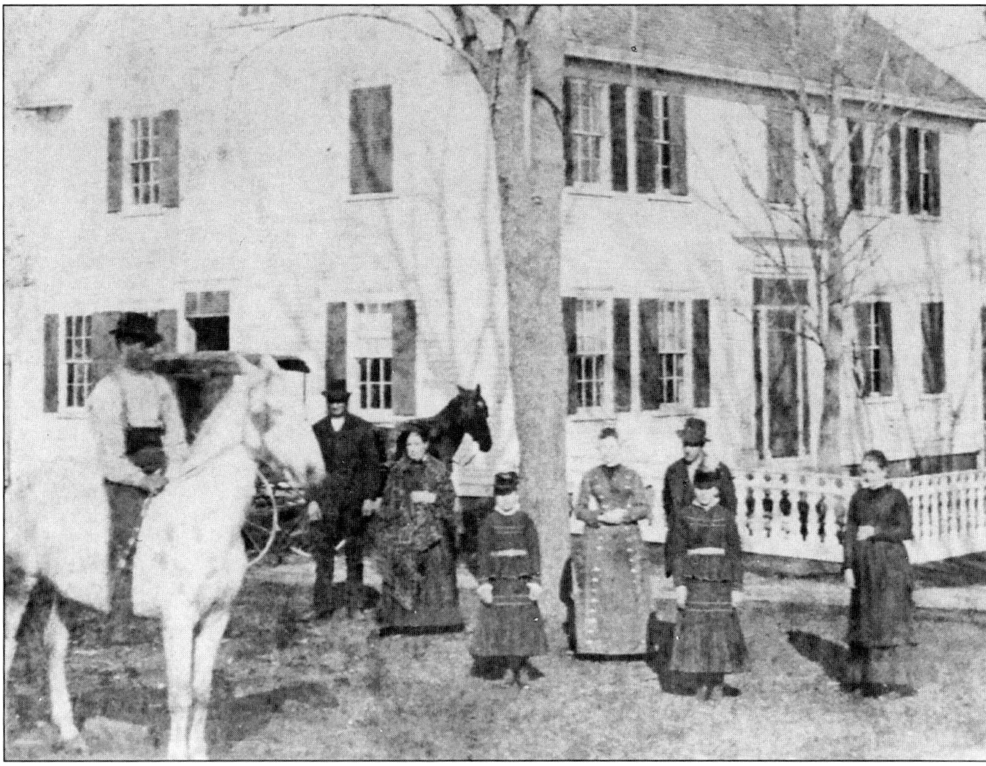

SEABROOK The Micajah Green homestead, Staid Road about 1880. (Courtesy of Eric Small)

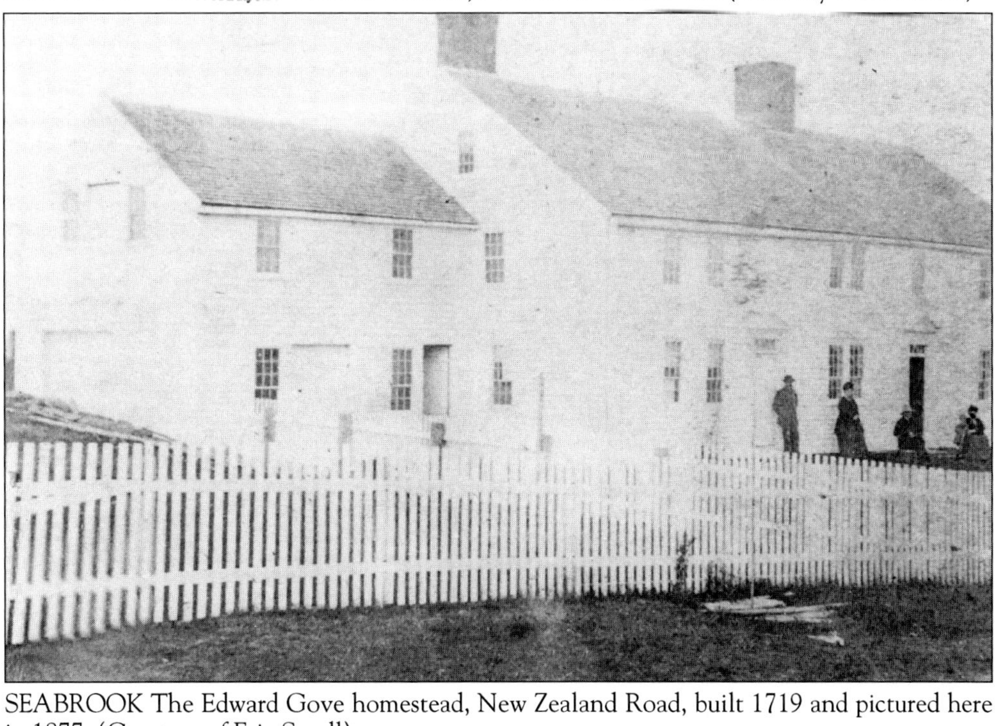

SEABROOK The Edward Gove homestead, New Zealand Road, built 1719 and pictured here in 1877. (Courtesy of Eric Small)

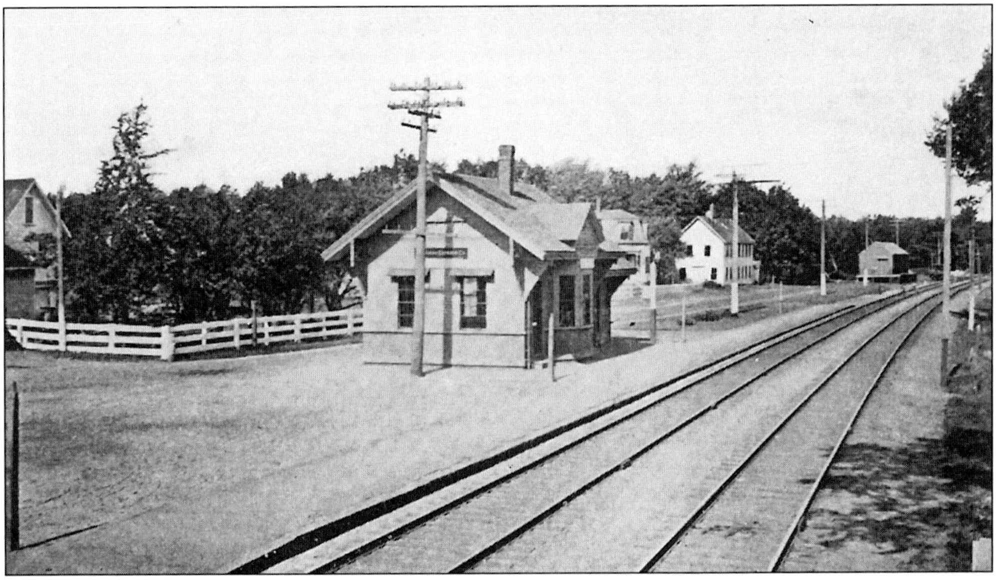

SEABROOK Seabrook depot about 1908. The depot was built in 1848 on the old Eastern and later the Boston and Maine railroad line. The depot was used until the early 1950s.

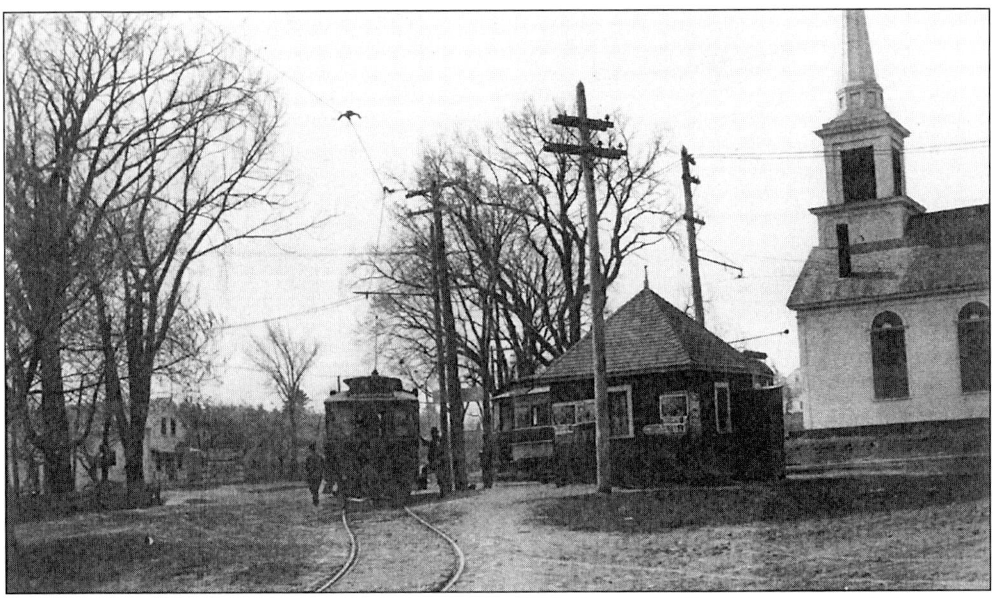

SEABROOK Smithtown Junction and Bert's Lunch, Route 1. The Hampton and Amesbury Street railway ran through Seabrook from 1899 until 1920.

Two

The Squamscott River and Great Bay

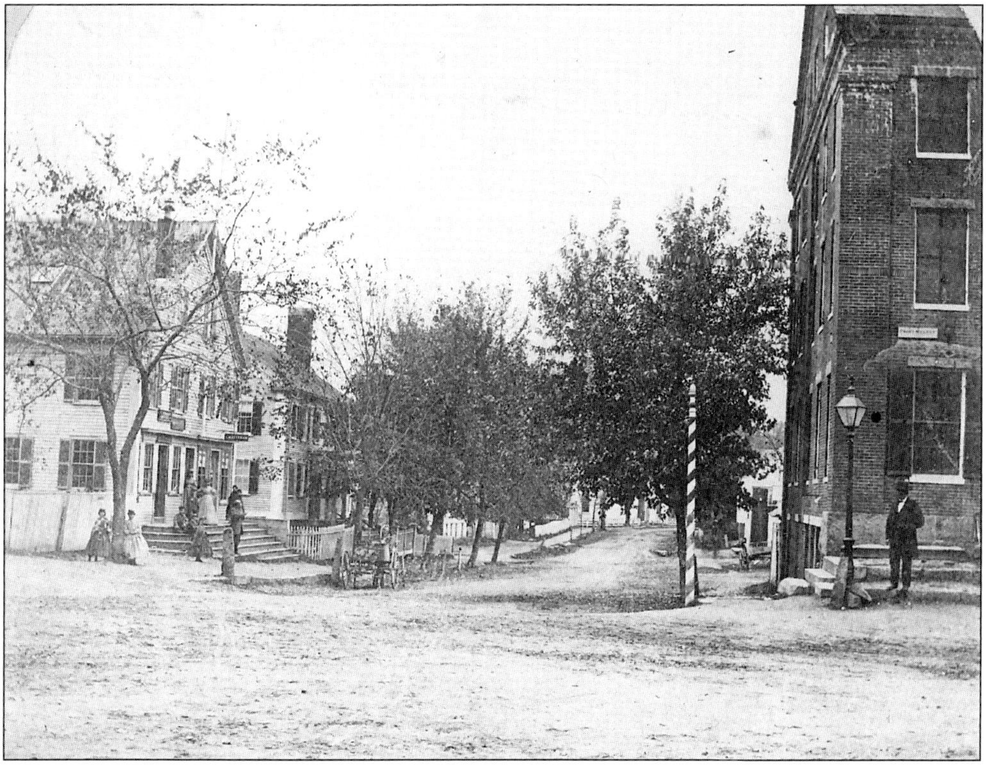

EXETER A view of Front and Court Streets looking south about 1870. The Squamscott Hotel, now Gorham Hall, is on the right as it appeared before extensive renovations in 1897 and 1908. (Courtesy Exeter Historical Society)

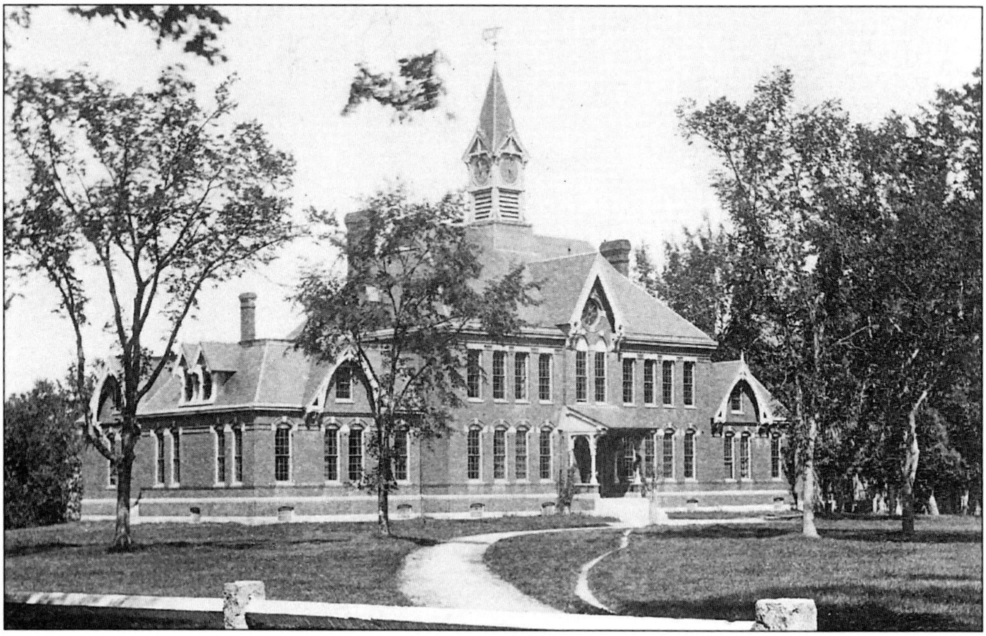

EXETER The third Phillips Exeter Academy building was built in 1872 and burned in 1914. Founded in 1781, Phillips Exeter is considered one of the most prestigious private schools in the United States. John Knowles set his novel, A Separate Peace, in a fictional preparatory school remarkably similar to Phillips Exeter. (Courtesy Exeter Historical Society)

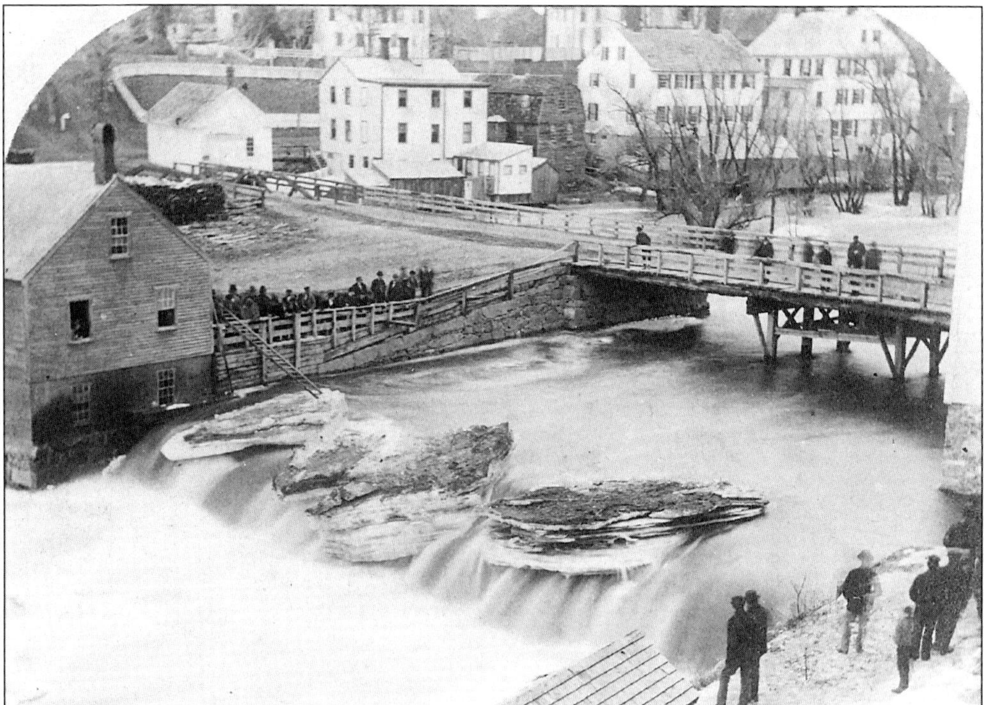

EXETER The falls of Squamscott River and String bridge about 1880. This was the site of Exeter's first mill built in 1640.

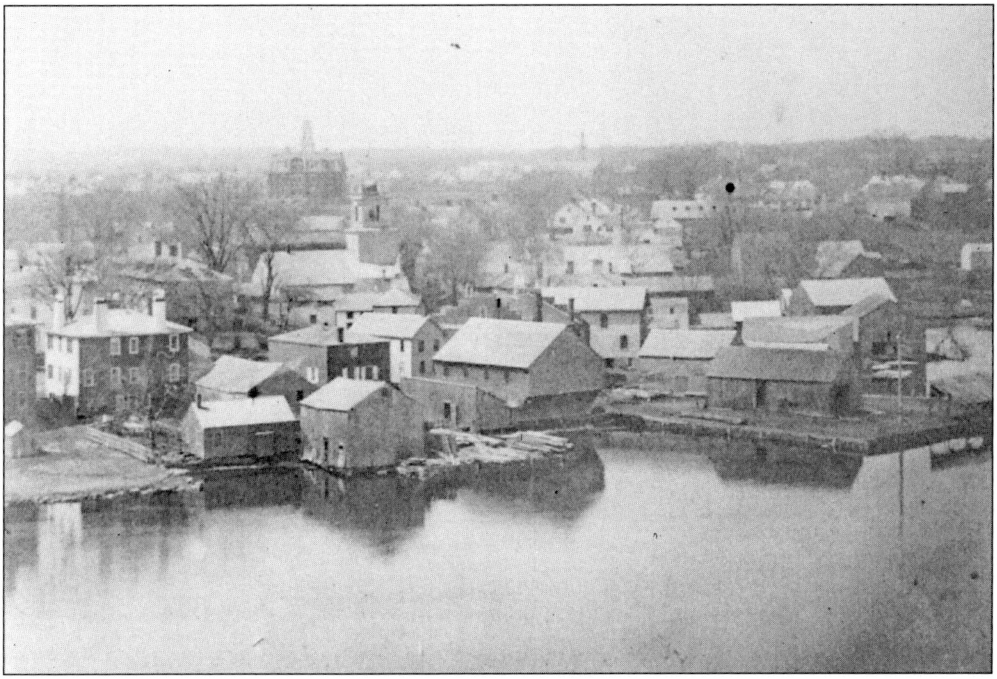

EXETER A rare view of Water Street looking toward Town Hill about 1870. Near the center of the photograph is the 1833 Water Street Baptist Church and in the distance is the Robinson Female Seminary built in 1869. (Courtesy Exeter Historical Society)

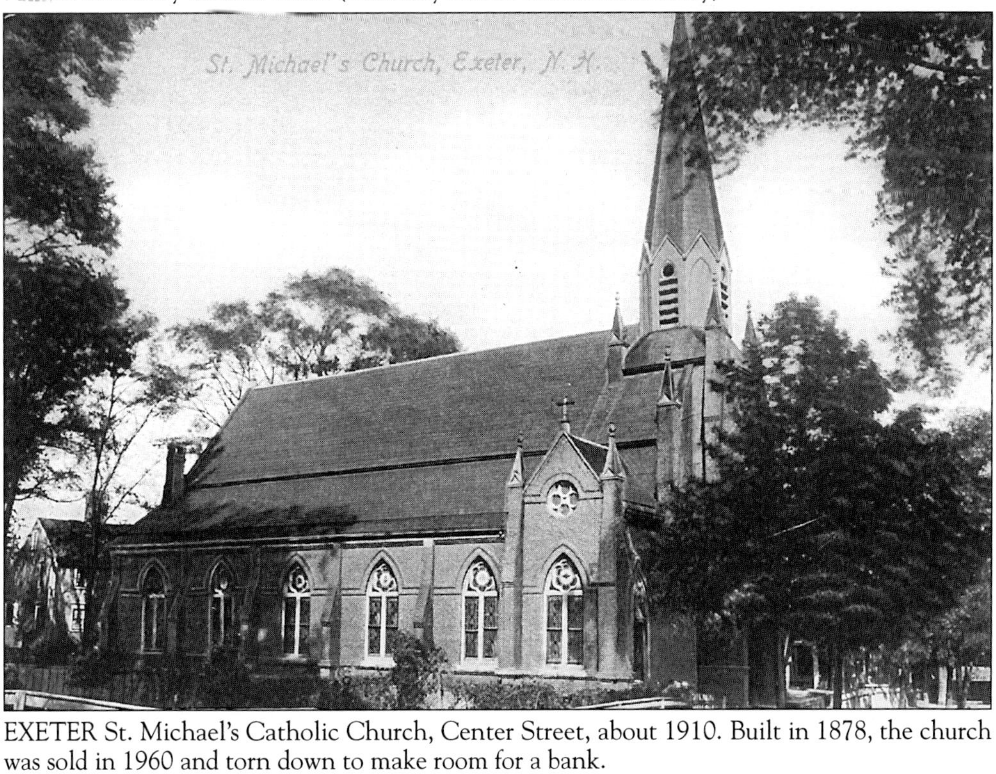

EXETER St. Michael's Catholic Church, Center Street, about 1910. Built in 1878, the church was sold in 1960 and torn down to make room for a bank.

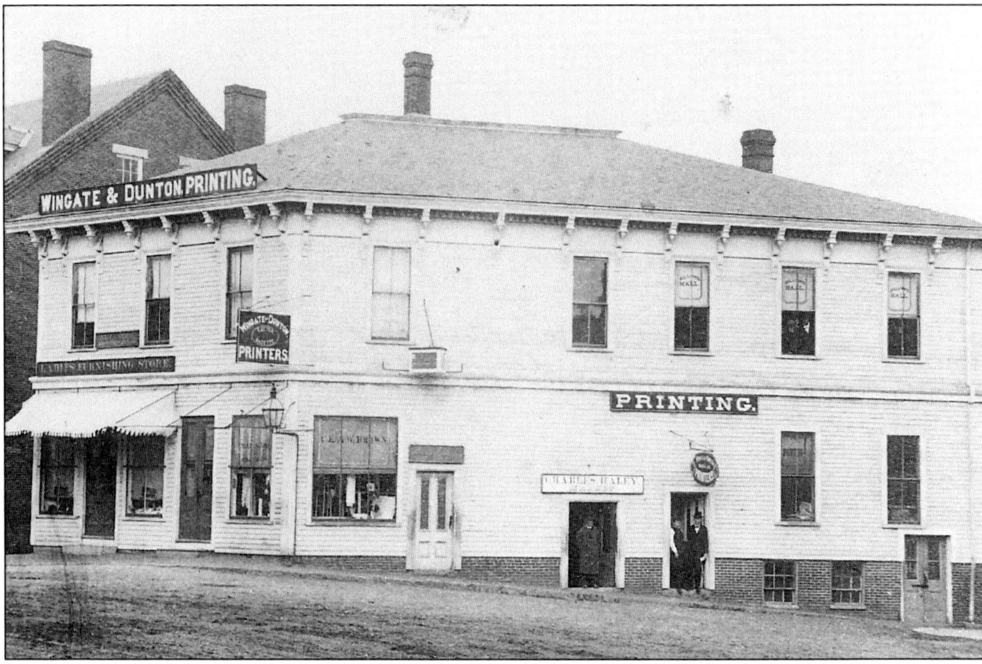

EXETER Wood's block, Water Street about 1878. Wingate and Dunton's Steam Printing business occupied the building at that time.

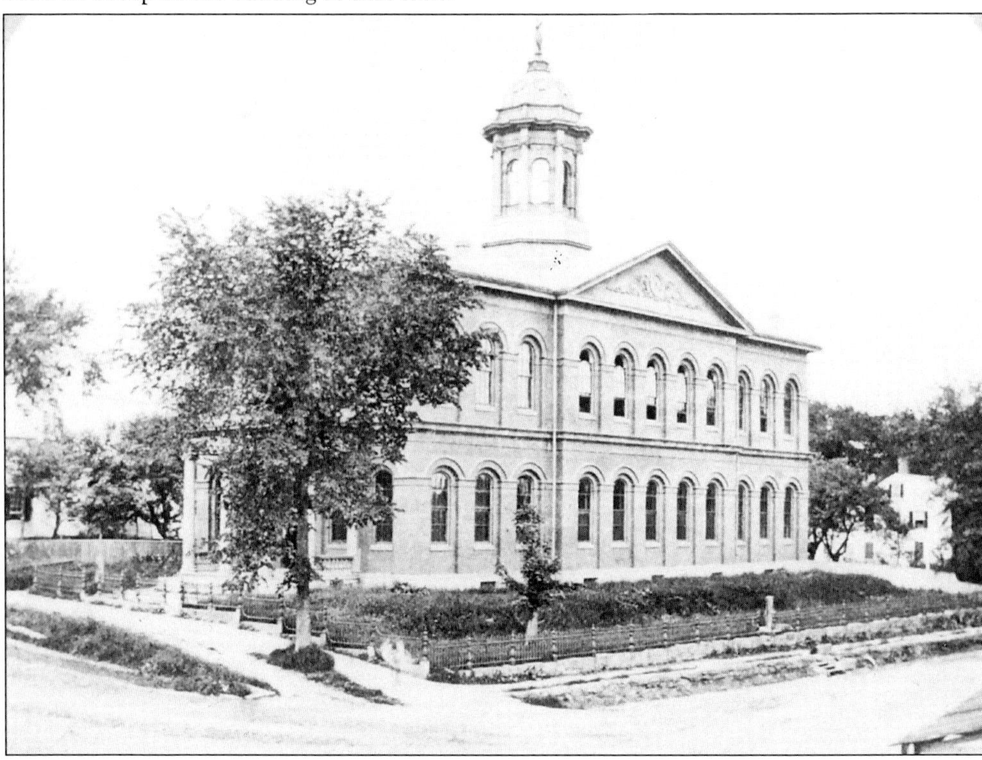

EXETER Exeter town hall built in 1855. This building is thought to be one of the most impressive examples of mid-nineteenth century architecture in New Hampshire.

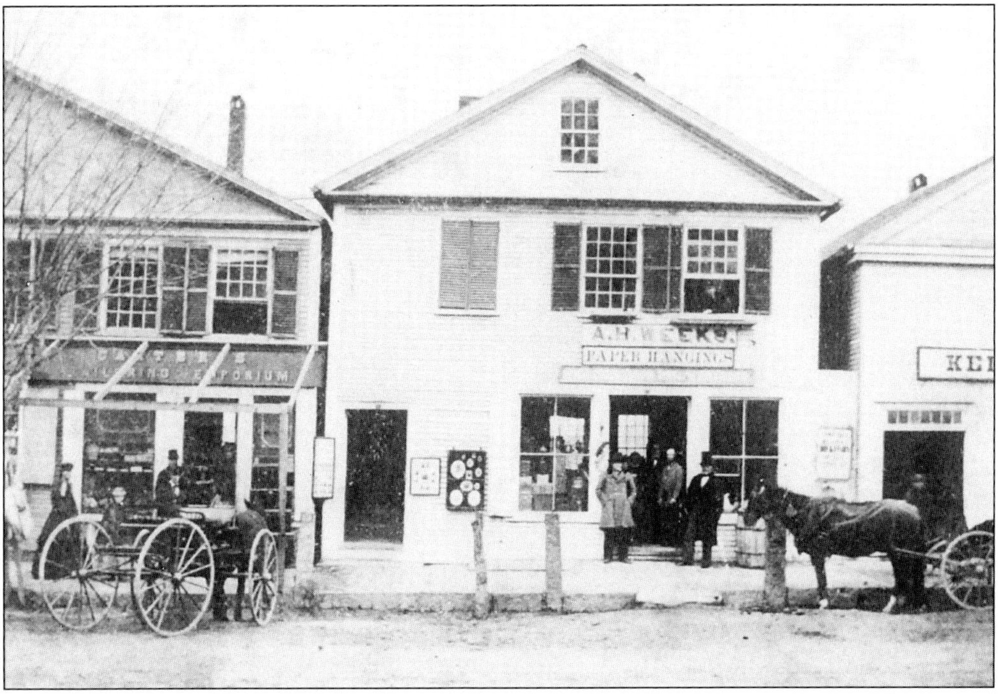

EXETER George Carter's Clothing Emporium and A.H. Weeks Paper Hangings at the time of the Civil War. Note the buckboard which was equivalent to today's pickup truck.

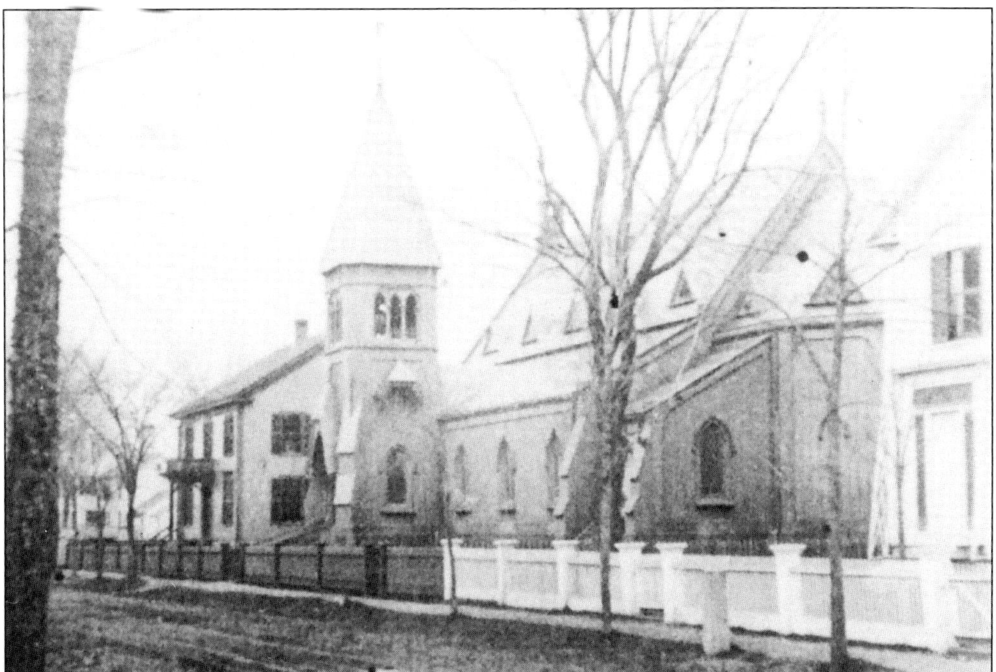

EXETER Elliot Street Episcopal Church, built in 1867 and photographed here shortly after construction. The fences in front of the houses served a number of purposes other than landscape, one of which was to slow the amount of mud thrown up from the dirt roads.

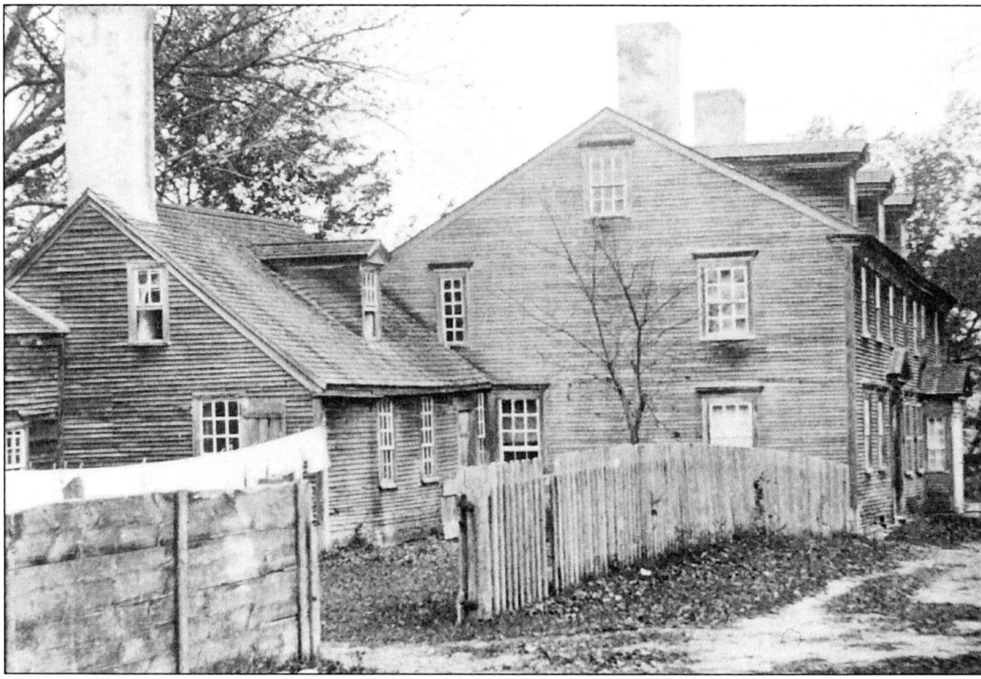

EXETER The Ladd-Gilman house, now the American Independence Museum, on Water Street about 1870. Built in 1721 and enlarged in 1747, this landmark served as the New Hampshire treasury during the Revolutionary War.

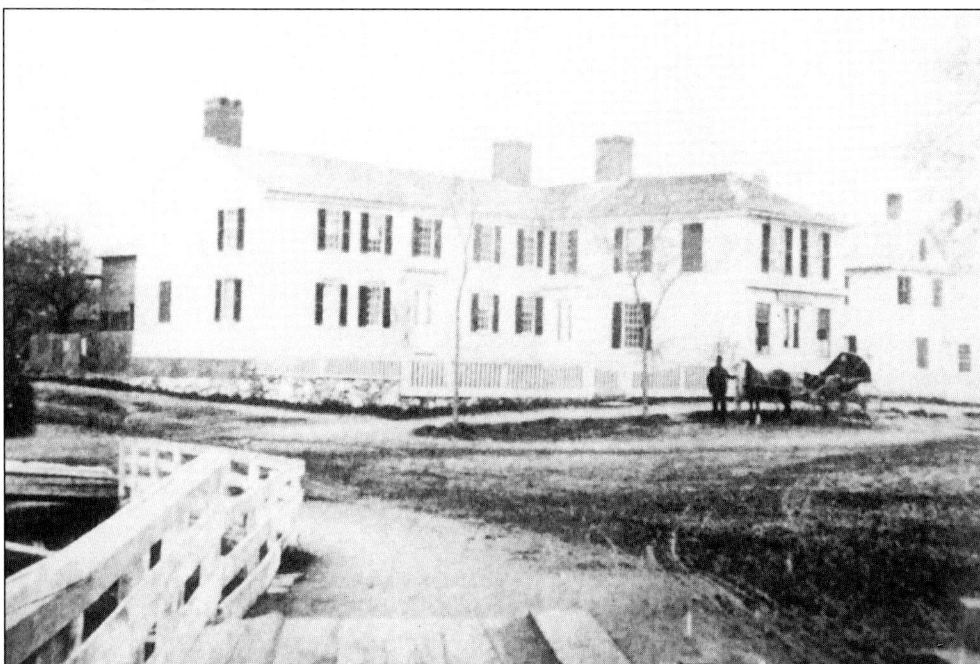

EXETER The Gilman garrison house, Water Street about 1870-75. This is one of the oldest garrison houses in New Hampshire. Built in 1675 it was one of the focal points of defense for the early settlers. (Courtesy Exeter Historical Society)

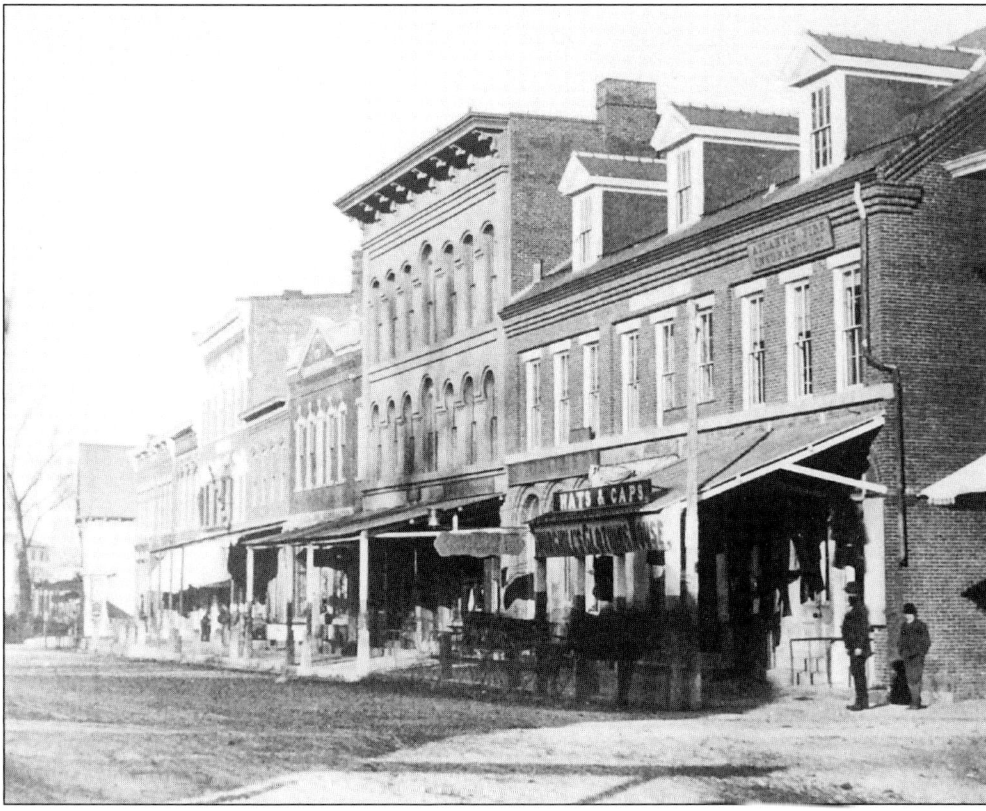

EXETER A Water Street scene showing the 1860 Janverin block in 1875. The architecture looks like something out of an old west town from the same era.

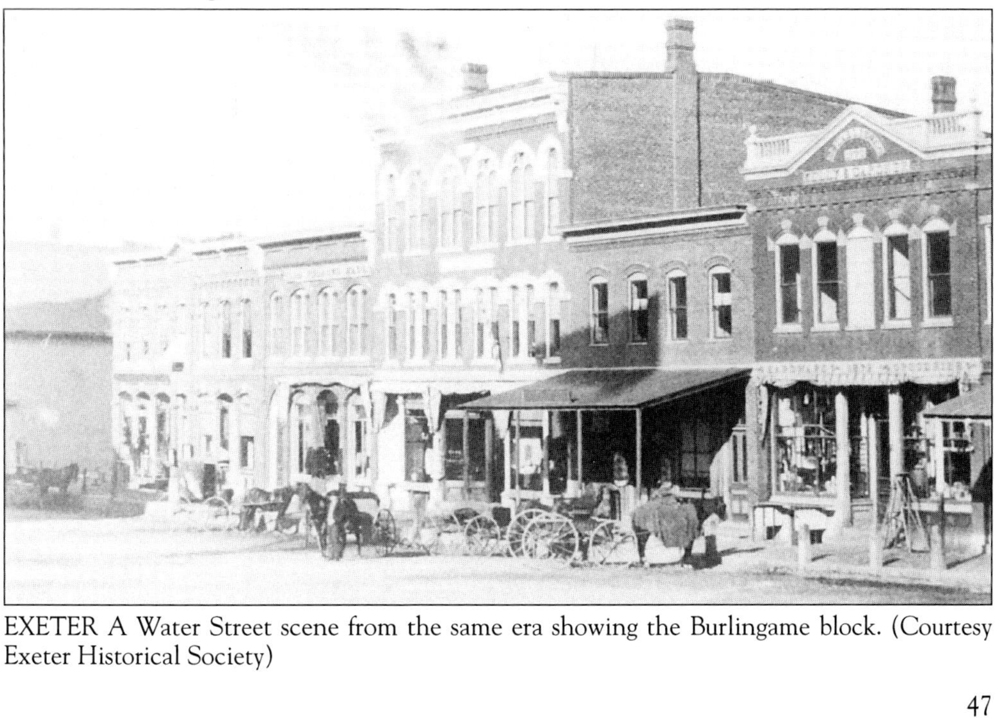

EXETER A Water Street scene from the same era showing the Burlingame block. (Courtesy Exeter Historical Society)

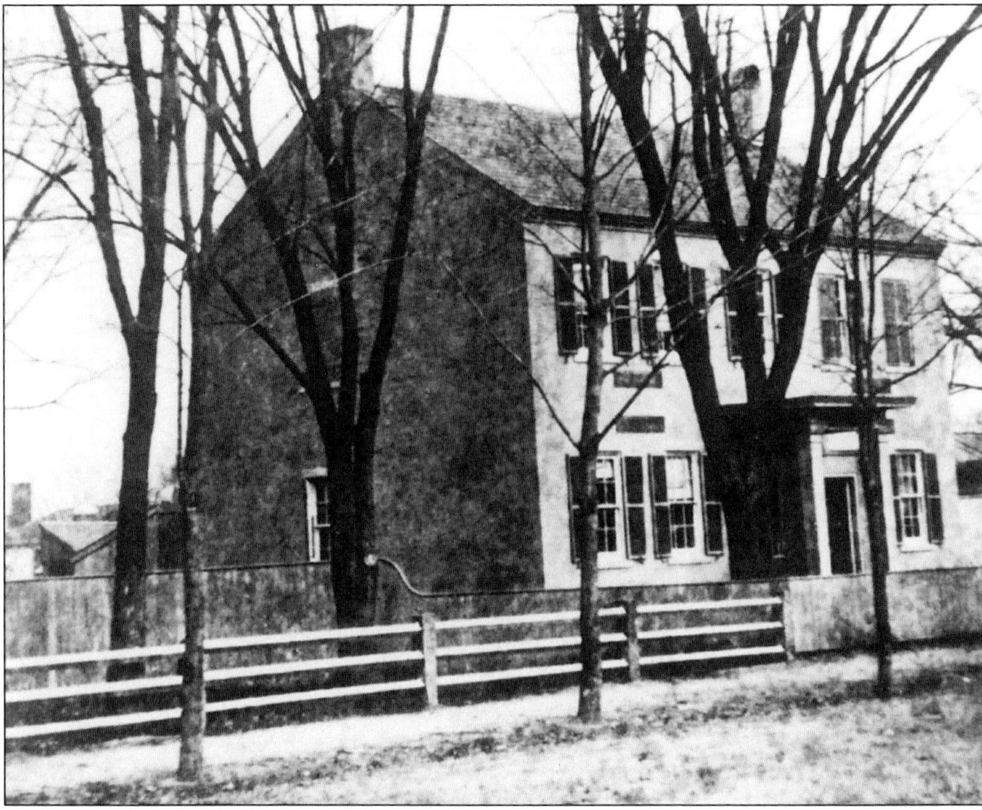

EXETER The old County Records building, Front Street about 1870-75. This building was torn down to make way for the 1894 Exeter Public Library. (Courtesy Exeter Historical Society)

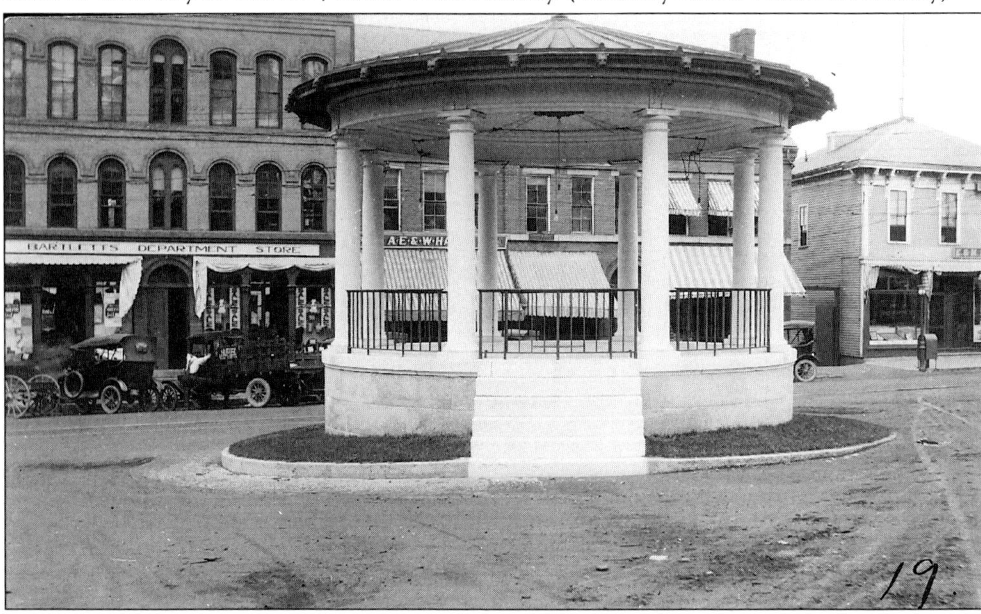

EXETER The Swasey bandstand at the corner of Water and Front Streets about 1920. This was given as a gift to the town of Exeter by Ambrose Swasey.

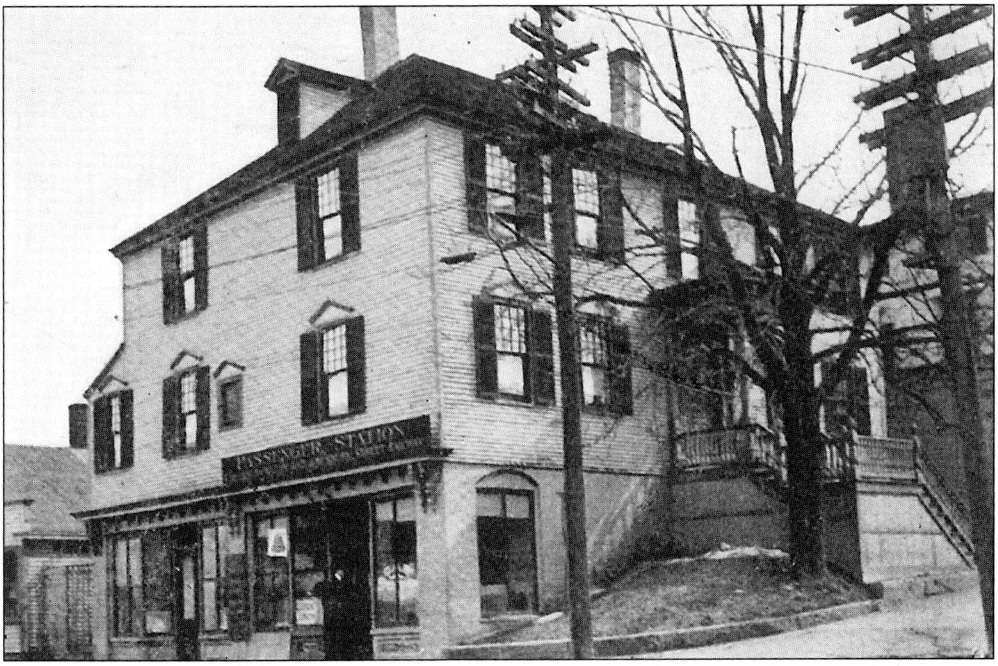

EXETER Folsom Tavern at the corner of Water and Front Streets about 1908. President George Washington ate breakfast here in 1789. Prior to being moved to Spring Street in 1929, it served as the passenger station for the Exeter and Hampton Electric trolley line.

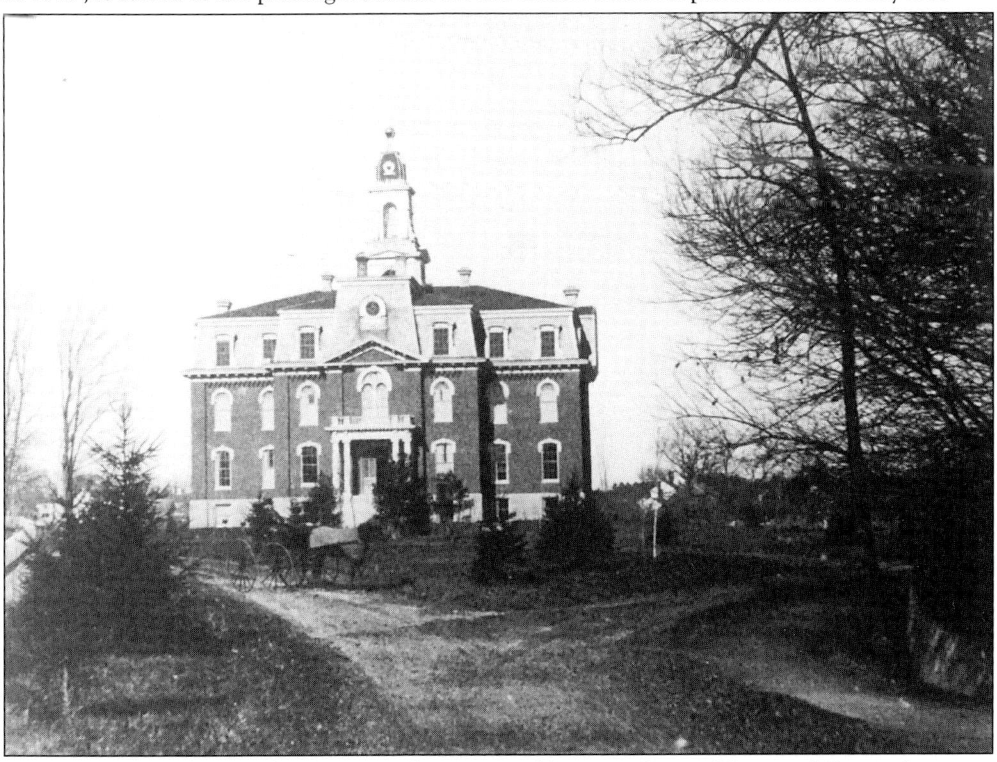

EXETER Robinson Female Seminary about 1870. (Courtesy Exeter Historical Society)

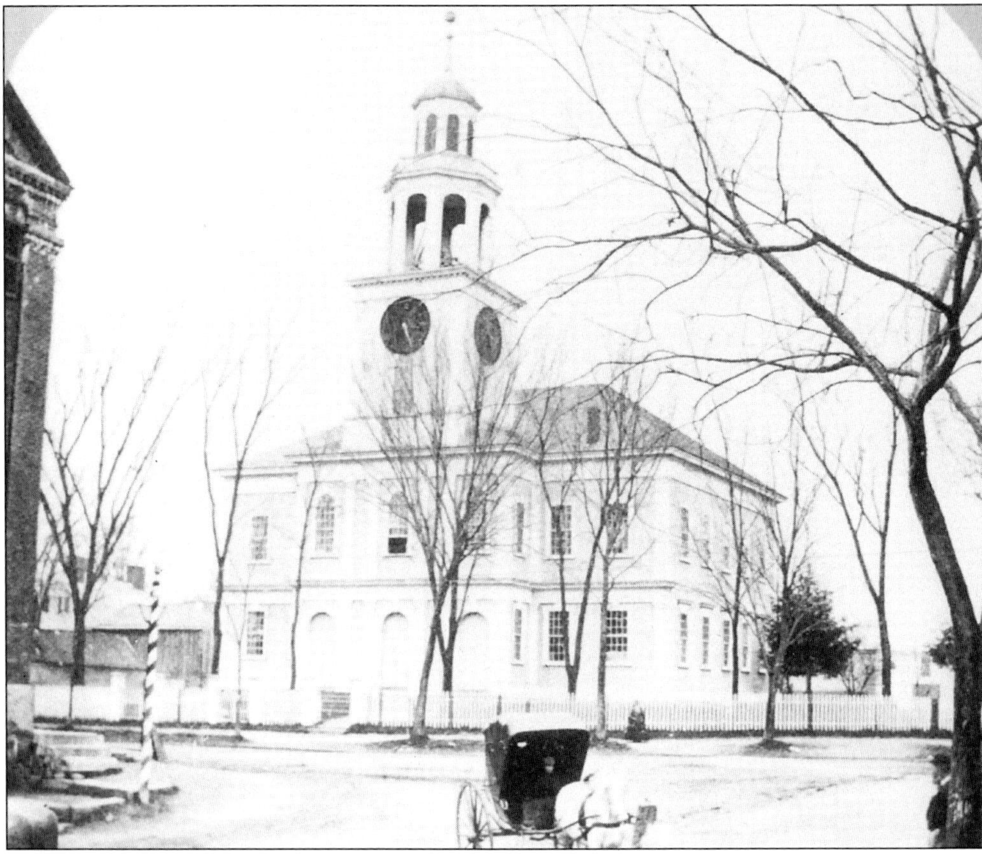

EXETER Congregational Church, Front Street about 1870. Built in 1798, it became the first hip-roof, Georgian style meeting house in New Hampshire. (Courtesy Exeter Historical Society)

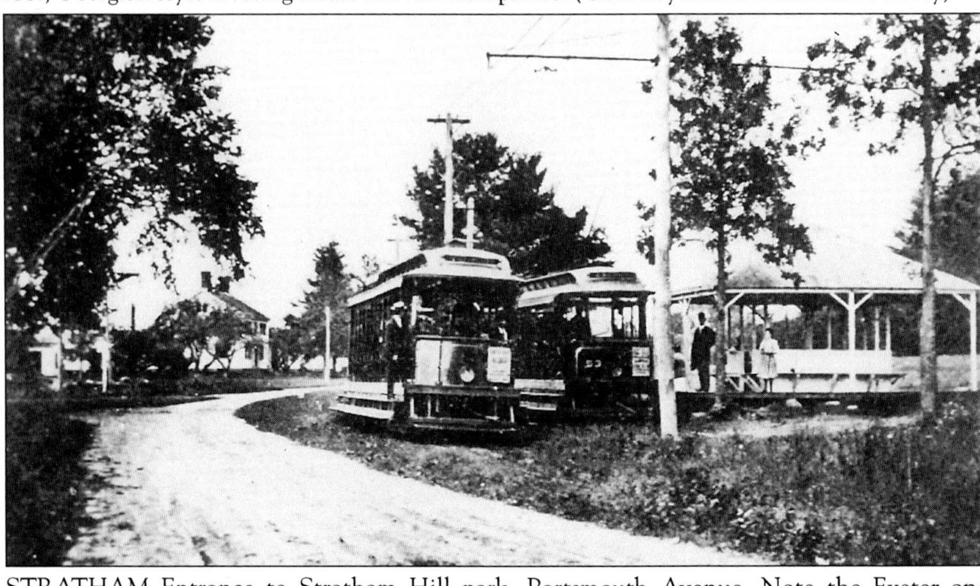

STRATHAM Entrance to Stratham Hill park, Portsmouth Avenue. Note the Exeter and Portsmouth Electric trolley cars which ran through the town from 1902 until 1913.

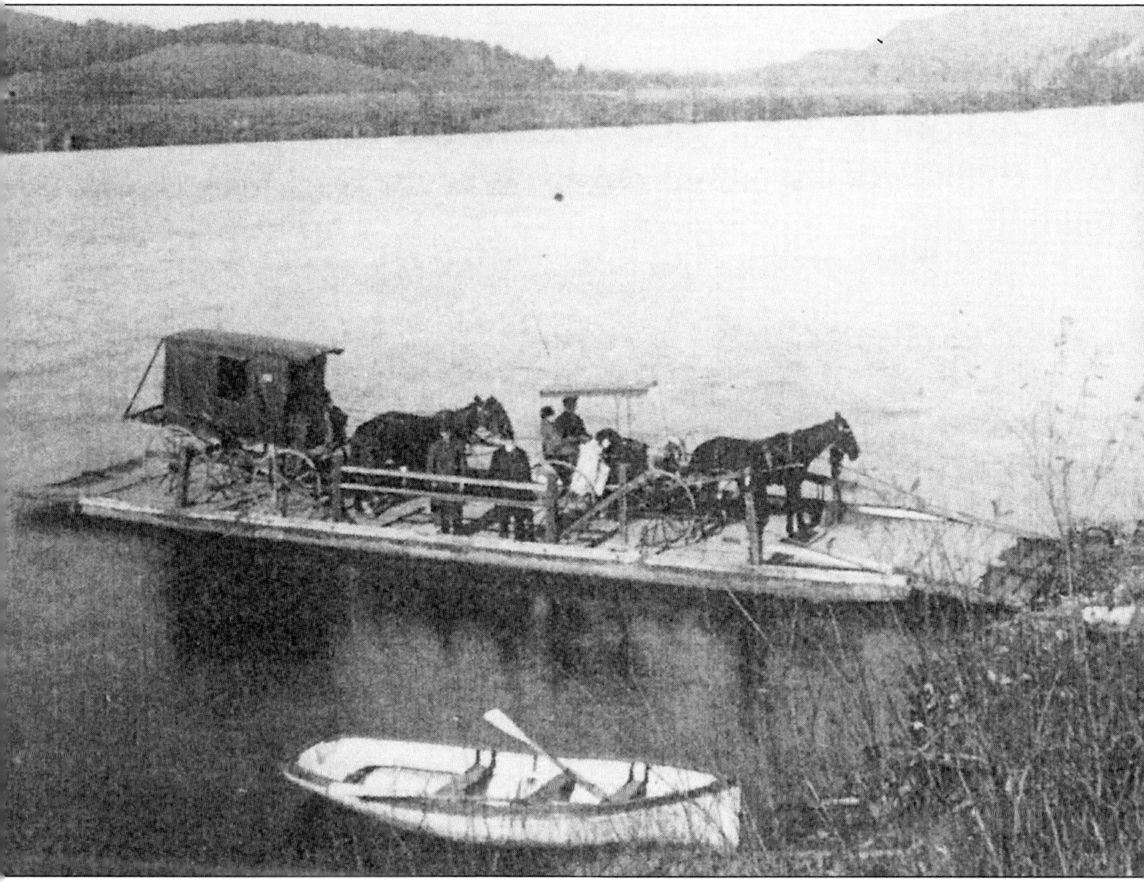

STRATHAM Ferrying across the Squamscott River about 1900.

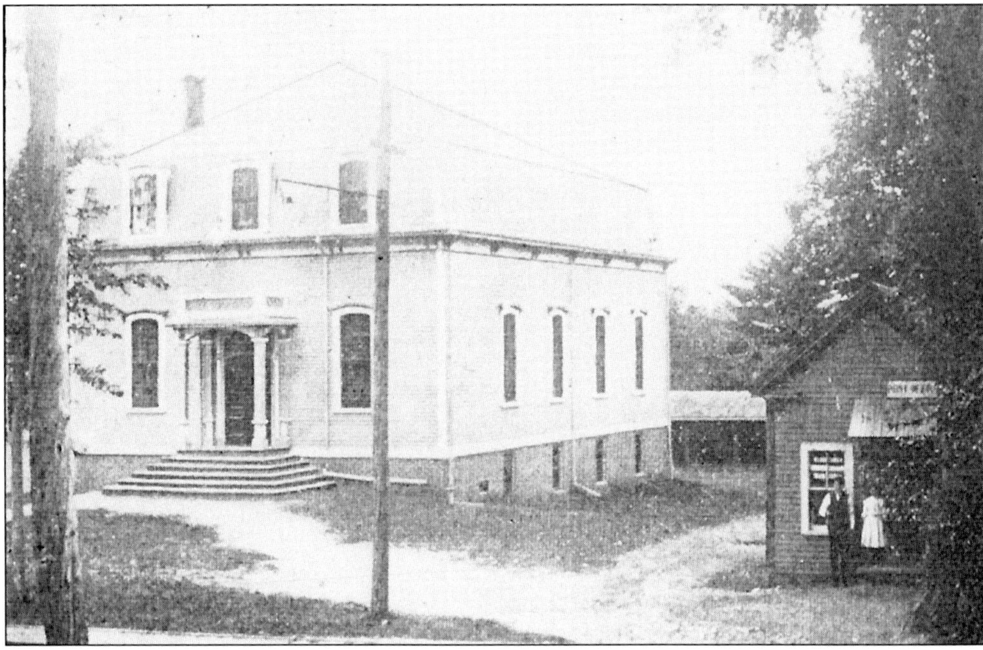

STRATHAM Town hall built in 1877 and the tiny post office on Portsmouth Avenue about 1916.

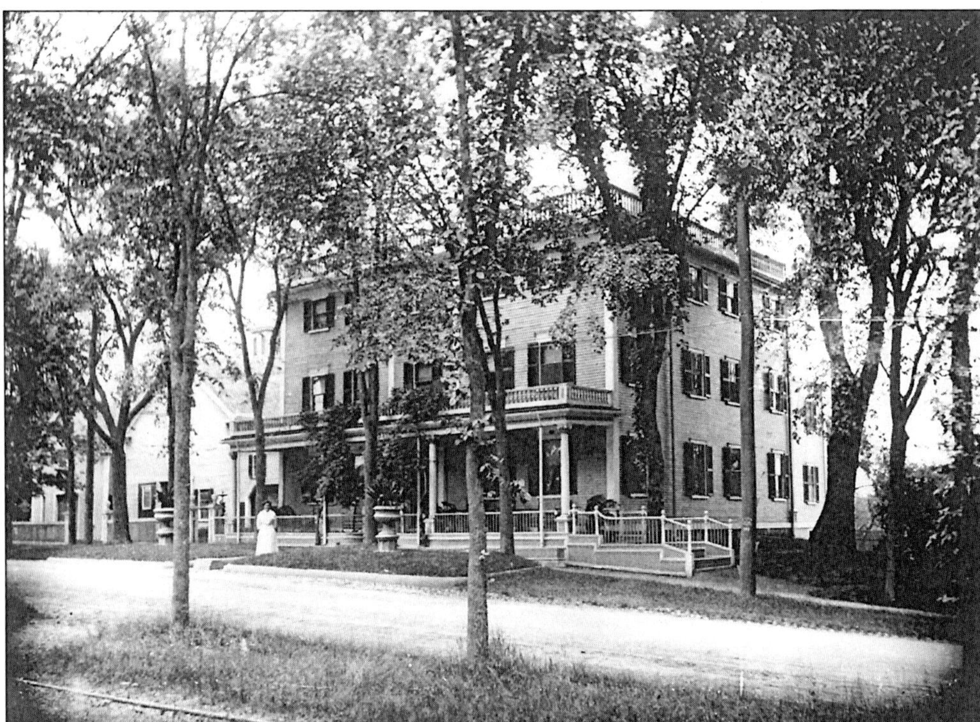

GREENLAND Folsom Tavern, built in 1810, Route 151 and Portsmouth Avenue. It is pictured here in 1905 when it was the old Frink mansion overlooking Greenland Parade. (Courtesy Paul F. Hughes, Jr.)

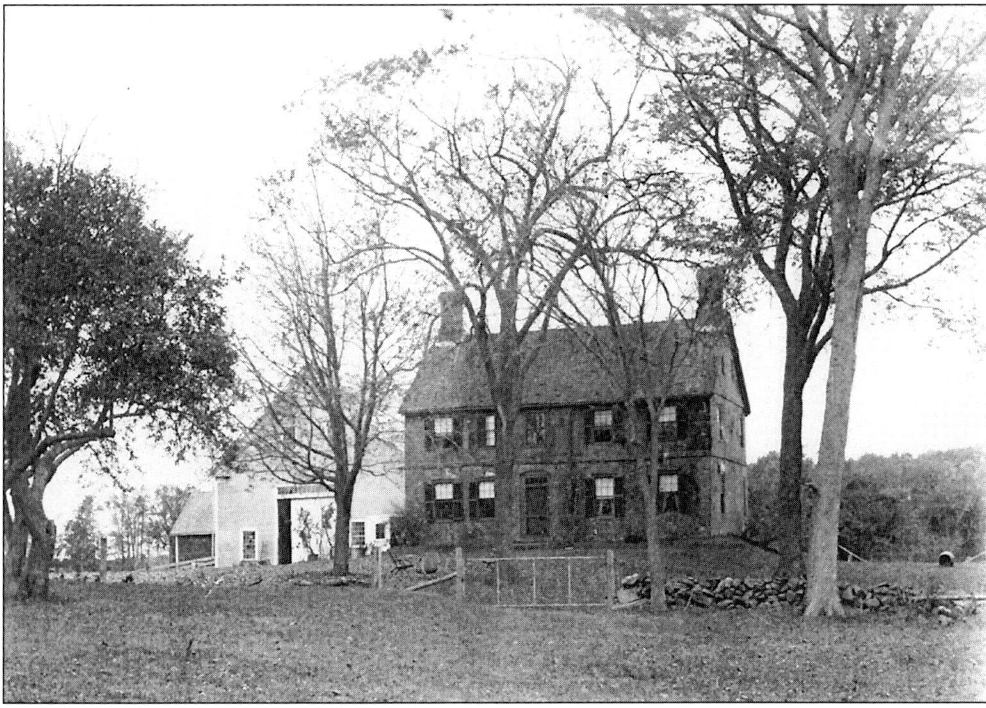

GREENLAND Weeks Brick house, Route 101, about 1890. Built around 1706, this is the oldest known brick house in New Hampshire. The outbuildings burned in 1938. (Courtesy Paul F. Hughes, Jr.)

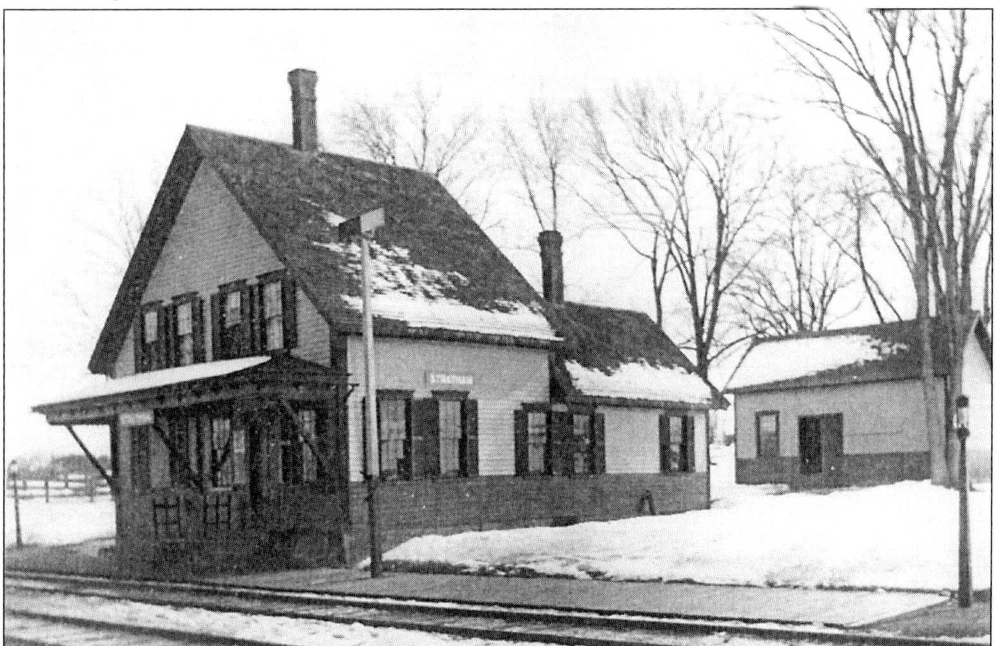

GREENLAND Stratham depot on the Portsmouth and Concord railroad about 1900. This depot is just over the line in Greenland and was built in 1870. (Courtesy Paul F. Hughes, Jr.)

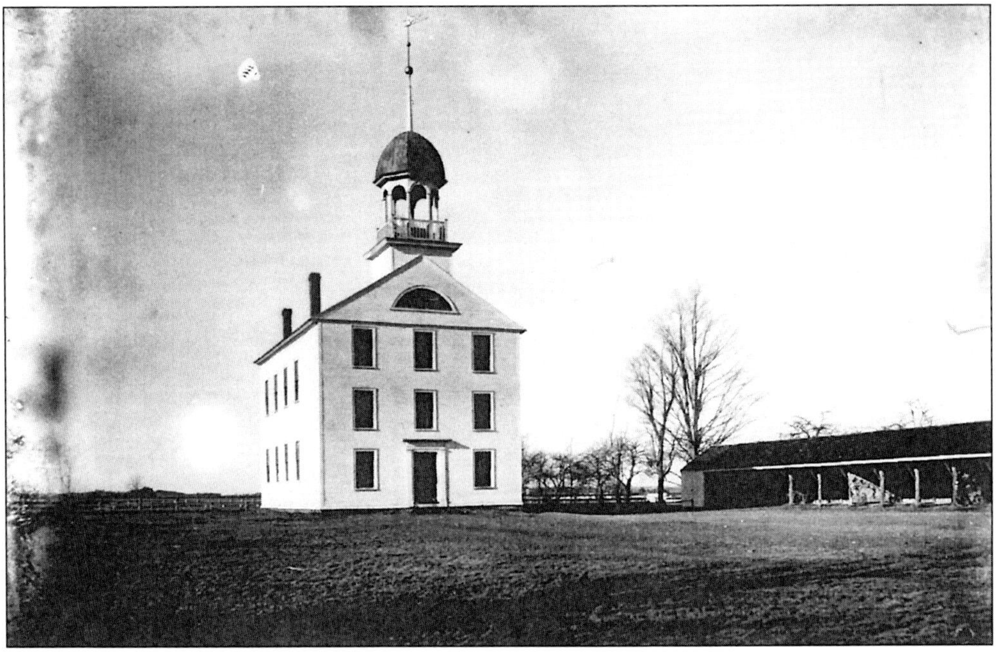

GREENLAND Brackett Academy was built in 1825 and burnt 1919. Note the horse shed on the right. This photograph was taken about 1900. (Courtesy Paul F. Hughes, Jr.)

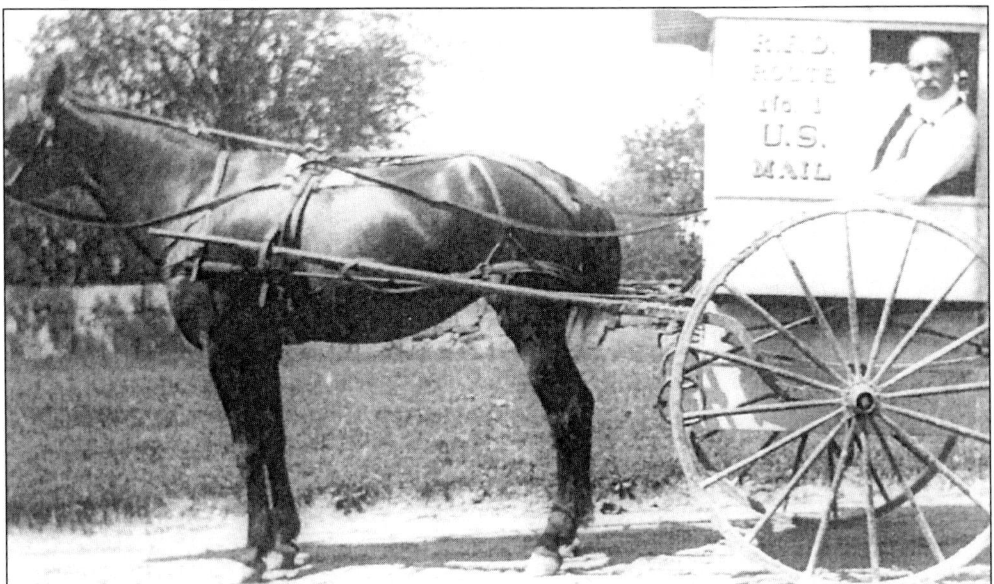

GREENLAND George W. Lord was the rural mail carrier from 1908 to 1925. This photograph is dated 10 May 1908. By the turn of the century the Post Office Department in the United States was one of the most powerful government agencies after the military. Postmasters were political appointments. Many towns had two individuals, one Republican, one Democrat, who alternated in the position depending upon the political party in power.

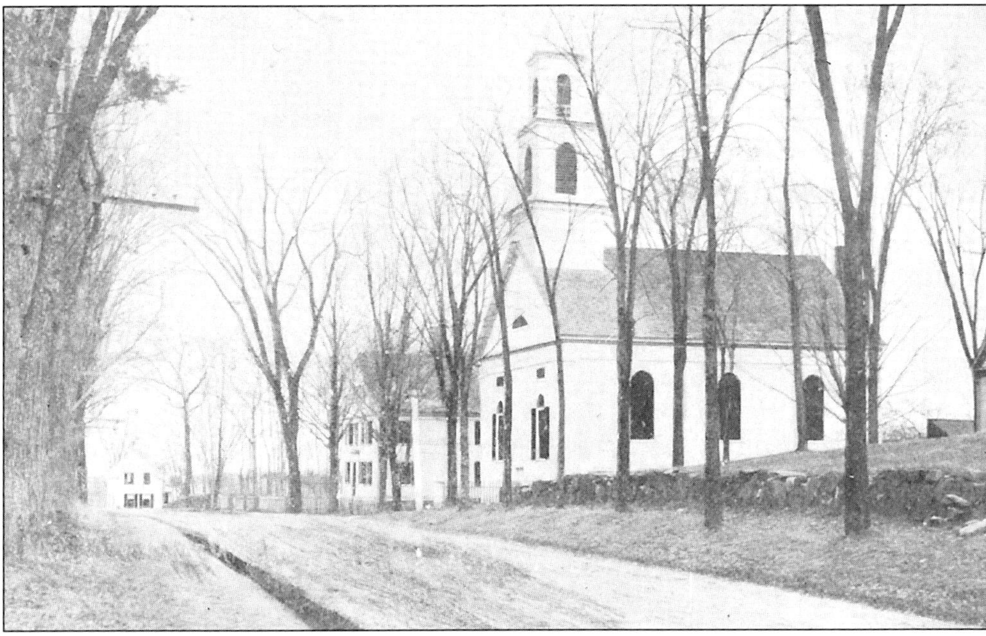

NEWFIELDS The Methodist Episcopal Church, Main Street, about 1911. The building burned in 1922.

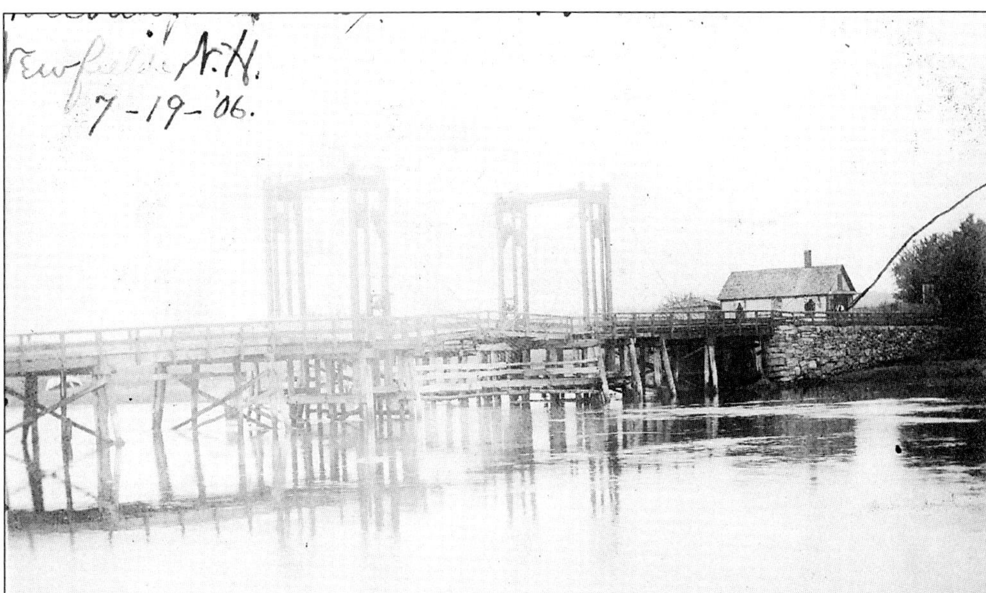

NEWFIELDS The first New Hampshire toll bridge was built about 1775 across the Squamscott River. It became a toll bridge in 1792.

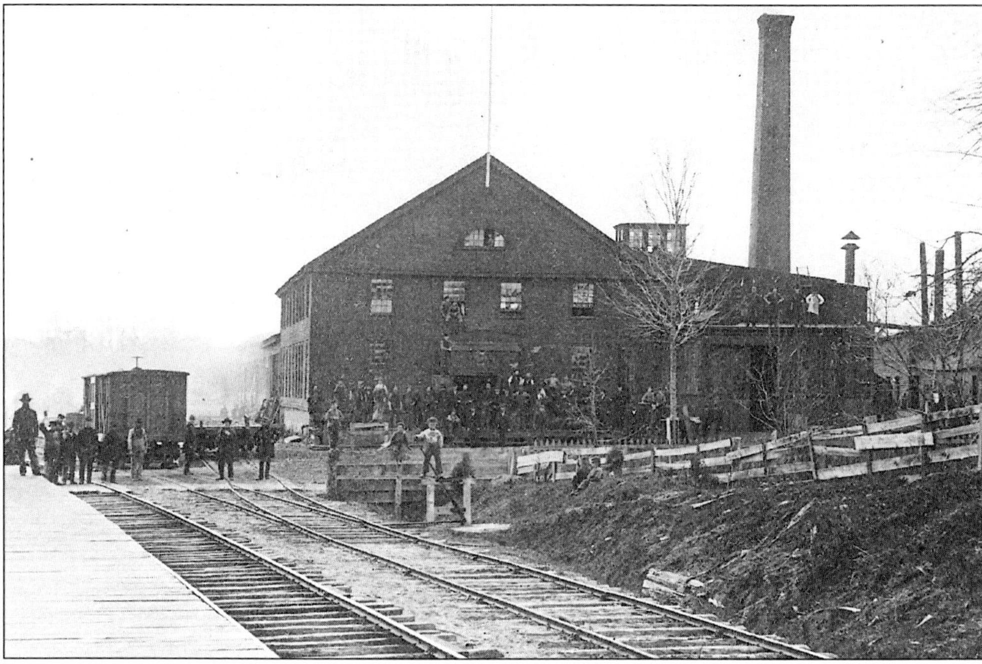

NEWFIELDS The Squamscott Machine Company was established in 1846. It produced iron castings for cotton and woolen mills. It was extremely successful throughout much of the nineteenth century, closing in 1893. The photograph in about 1875.

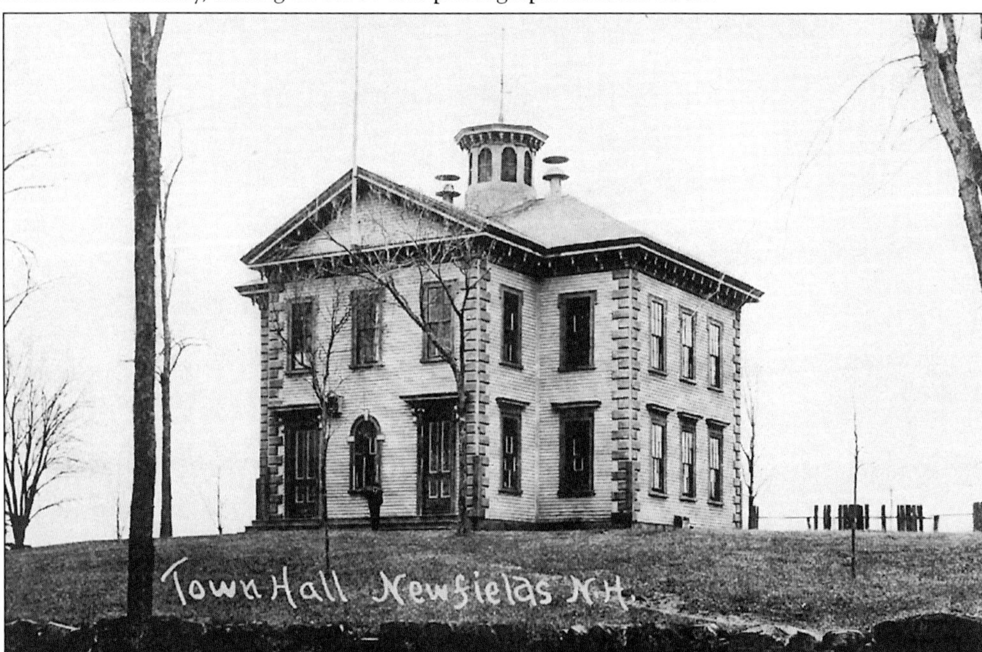

NEWFIELDS Newfields town hall and school, built 1854, and burned in 1907. The rash of buildings which burned between the Civil War and the First World War was due in large part to heating and lighting needs of the population. The result was often unsafe practices in public buildings.

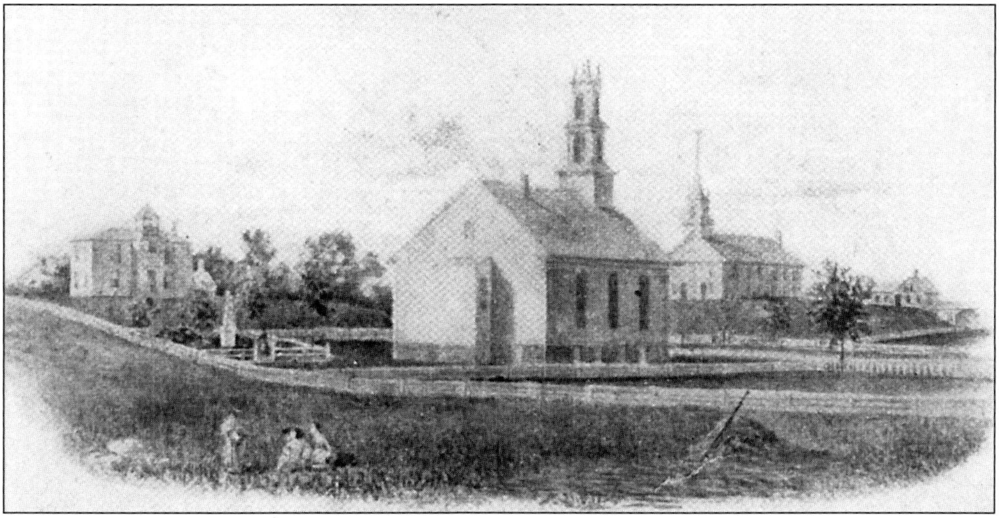

NEWFIELDS From left to right this photograph shows the Franklin Academy, built in 1835, the Methodist Episcopal Church, built in 1837, and the Newmarket Wesleyan Methodist Academy, built in 1817 and the first of its type in New England.

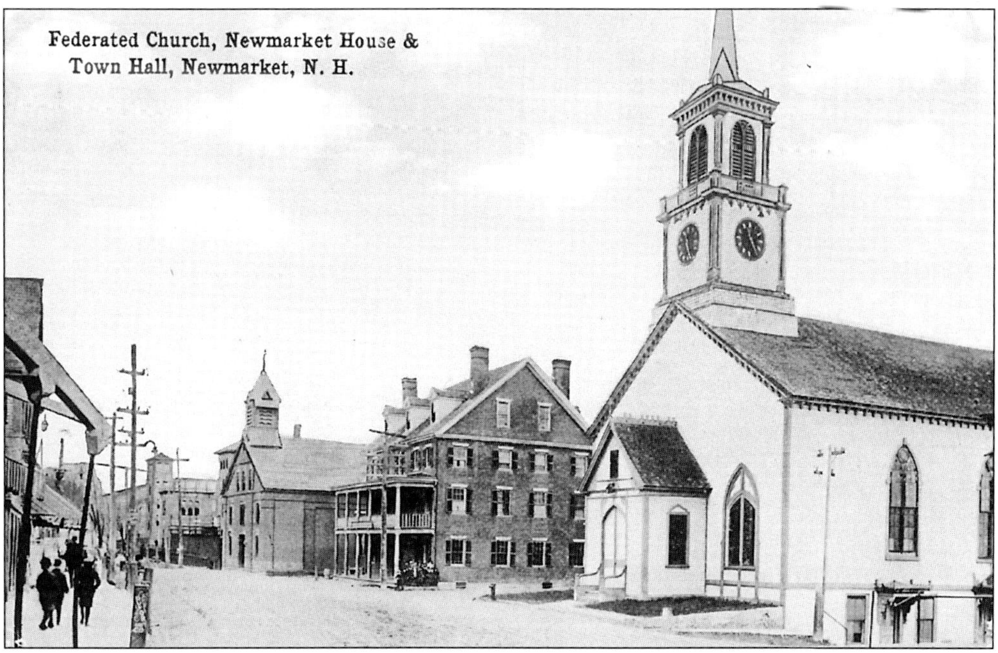

NEWMARKET A view of the town center about 1905. The Federated Congregational Church was built in 1828 and the Newmarket House in 1847. The town hall which no longer stands was built in 1847.

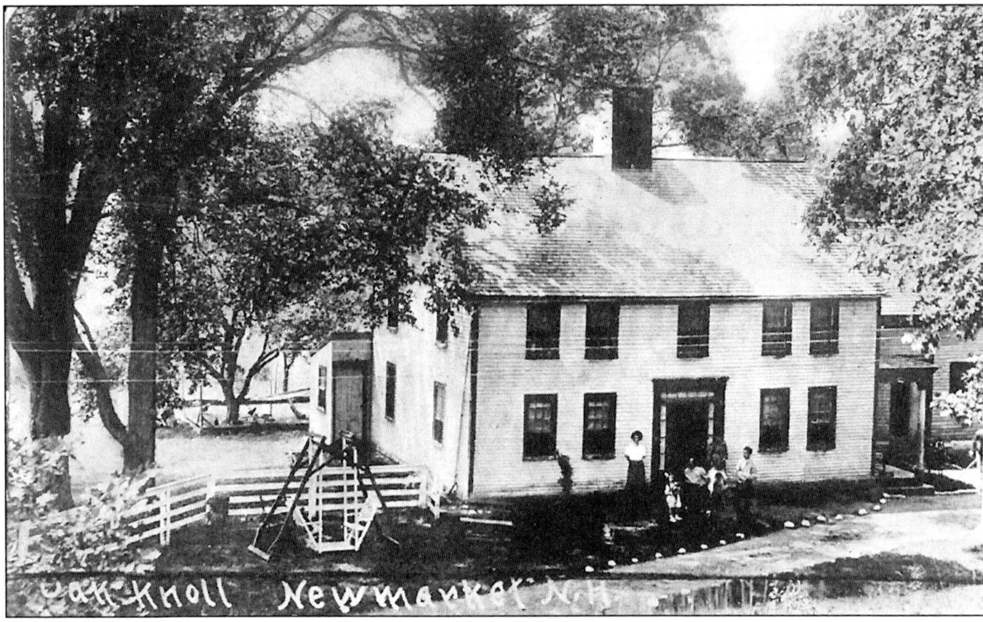

NEWMARKET It was a popular custom around the turn of the century to give place names to old farm houses. This is Oak Knoll about 1910. Note the swing in the front yard.

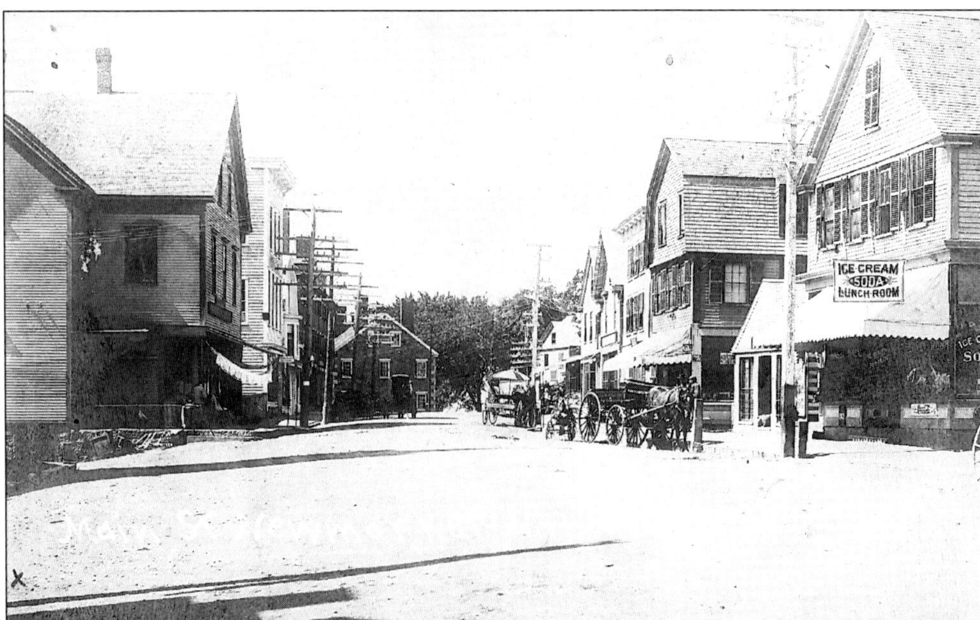

NEWMARKET Bustling downtown Newmarket about 1908. The main street is still unpaved. To cut dust the main streets were often watered down in the summer. In the winter snow was removed either by shoveling or rolled flat by horse-drawn apparatuses.

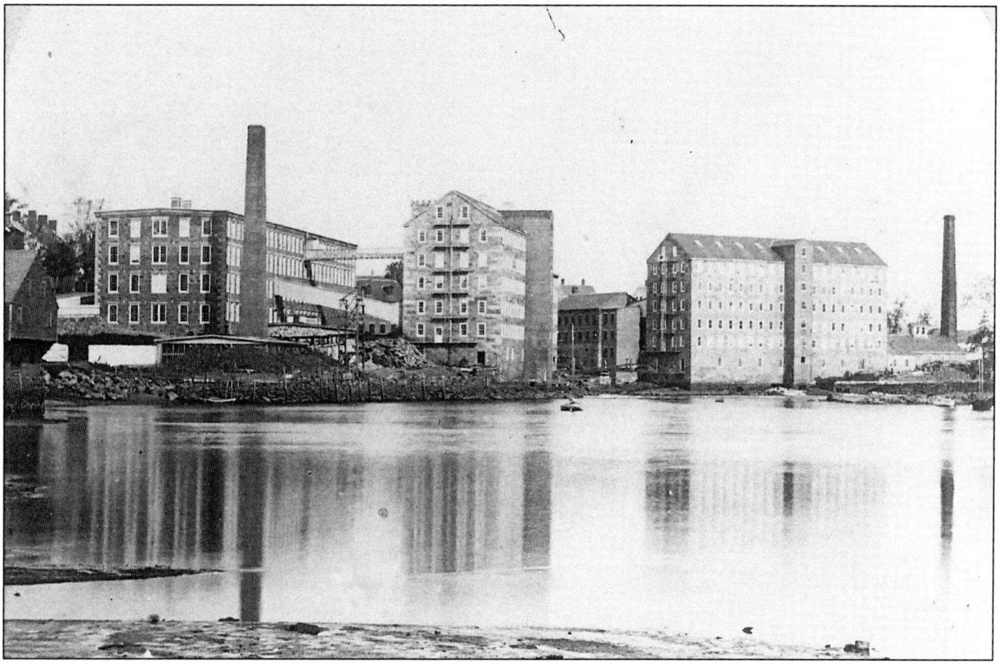

NEWMARKET The Newmarket Manufacturing Company stone mill buildings. Built in the mid-1820s this is how they looked in the 1880s as viewed from "the Flats".

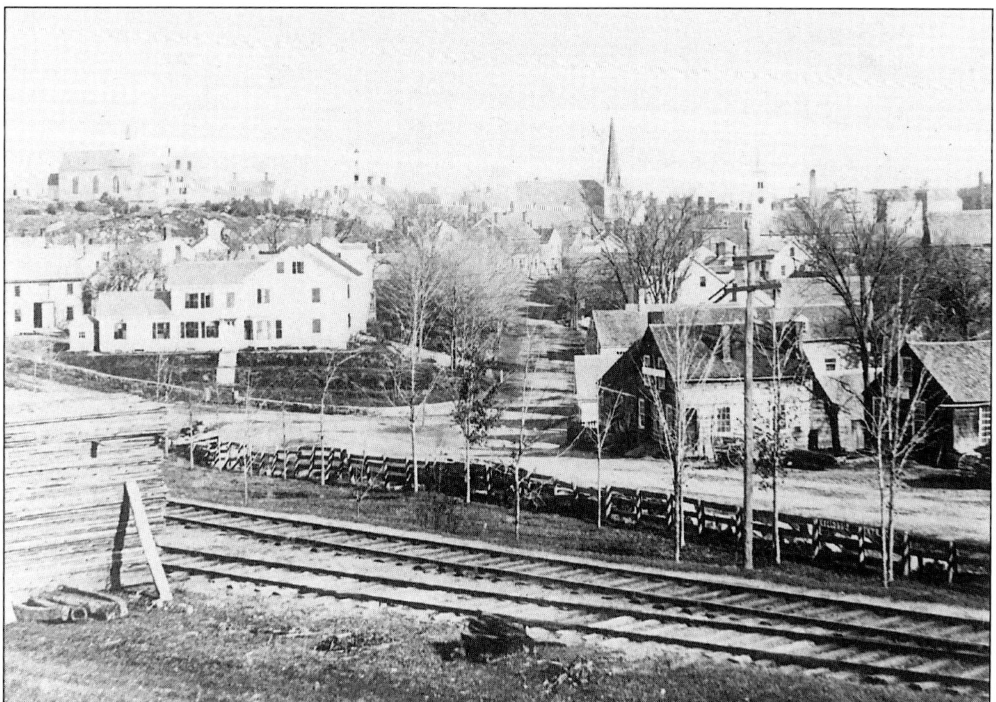

NEWMARKET View of Newmarket Village from the railroad crossing about 1885. By the mid-1880s, Newmarket citizens could ride the train to Boston in considerable comfort.

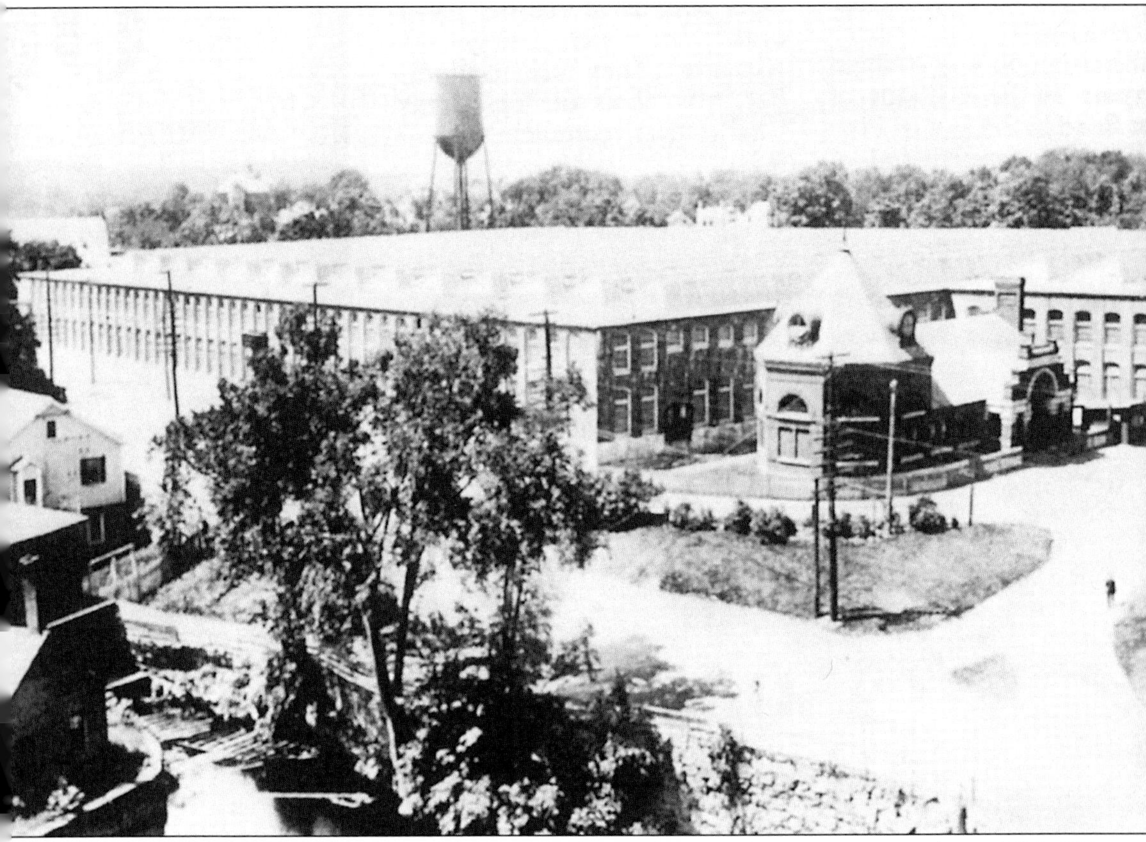

NEWMARKET. The Newmarket Manufacturing Company's weaving room about 1925. This was the largest single room manufacturing building in the world. It has since disappeared with the exception of the circular portion which is now the Newmarket town library.

Three

Southern Rockingham County

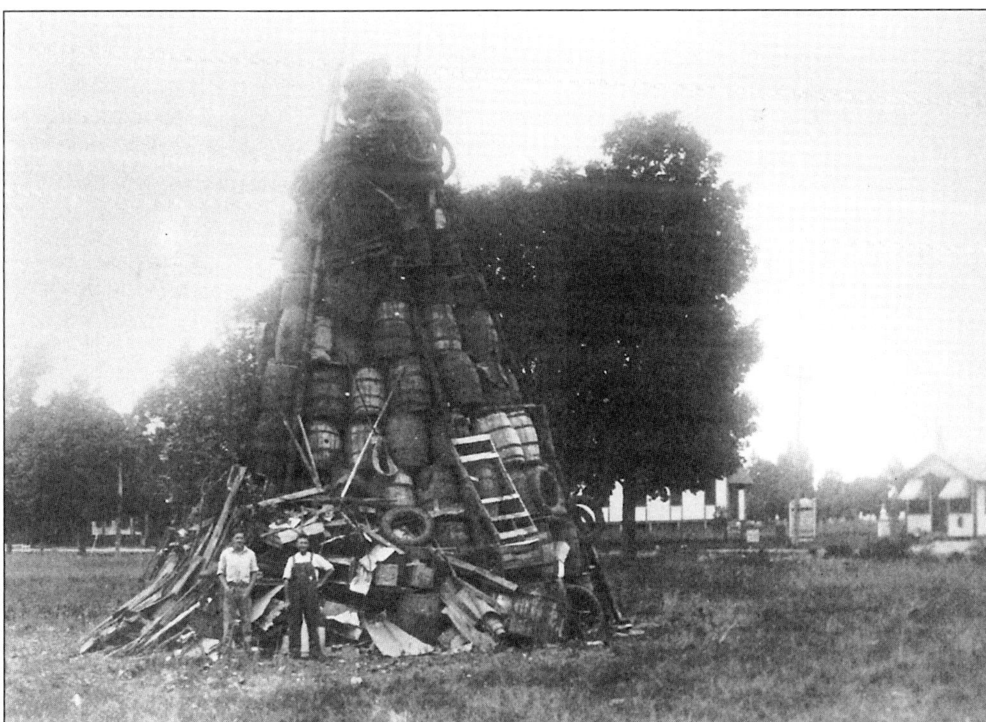

KINGSTON A Fourth of July bonfire on Kingston Plains in 1936. Such fires, made up primarily from wooden barrels and an occasional scavenged outhouse, were common prior to the Second World War.

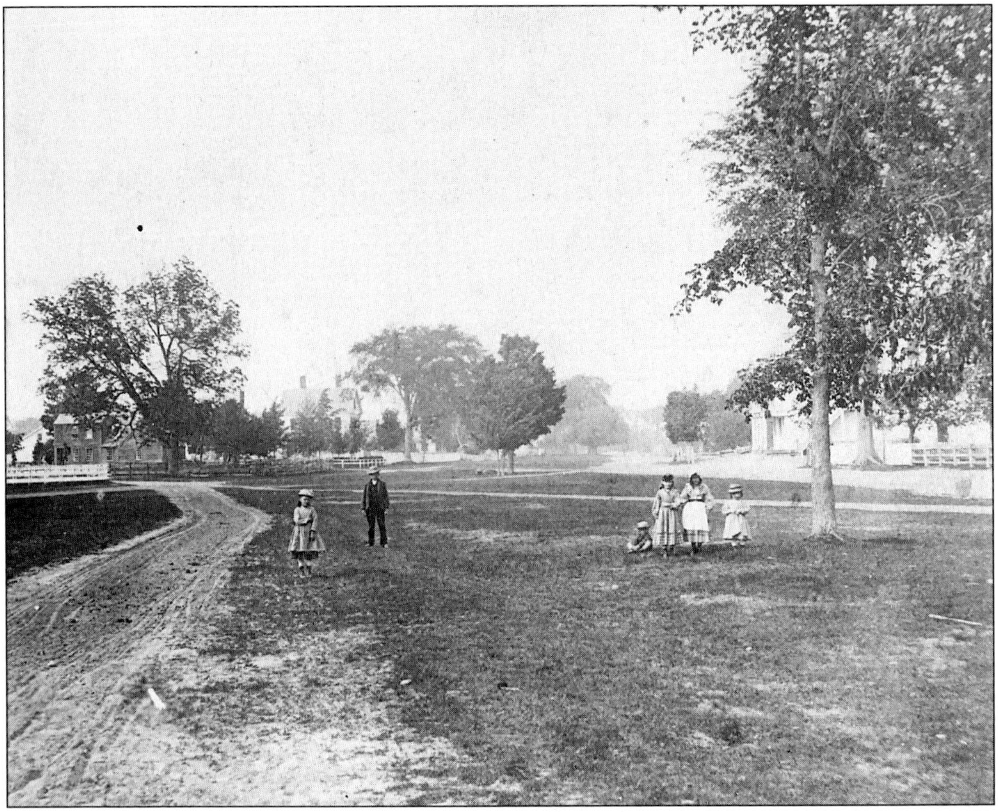

KINGSTON A view of the north end of Kingston Plains about 1870-75.

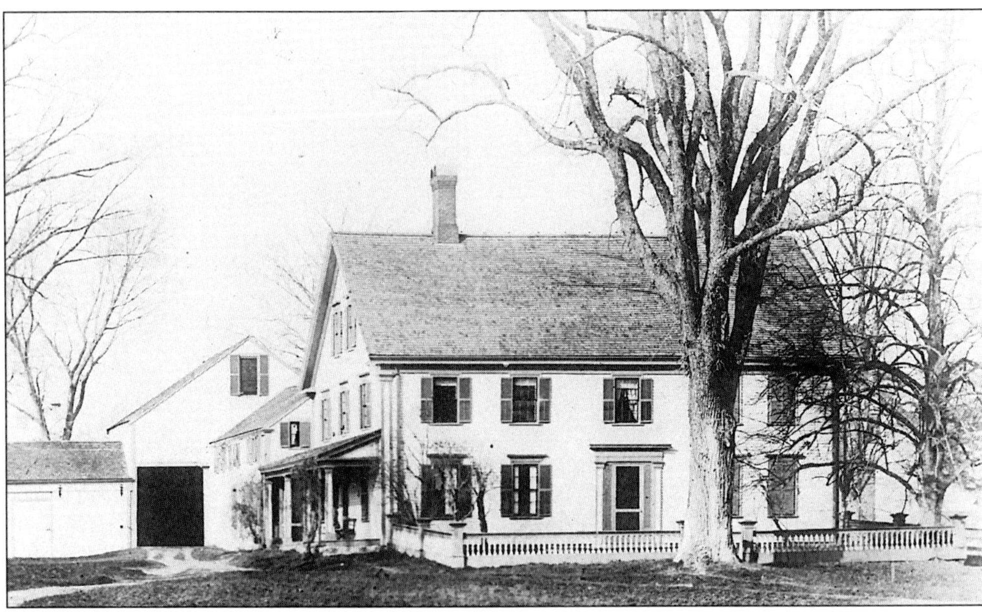

KINGSTON The Dr. Josiah Bartlett house on Route 111. Bartlett was a signer of the Declaration of Independence. The house, which was built in 1774, is still occupied by his descendants.

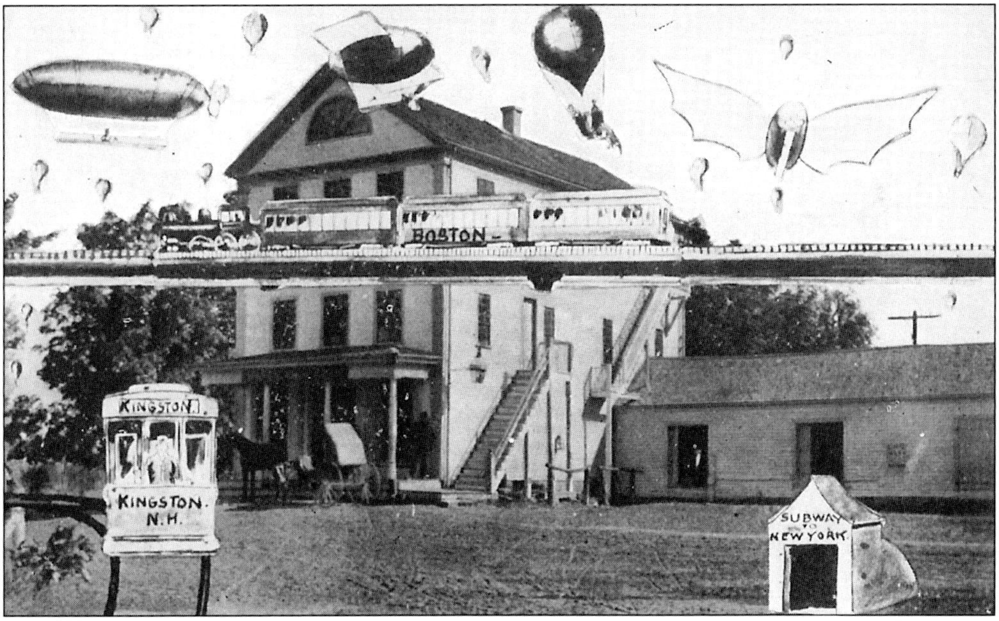

KINGSTON A postcard impression of what the future view of Kingston might be with the Peaslee store as backdrop. It is interesting that the future vision saw dirigibles rather than jet planes as the wave of the future.

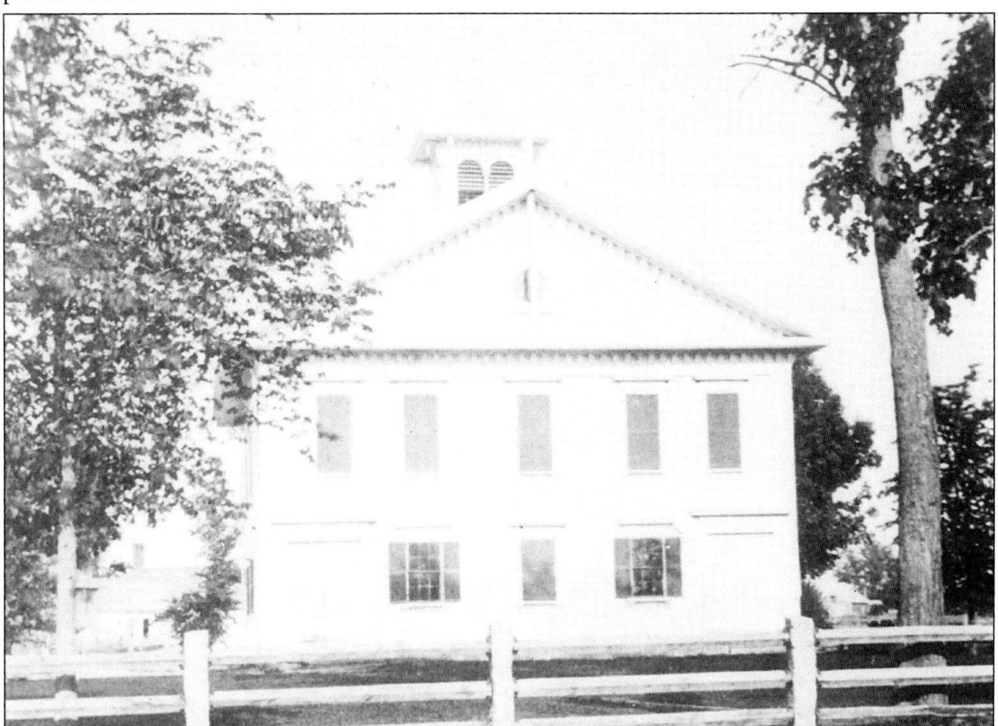
KINGSTON The Kingston Academy built in 1819 stood where the present town hall now stands on Route 111. It ceased operation as an academy about 1900 and was destroyed by fire in 1928. (Courtesy of Ruth R. Alberts)

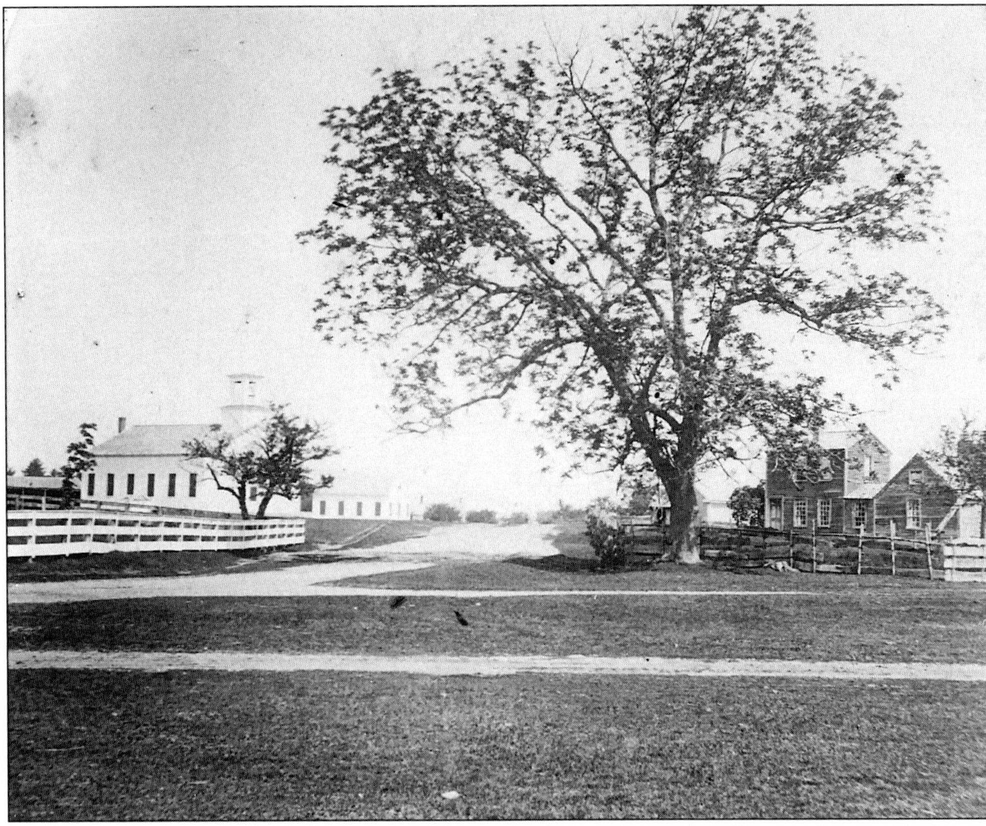

KINGSTON The 1825 Congregational Church and the Plains schoolhouse about 1870.

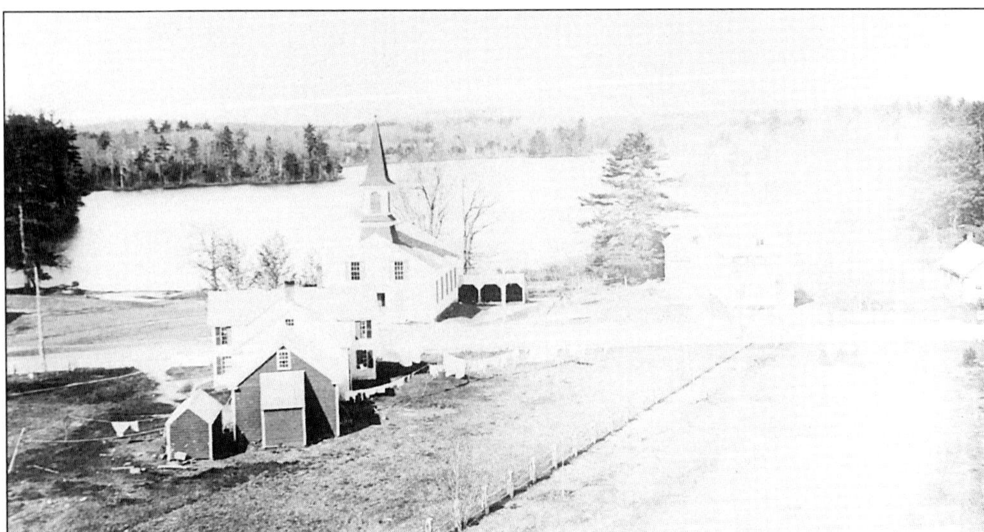

KINGSTON The Methodist Church on Church Street about 1890. The church was built in 1846 and the steeple added in 1878. Little Pond, now Greenwood Pond, is behind the church which now serves as a day care center.

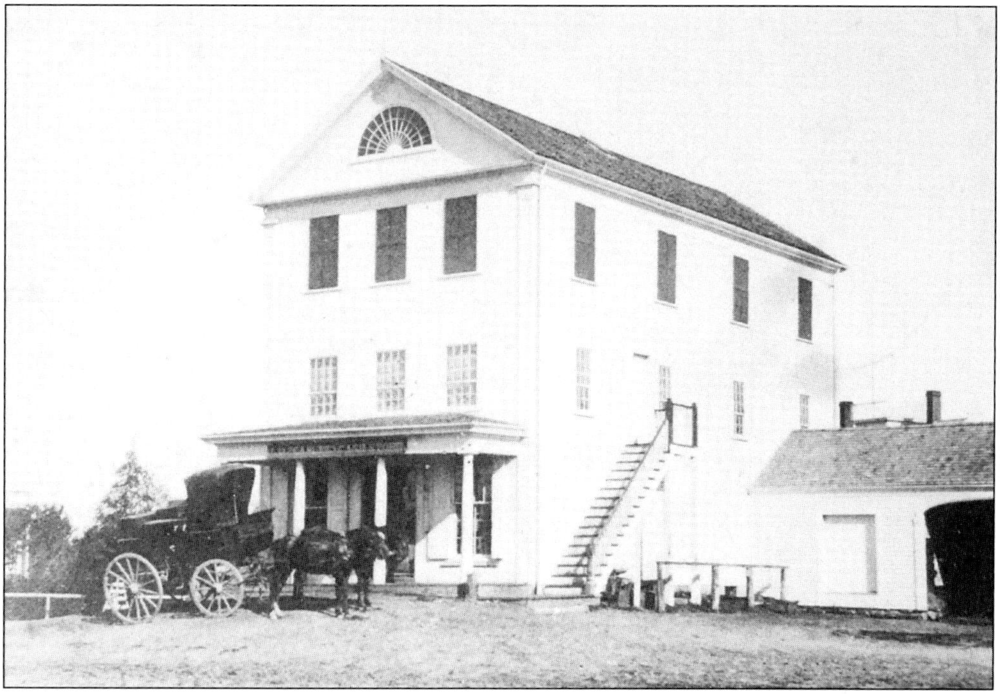

KINGSTON The Luther D. Peaslee store and Masonic hall, Route 111 about 1870-75. The store eventually became the Bakie Brothers store. Presently it is known as the Kingston Village Store.

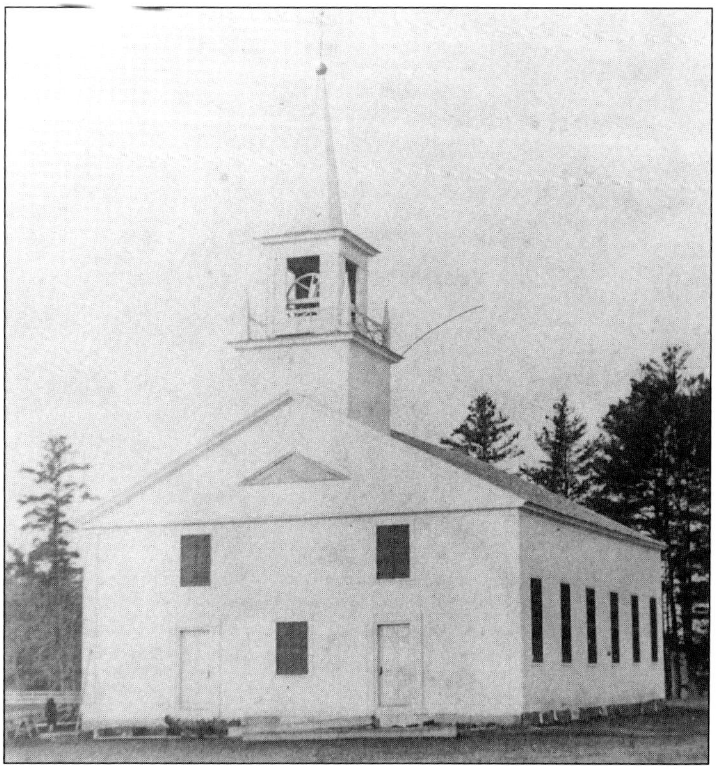

KINGSTON The Congregational Church on Church Street. The church was extensively remodeled in 1840, 1879 and 1952. It is the oldest two-aisle church in Rockingham County. (Courtesy Ruth R. Alberts)

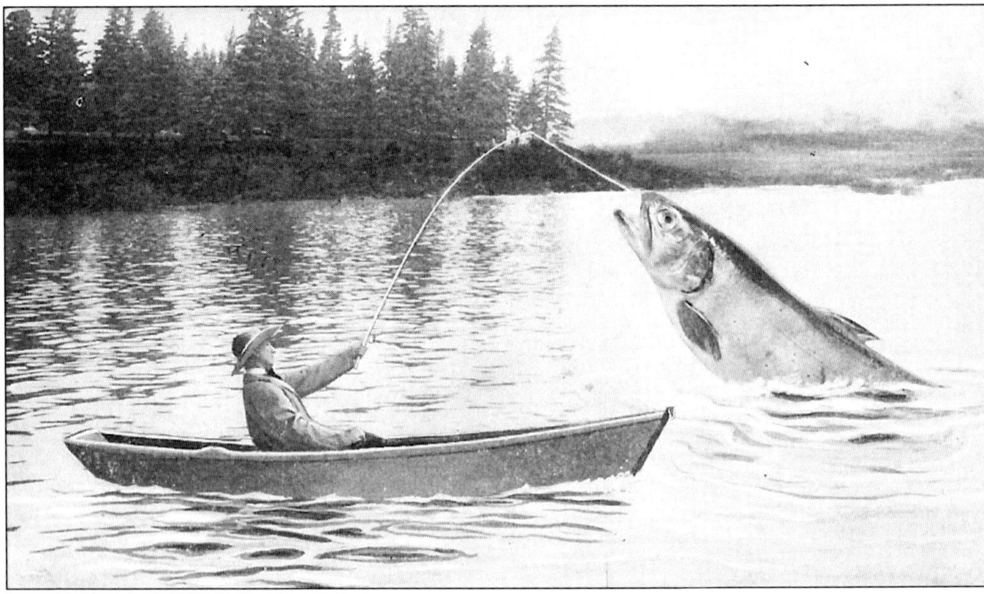

KINGSTON An amusing view of Greenwood Pond as it looked just before the First World War.

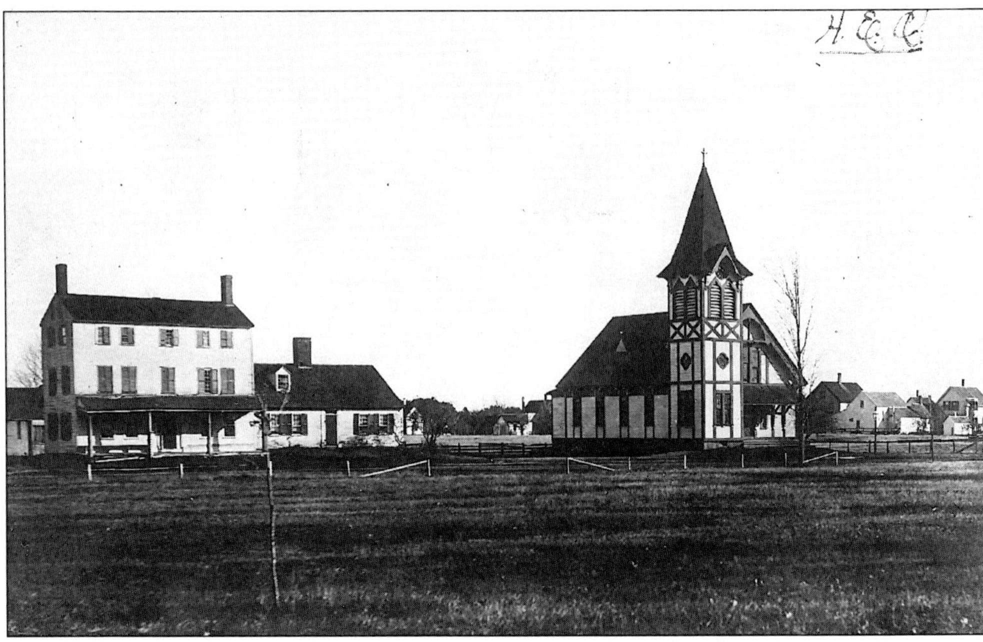

KINGSTON The 1763 Calf Inn, and the 1879 Universalist Church, on Route 111 pictured about 1905. The Calf Inn has since been reduced to a two-story building.

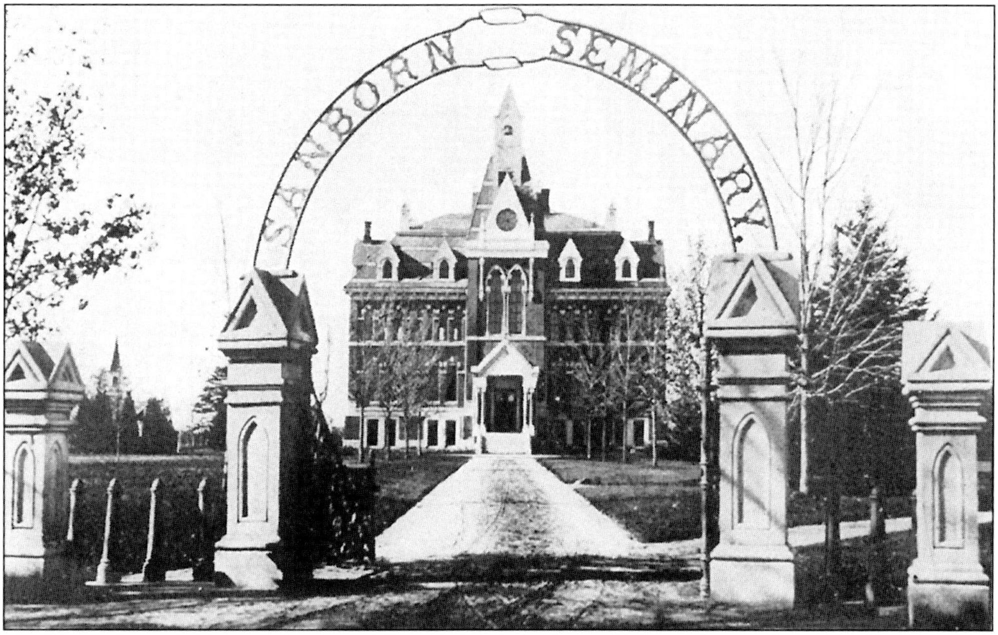

KINGSTON Sanborn Seminary, built in 1888, on Route 111. One of the outstanding examples of Gothic architecture in New Hampshire, it now houses Sanborn Regional High School.

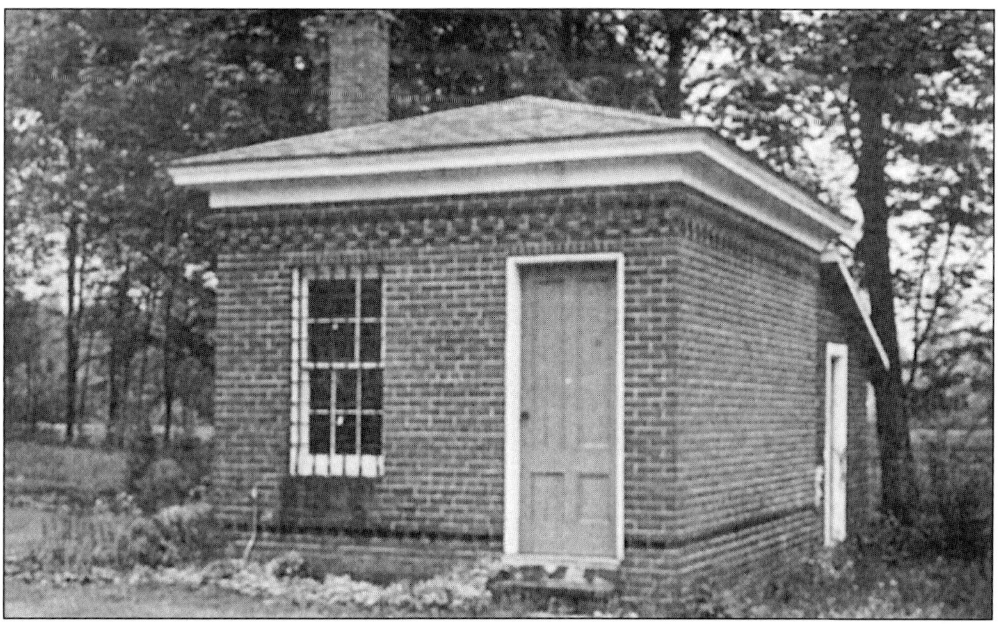

KINGSTON The Tramp house built in 1907 behind the town hall on Route 111. An early form of homeless shelter, the tramp houses were built by the individual towns to house wandering homeless people overnight.

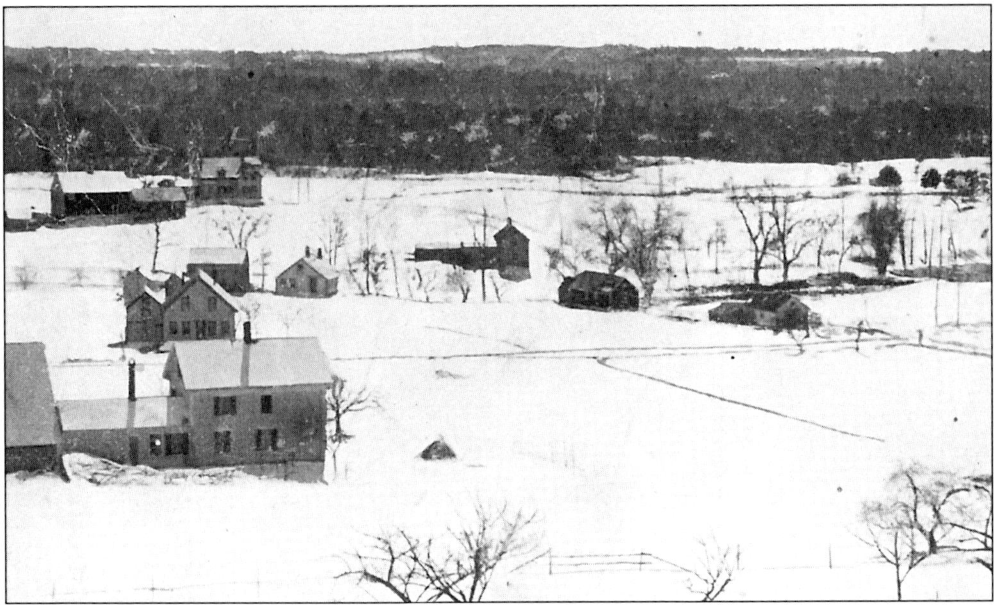

EAST KINGSTON East Kingston looking south from Falls Hill shortly after the turn of the century.

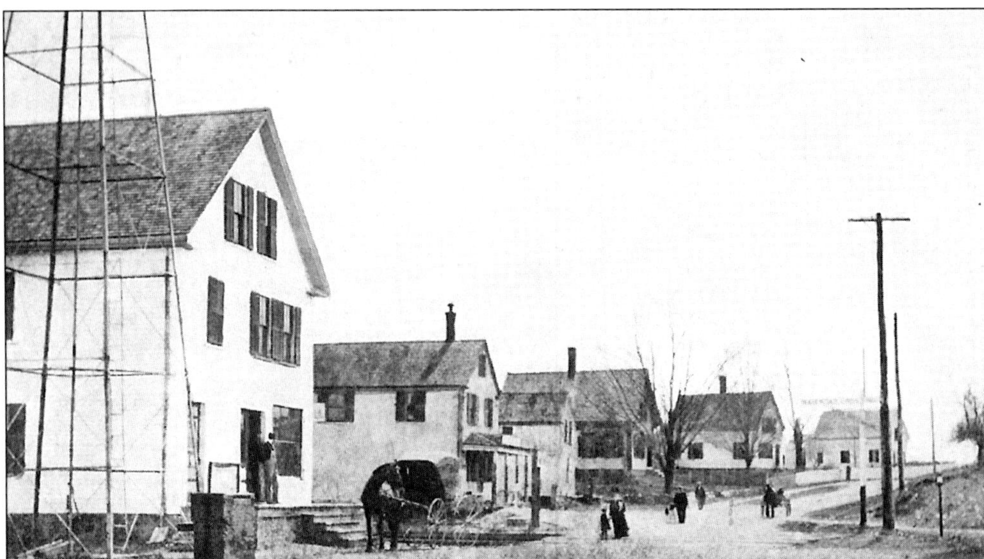

EAST KINGSTON Falls Road looking east toward the Powwow railroad station shortly after the turn of the century.

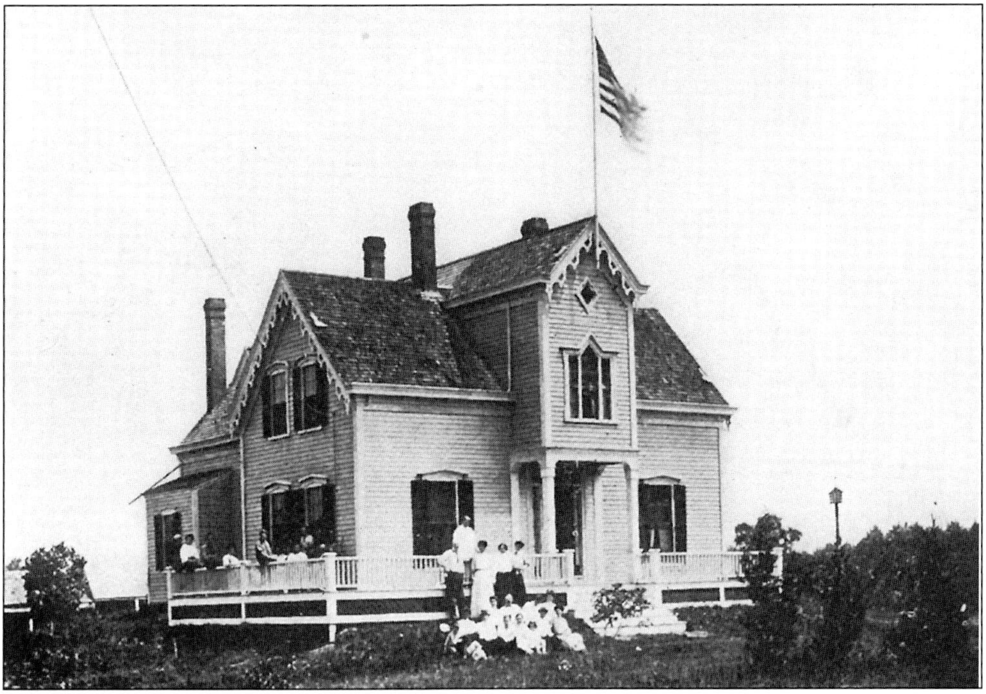

EAST KINGSTON Thelma cottage at Powwow River about 1902. This was one of several tourist boarding houses in East Kingston.

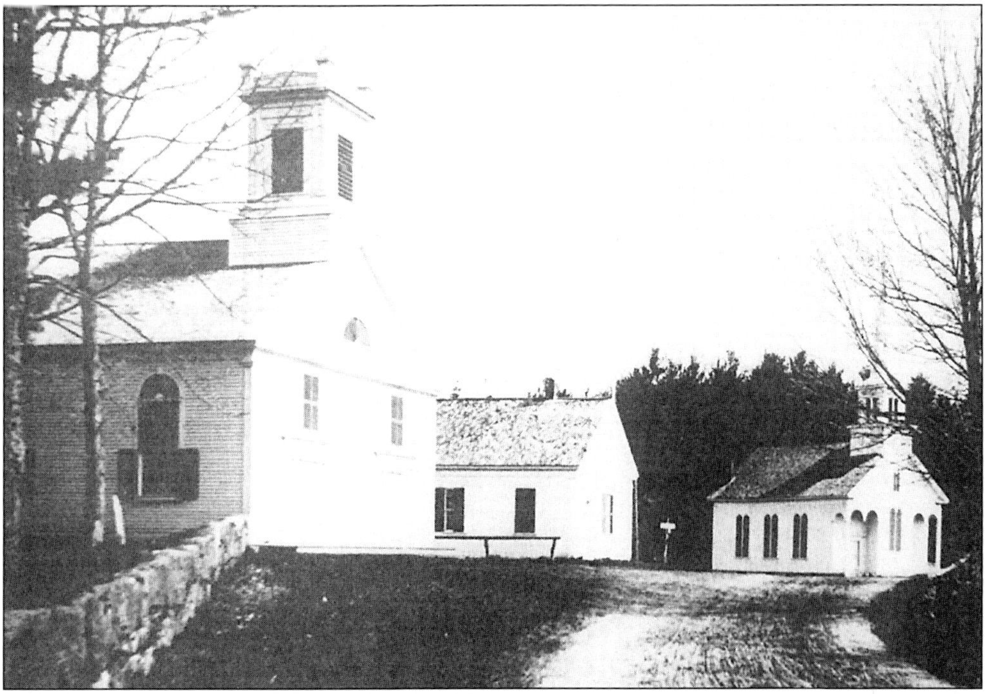

KENSINGTON A view of Kensington village in 1898. Seen left to right are the Union meeting house built in 1840, the town hall built in 1846, and the Congregational Church built at the end of the Civil War.

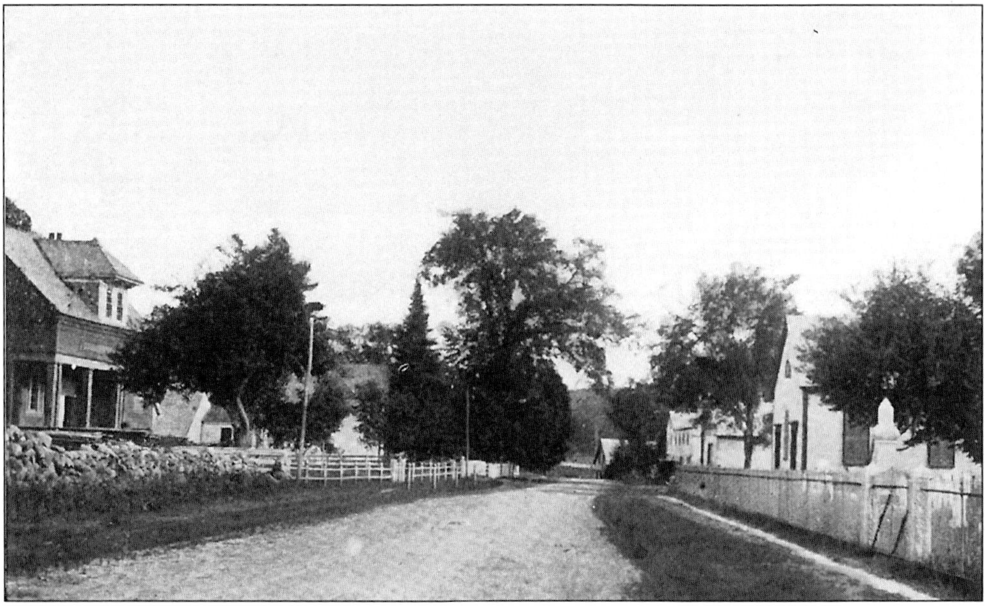

KENSINGTON The Social Library built about 1894 is on the left and the Lower Cemetery and Christian Church built in 1838 are on the right in this 1907 photograph.

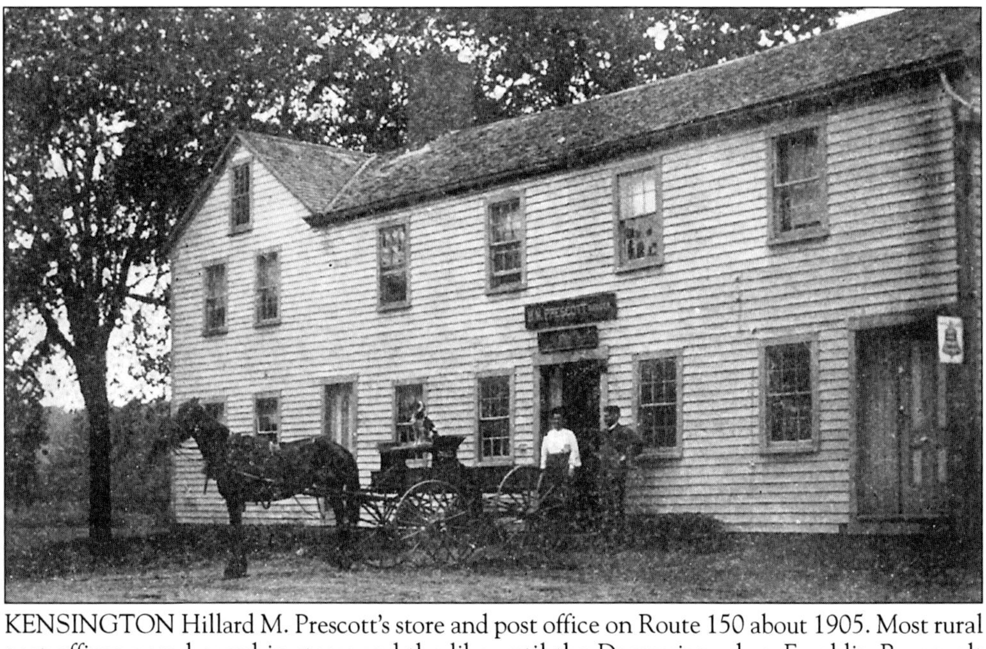

KENSINGTON Hillard M. Prescott's store and post office on Route 150 about 1905. Most rural post offices were housed in stores and the like until the Depression when Franklin Roosevelt authorized a massive program of post office construction.

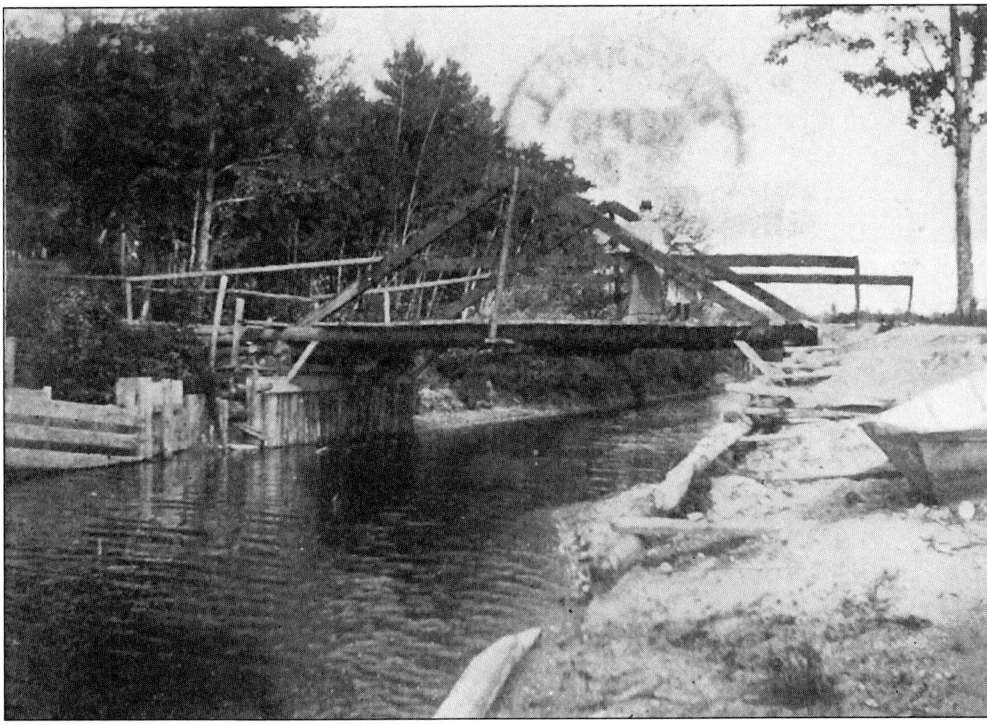

NEWTON The bridge at Silver Lake about 1910.

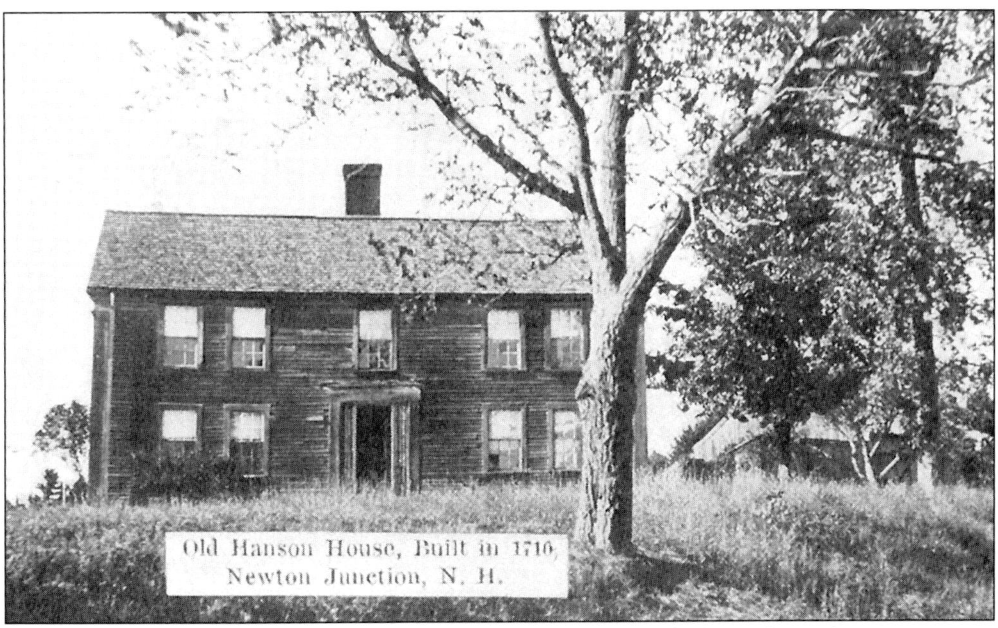

NEWTON The Hanson house built in 1710 at Newton Junction shown here about 1907.

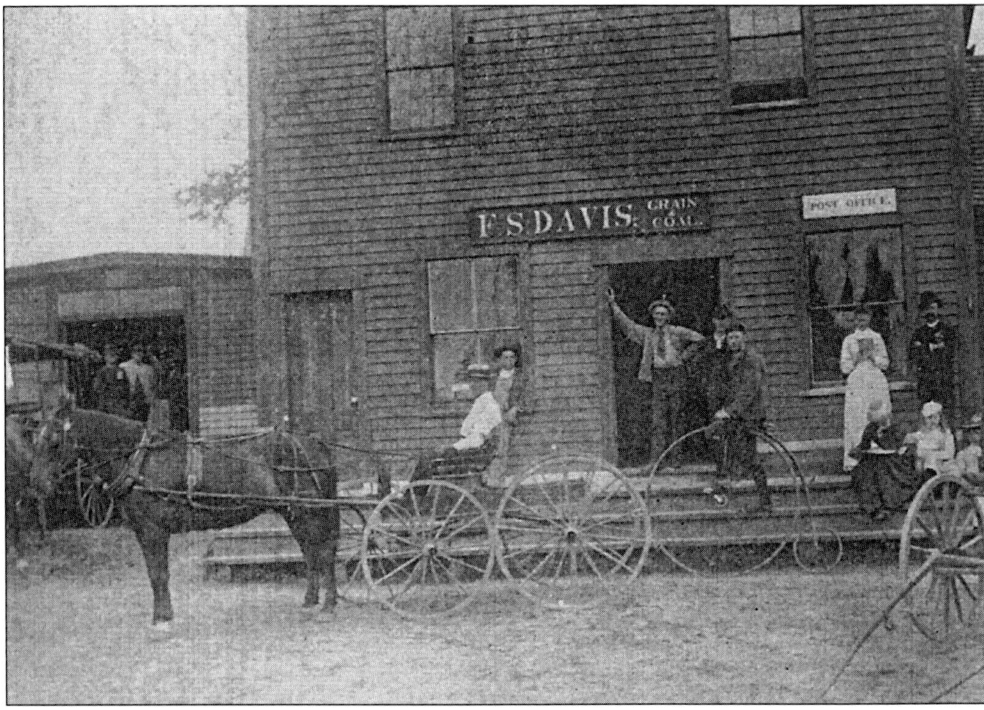

PLAISTOW F. S. Davis' store and post office.

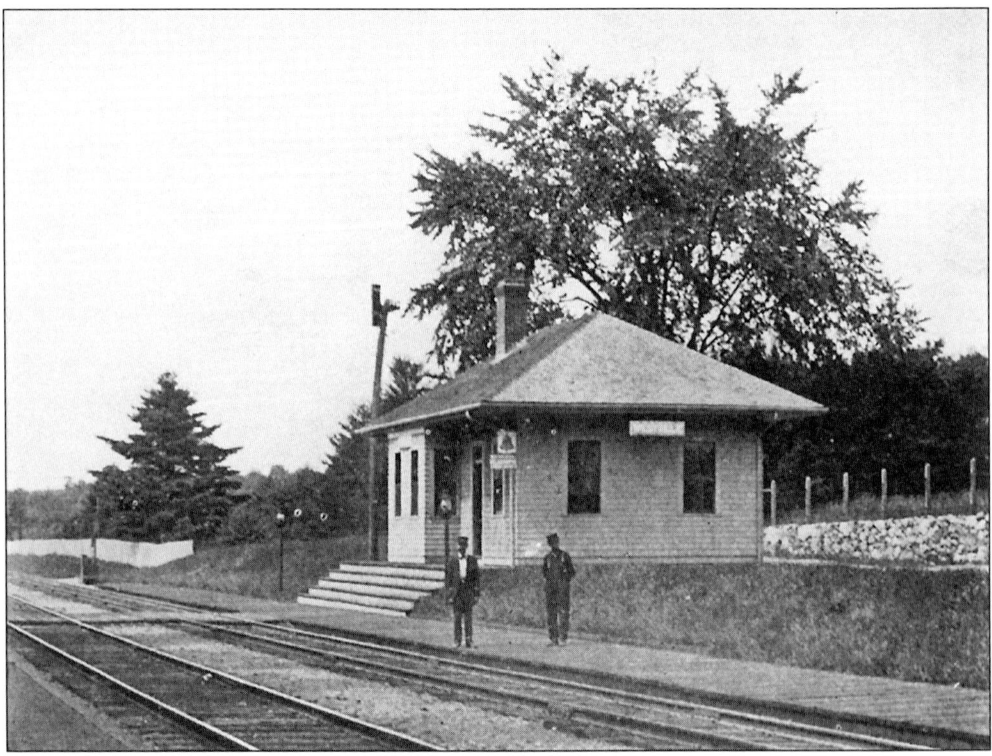
PLAISTOW The Westville Boston and Maine railroad station about 1910.

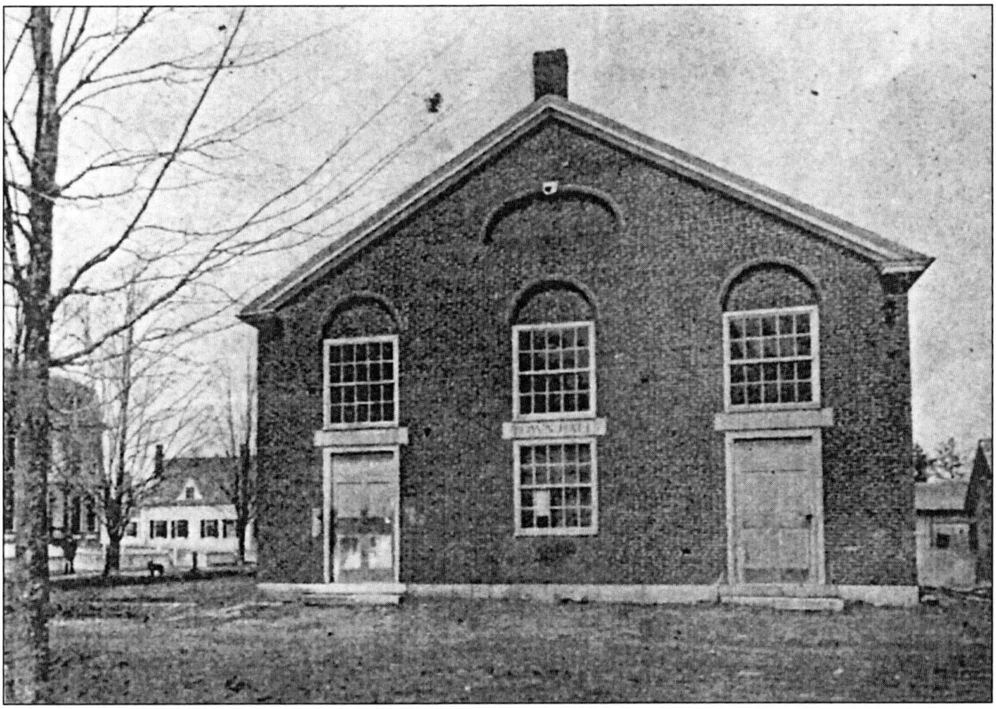

PLAISTOW The town hall built in 1831 was one of the earliest town halls in Rockingham County. It occupied the site of the current town hall which was built in 1895.

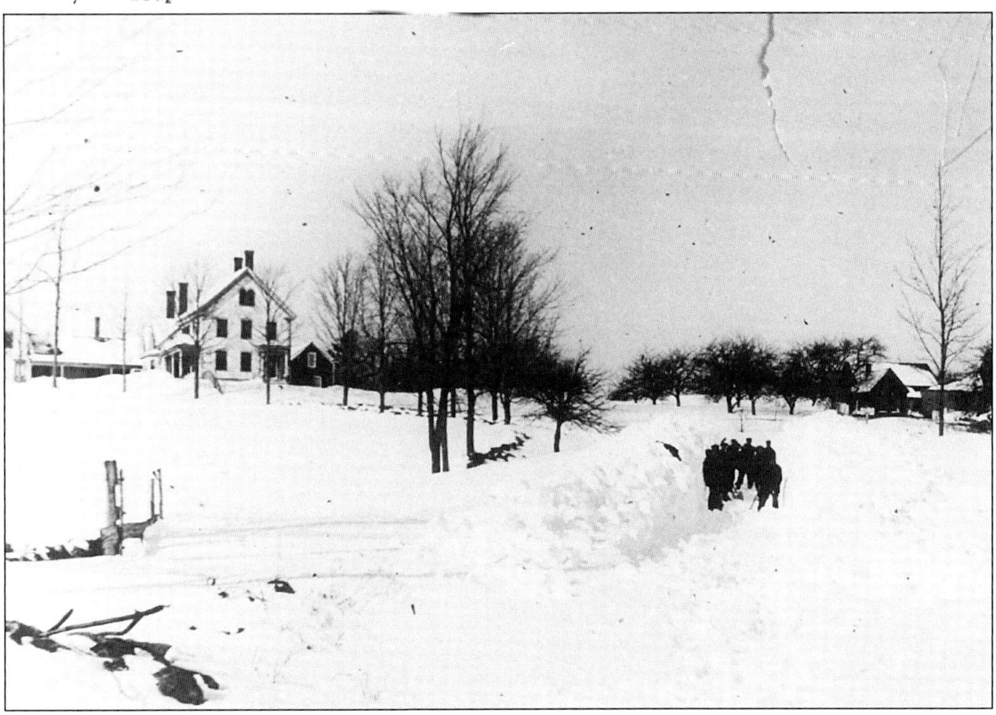

DANVILLE Danville residents shoveling out snowdrifts on Beach Plain Road about 1890. This was a common practice in which all able-bodied men were expected to participate.

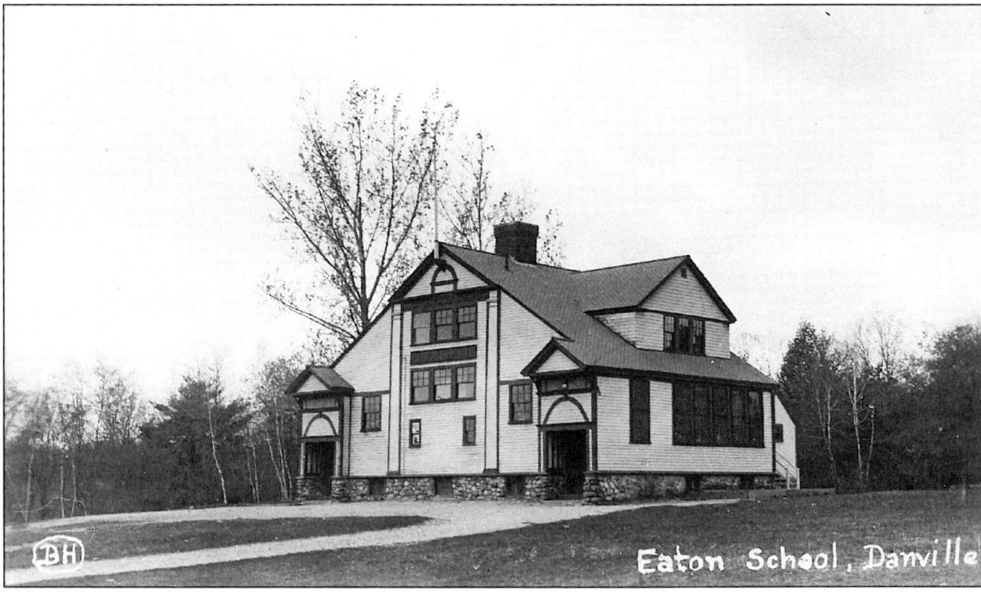

DANVILLE The Eaton School about 1930. Built as a high school in 1912 for freshmen and sophomores only, it later became an elementary school which continued until 1961. It was destroyed by fire shortly thereafter.

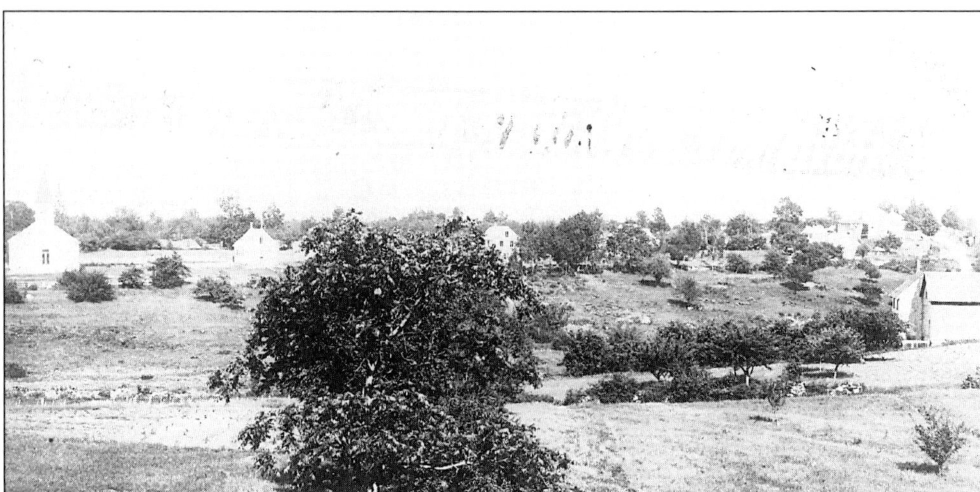
DANVILLE A view off Route 111A looking toward the Union Church, built in 1850, and the schoolhouse, built in 1895, on Beach Plain Road. This photograph was taken shortly after the turn of the century.

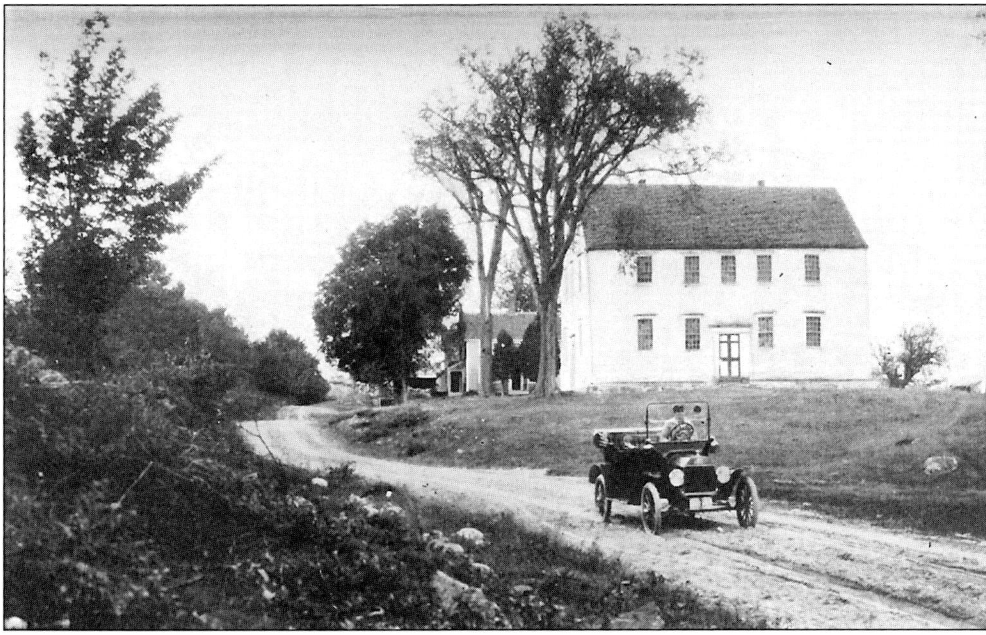

DANVILLE The old meeting house on Route 111A about 1912. Built in 1760, this is the oldest of the three spireless eighteenth century meeting houses in Rockingham County. Restored in 1936 it contains the oldest elevated pulpit in New Hampshire. Such pulpits were common in Congregational and Puritan churches built around the Revolution.

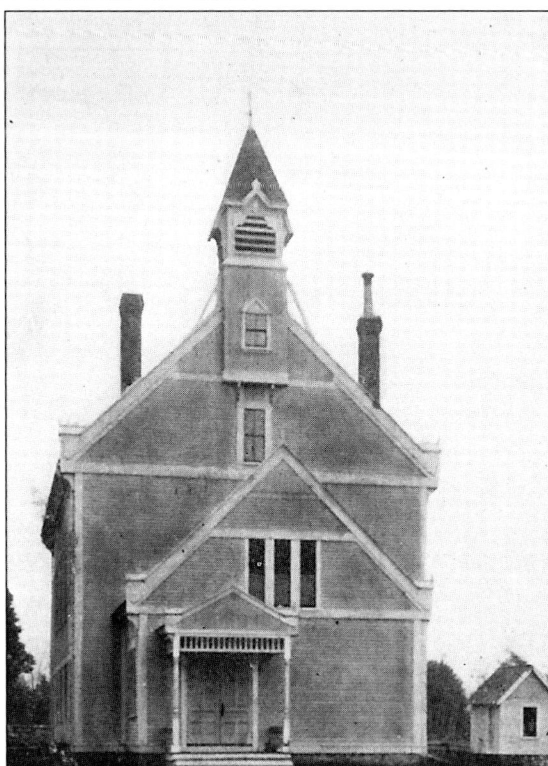

DANVILLE The town hall on Route 111A which was built in 1886. The location and style of this building did not appeal to many townspeople, one of whom attempted to burn it down before its dedication on January 13, 1887. It originally contained a local jail for vagrants and local criminals.

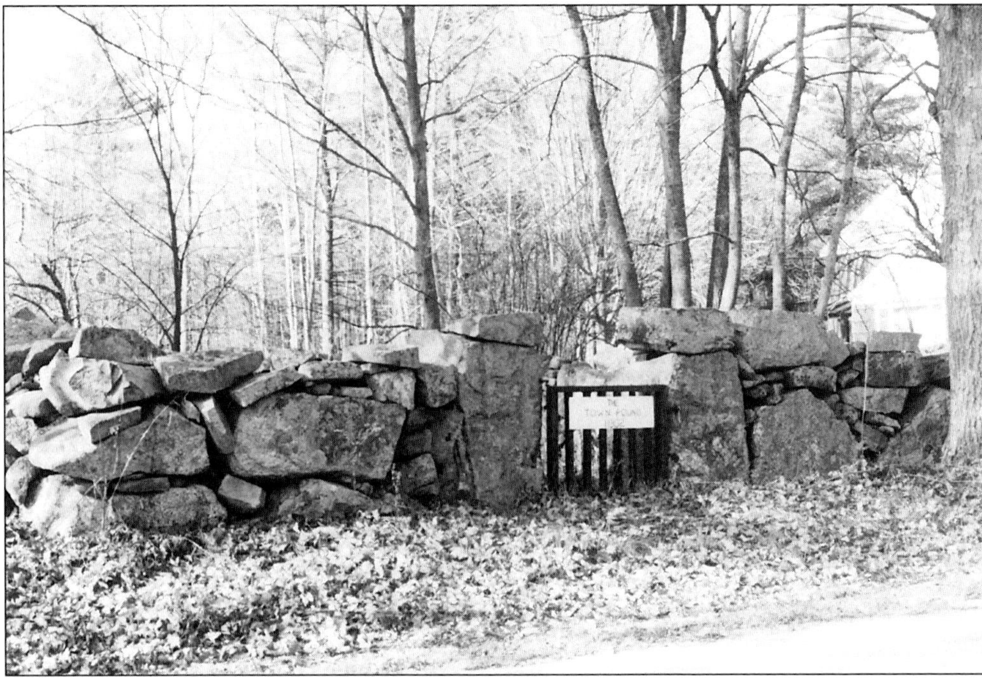

DANVILLE The town animal pound built in 1802 on Route 111A. This was used to confine livestock found roaming at large on town roads. Fines were levied against the owners by the town poundkeeper who was an elected official.

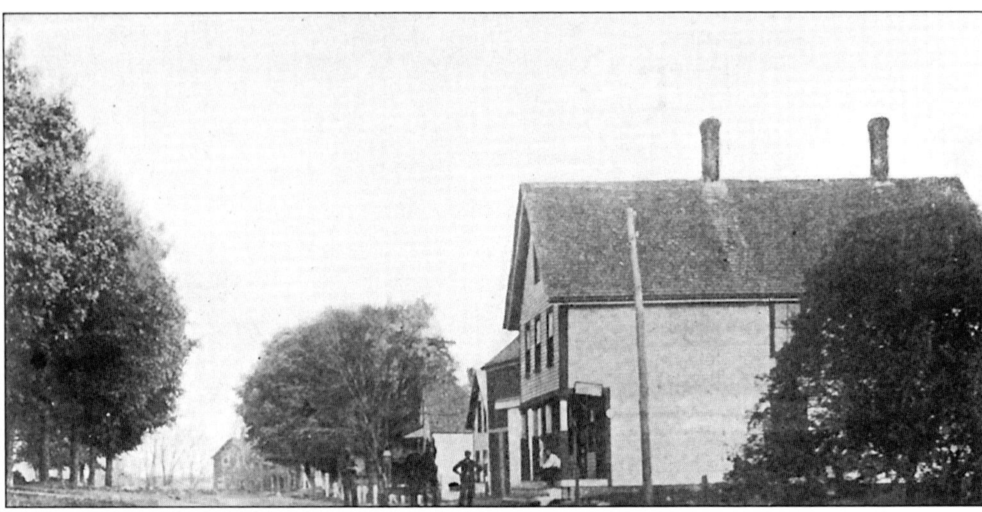

DANVILLE George B. Hines' corner store about 1910. This store formerly stood near the corner of Route 111A and Garrison, now Kingston, Road.

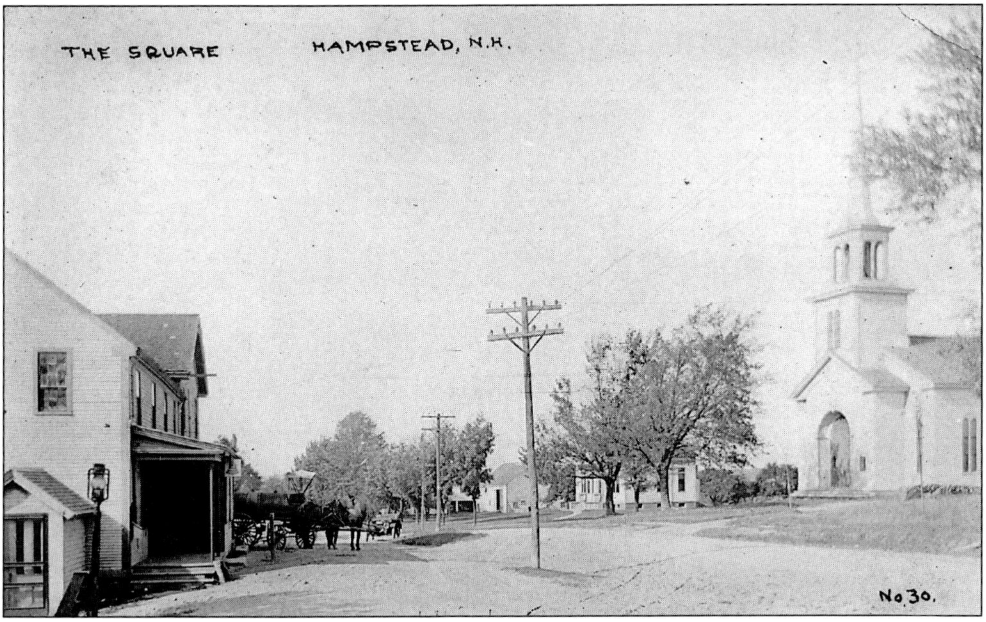

HAMPSTEAD The village square about 1908-12. Isaac Randall's store on the left burned in 1917. On the right is the Congregational Church built in 1861.

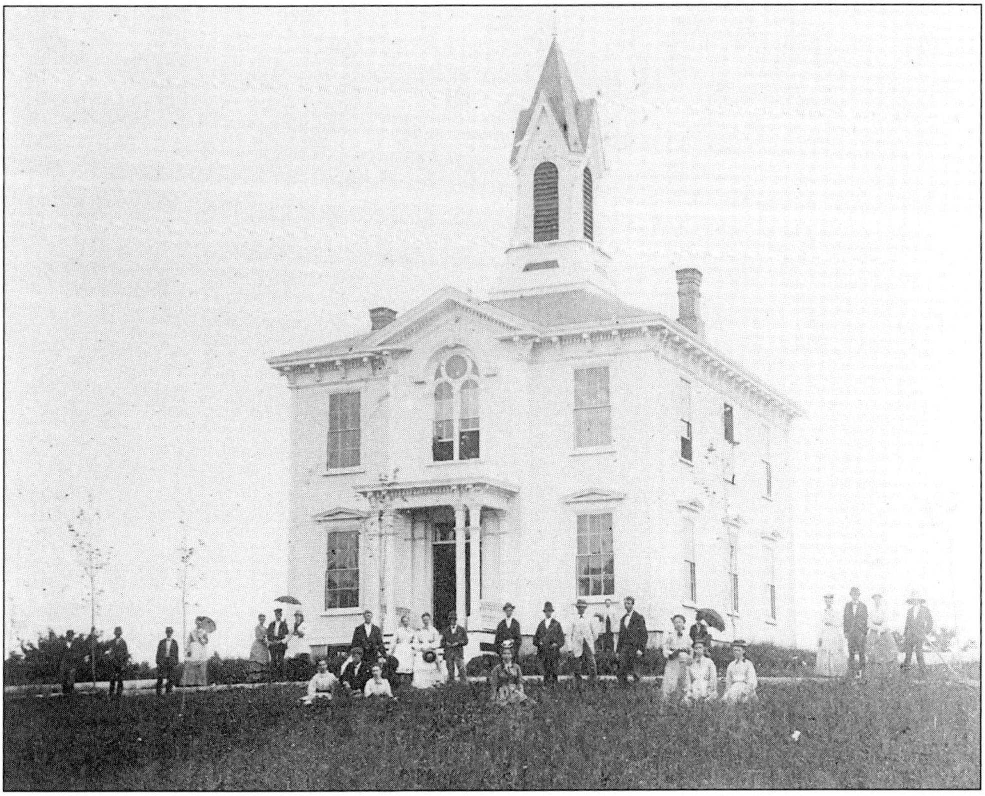

HAMPSTEAD The high school, built in 1874 and used until 1958. The building on Route 121 is now used as the town office building. This photograph was taken in 1876.

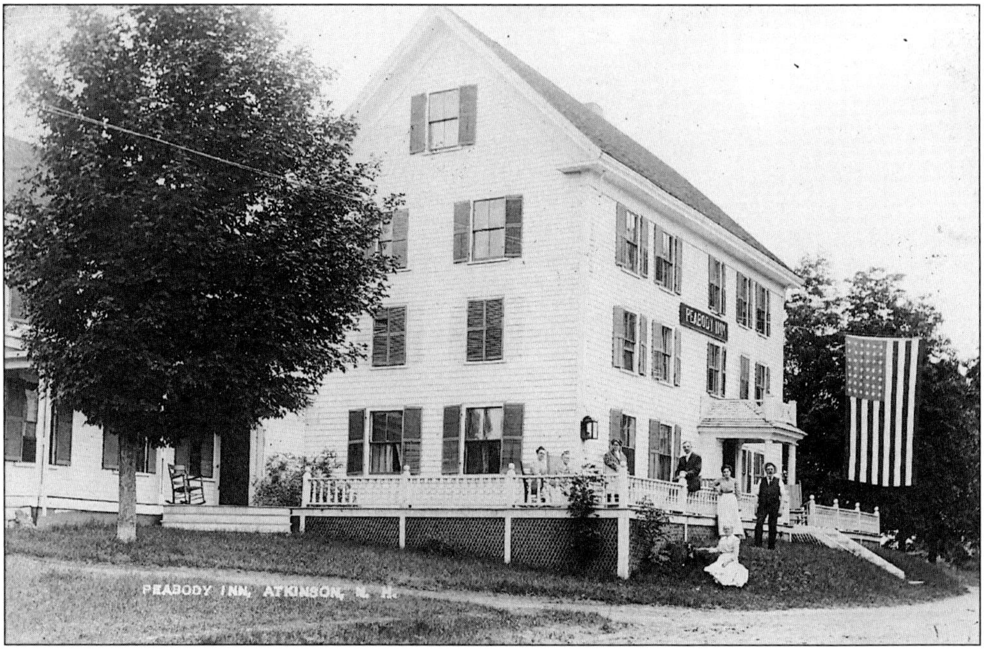

ATKINSON Peabody Inn about 1910. It was once home to Revolutionary War General Nathaniel Peabody, who died in debtor's prison in 1823. The house was also known as the Hotel Clay at the turn of the century. (Courtesy of Una Collins)

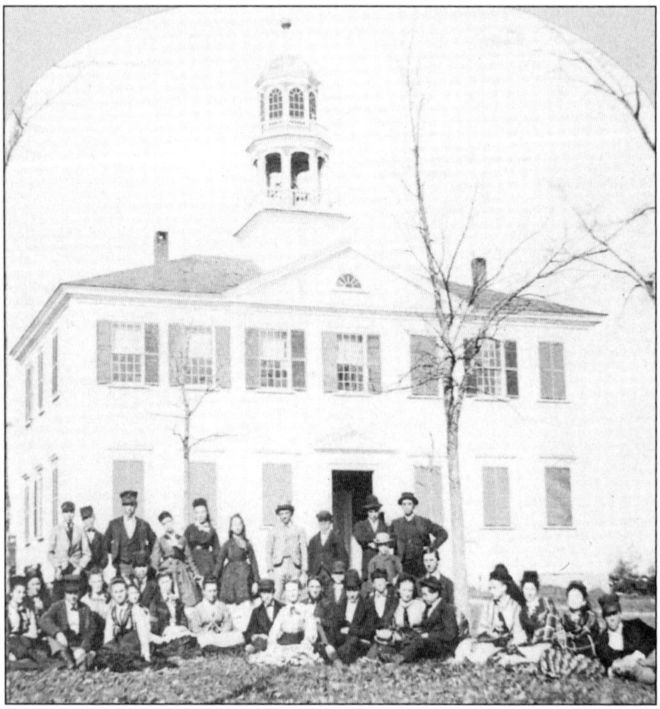

ATKINSON The second Atkinson Academy building on Academy Street, built in 1803 and pictured here in 1870. Incorporated in 1791, this academy was the second co-educational academy in the United States. The building was designed by Ebenezer Clifford, a noted New Hampshire architect.

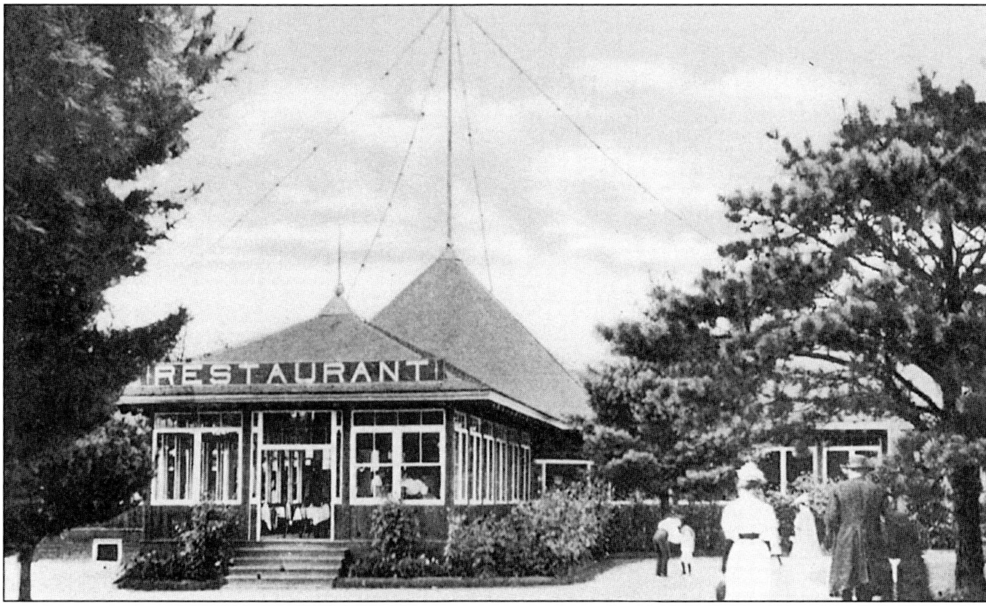

SALEM Canobie Lake Park Restaurant in 1907. The lakeside amusement park opened to the public in 1902. Nearing its centenary, the park is still a major summer tourist attraction as well as a place of enjoyment for generations of children.

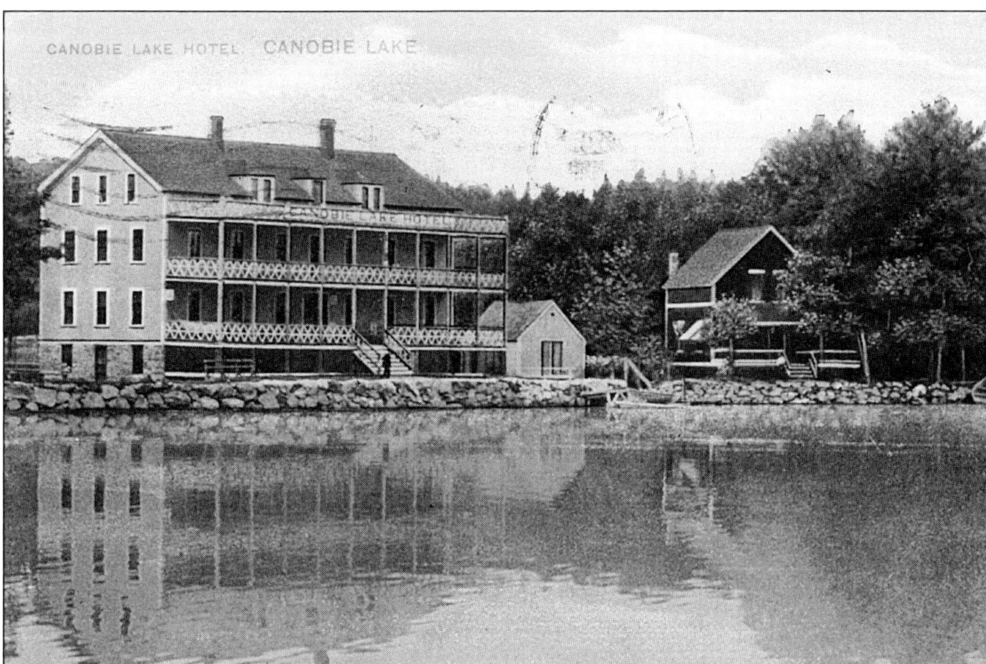

SALEM The Canobie Lake Amusement Park Hotel just before the First World War.

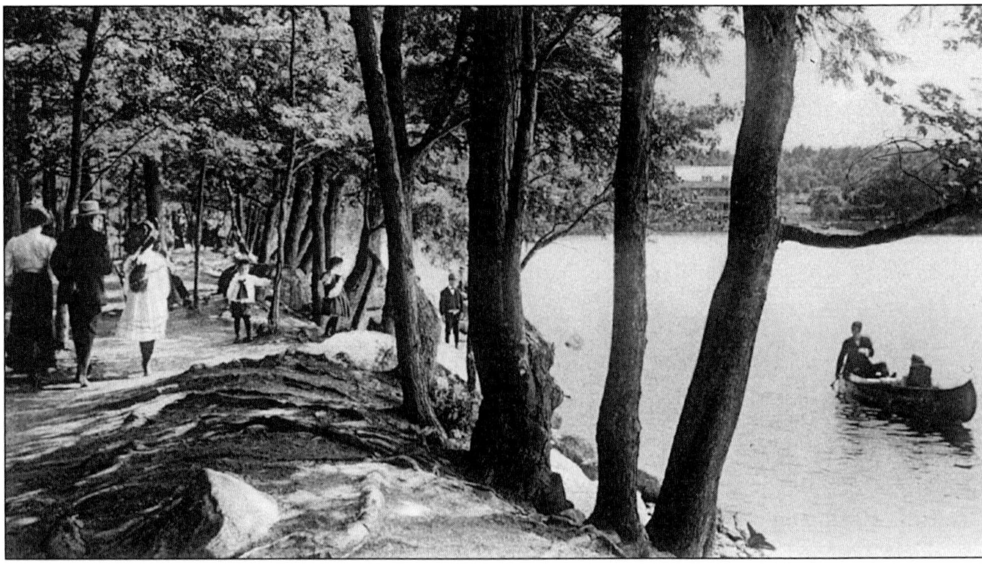

SALEM Lover's Walk at Canobie Lake Amusement Park about 1910.

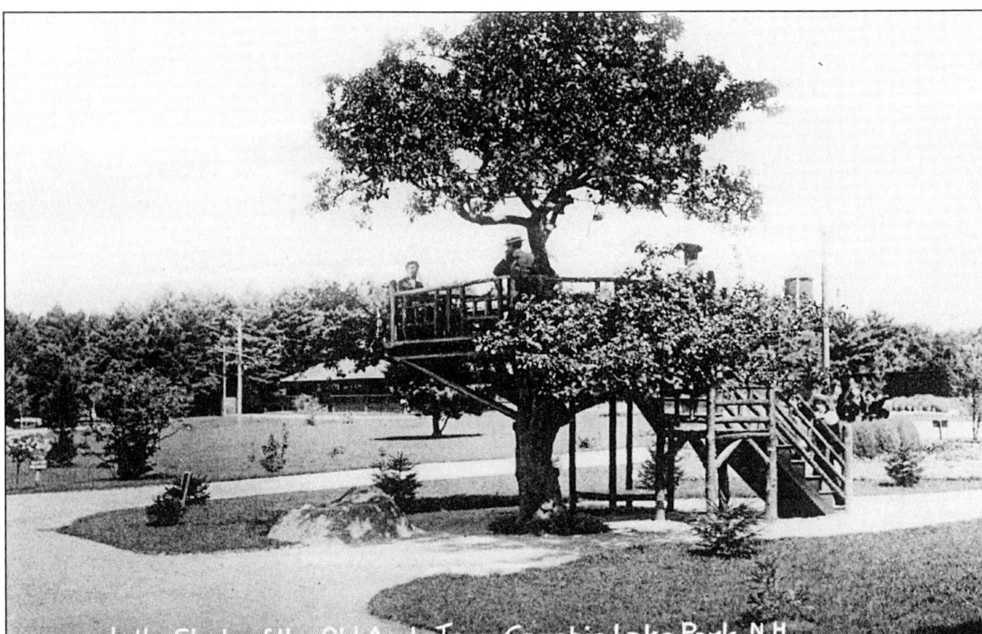

SALEM In the shade of the old apple tree at Canobie about 1910.

Four

The Heart of Rockingham County

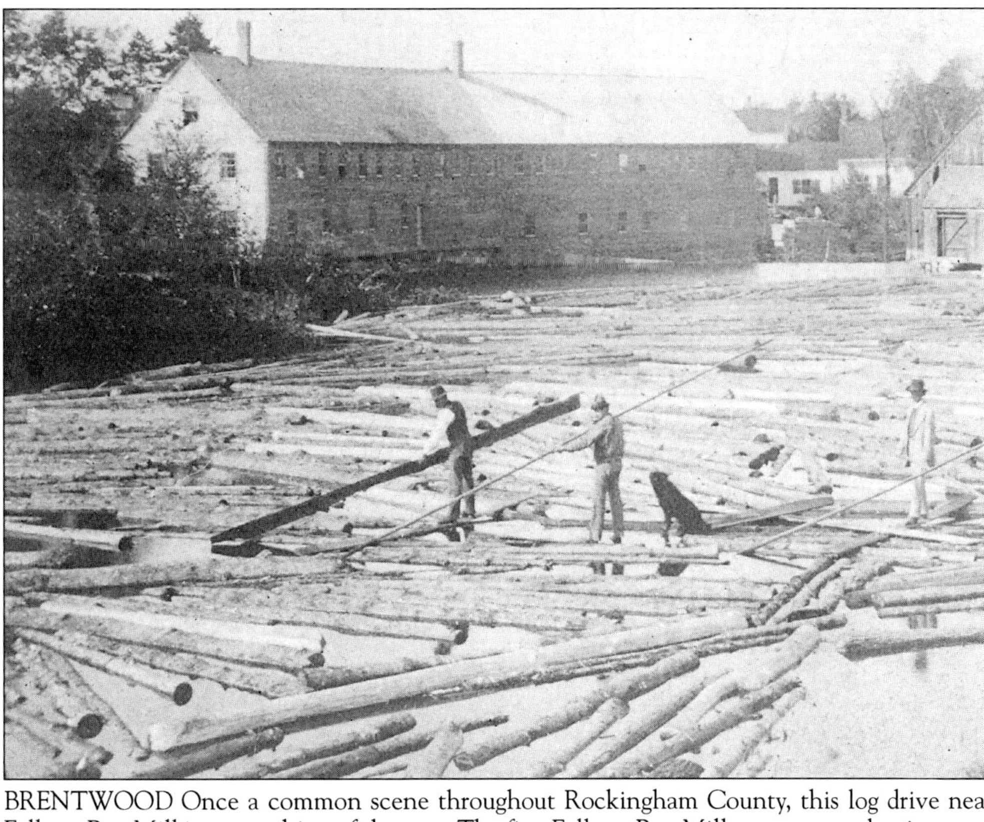

BRENTWOOD Once a common scene throughout Rockingham County, this log drive near Fellows Box Mill is now a thing of the past. The first Fellows Box Mill, seen across the river, was built in 1860 and burnt early in 1864.

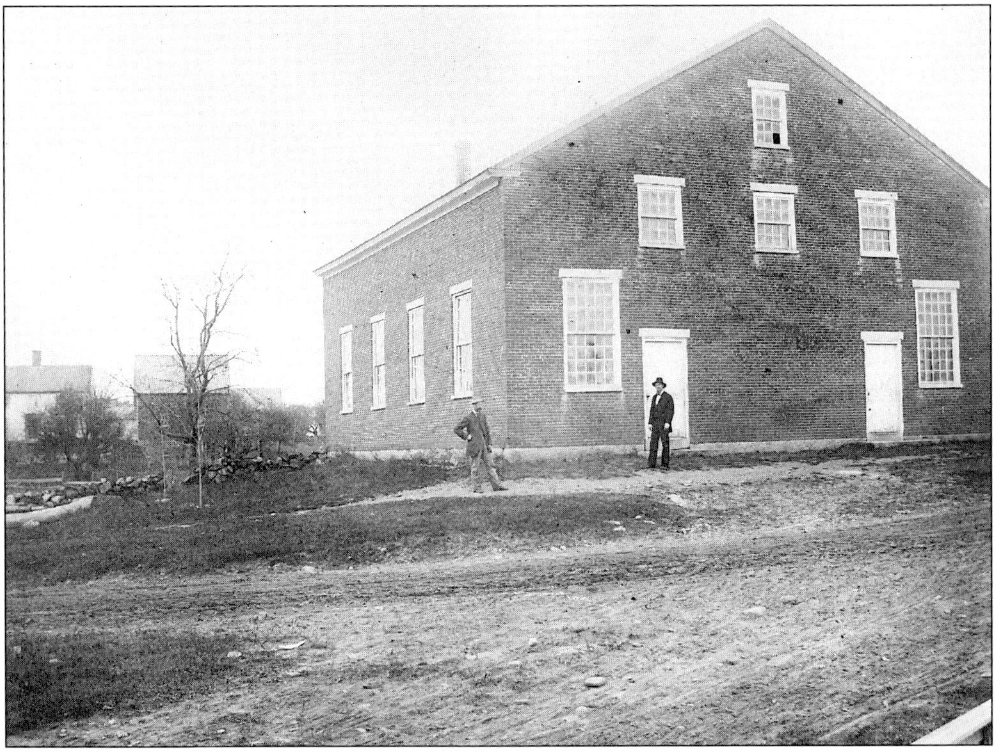

BRENTWOOD The Baptist Church on North Road about 1881. Built in 1828, the steeple was added in 1886. The Rev. Samuel Shepard established this church in 1771. The original meeting house was a wooden structure that stood directly across the road.

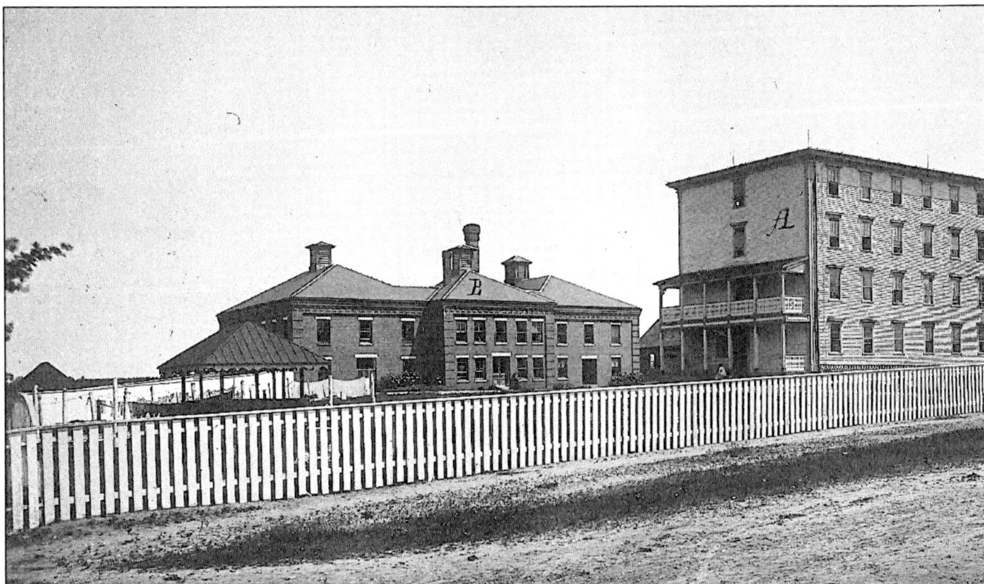

BRENTWOOD The Rockingham County alms house and insane asylum on North Road in 1888. It is interesting to note the attitude of the times which saw nothing wrong with housing the indigent who were usually elderly in the same building with the mentally ill.

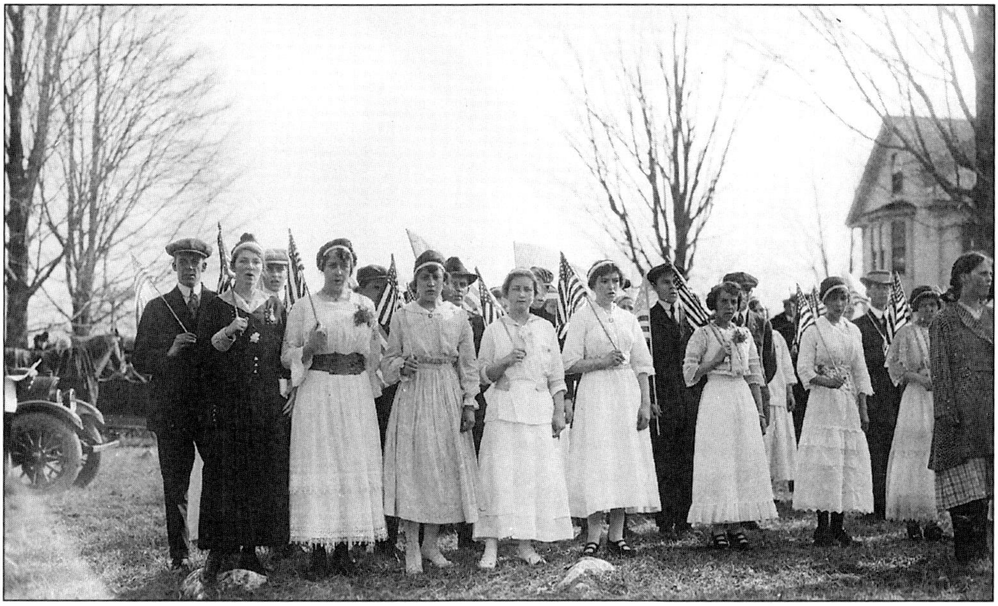

BRENTWOOD In November 1917 a flag raising ceremony took place at the Fellows Box Mill in support of the the First World War effort. These ladies were part of the program which was typical of the home front effort.

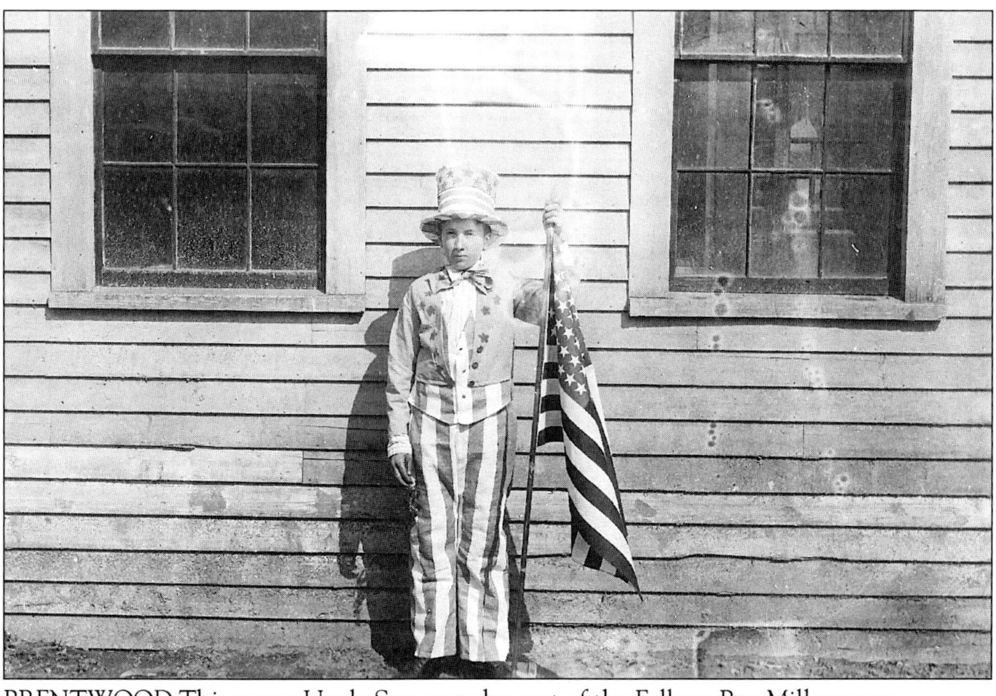

BRENTWOOD This young Uncle Sam was also part of the Fellows Box Mill program.

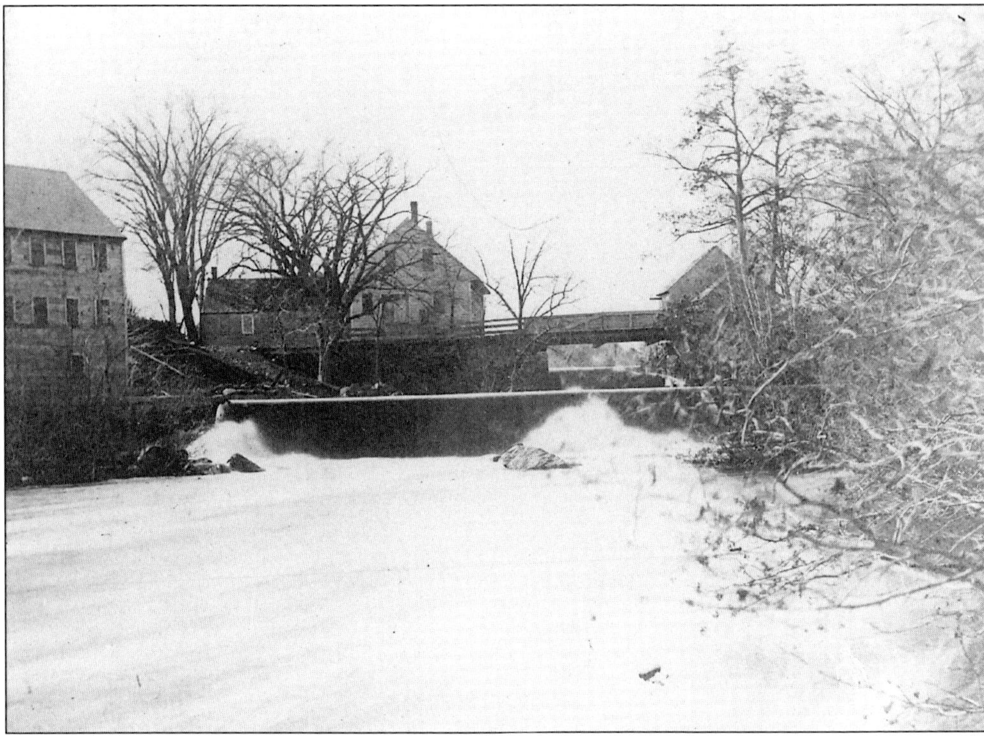

BRENTWOOD Mill buildings at Crawley's Mills on Middle Road shortly after the Civil War. Thomas Crawley had been given permission in the early 1650s to erect a sawmill near this point. Mills continued near here for over three centuries.

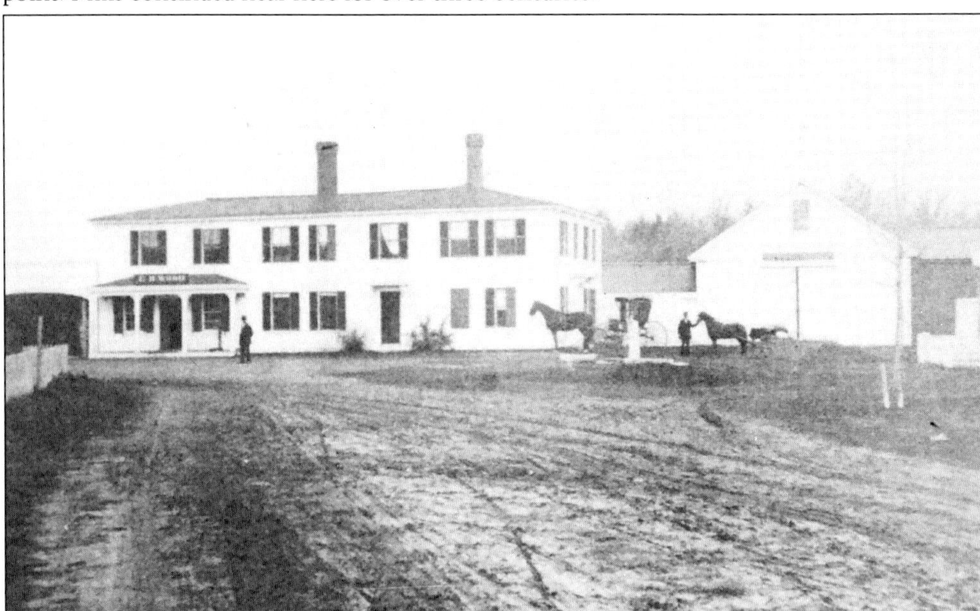

BRENTWOOD Eliphalet B. Wood's store on Ladd's Lane in the early 1870s. This building dates back to about 1806 and served as Asa Wood's tavern in the 1820s. Eliphalet and his son Frank operated the store between 1835 and the early 1920s.

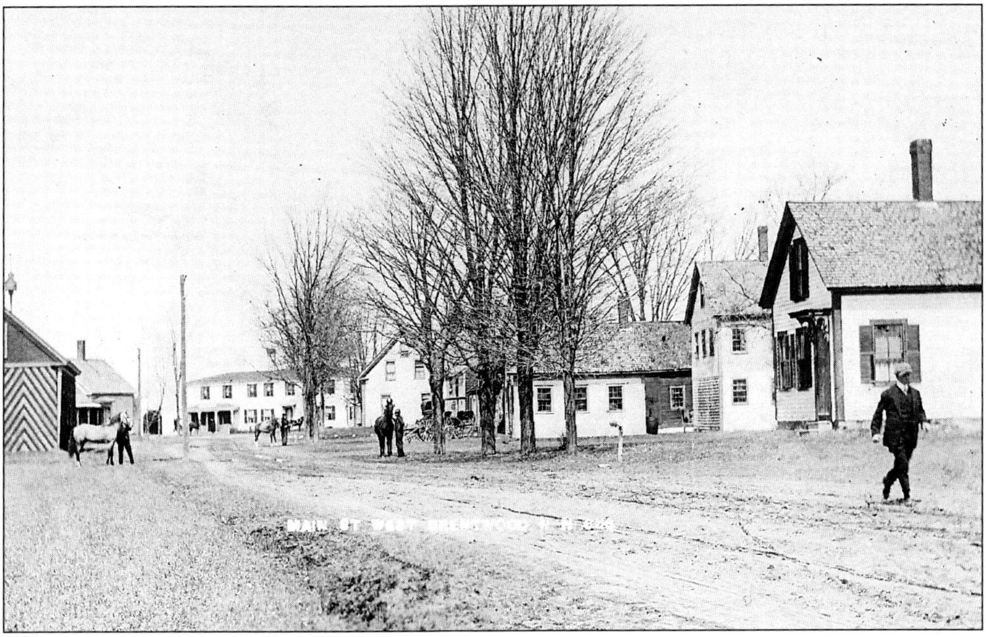

BRENTWOOD A rare view of Wood's Corner, now Ladd's Lane, about 1910. Arthur A Burnap's Carriage Painting and Blacksmith business operated here from 1899 until the early 1940s.

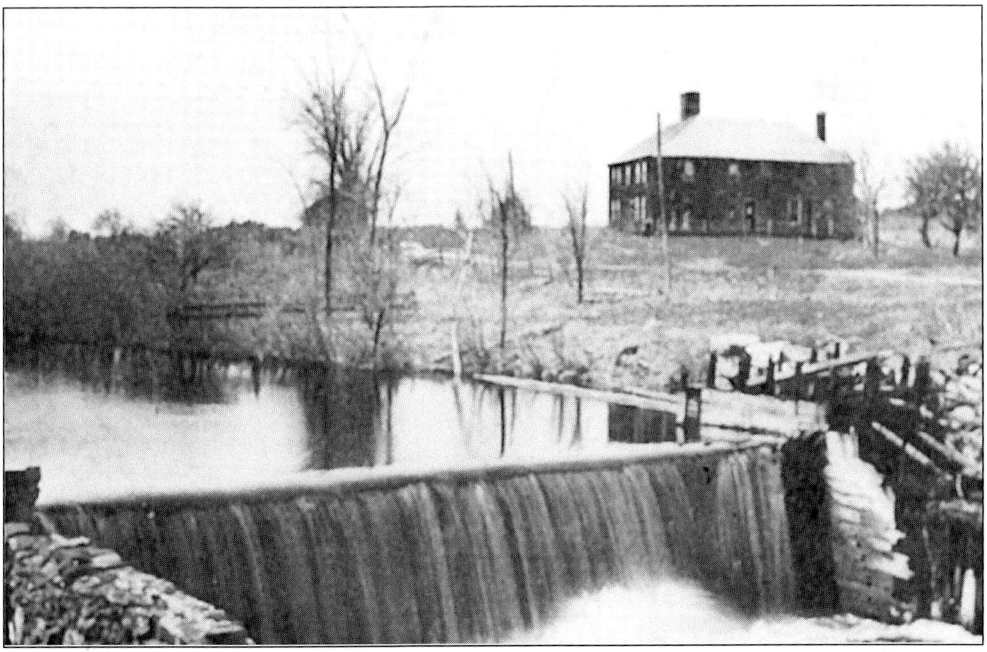

BRENTWOOD The upper dam at Crawley's Falls on Middle Road. The old Morrill house in the background was razed in the 1950s to make way for the current Route 125.

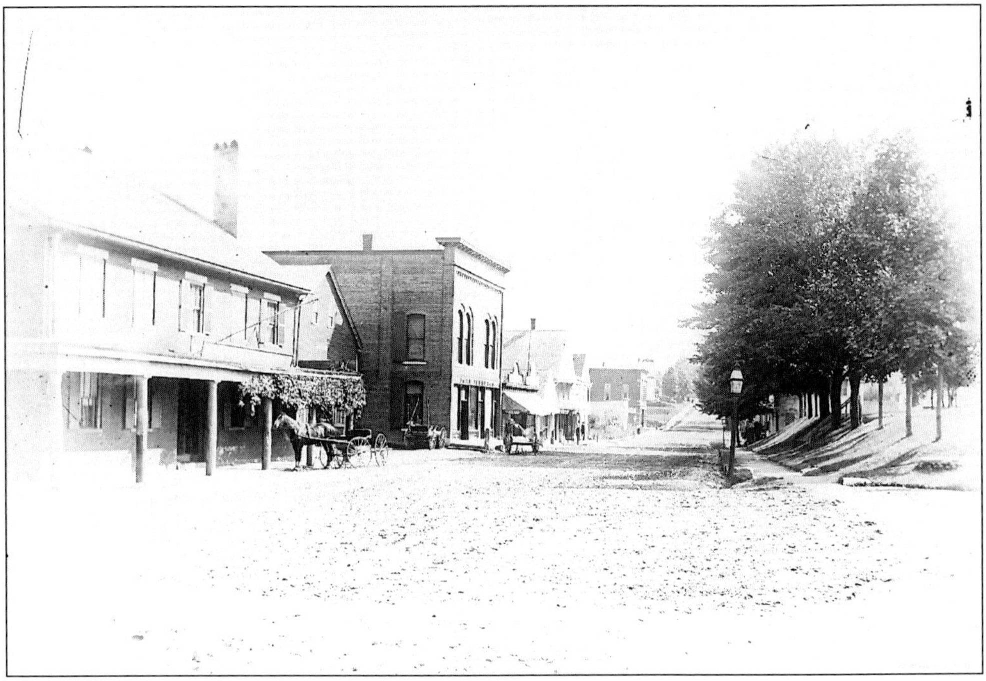

EPPING A view of Main Street about 1910. Epping became a prosperous brick and shoe-making community by the turn of the century. Millions of bricks were manufactured here between 1860 and 1960.

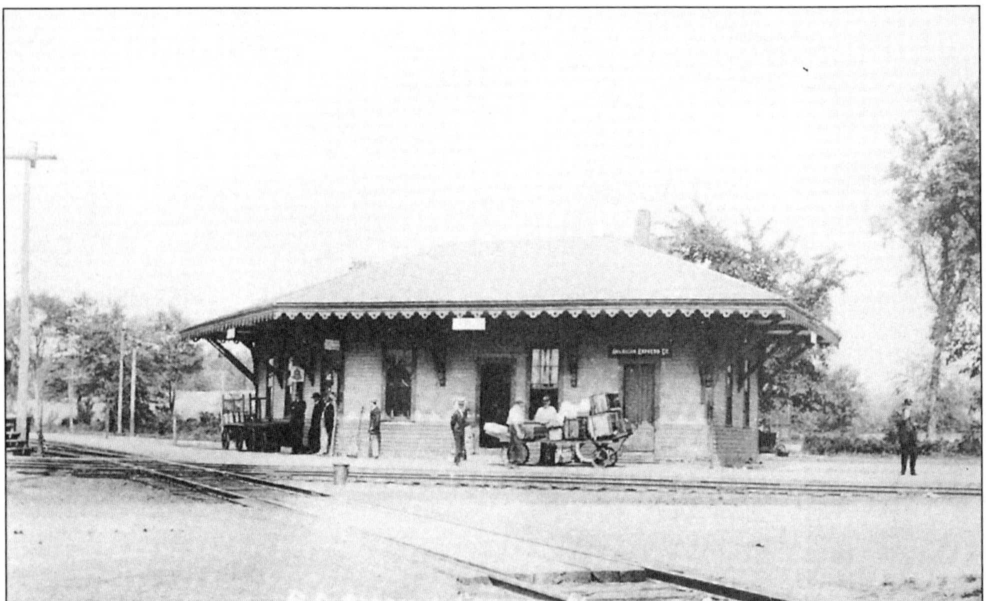

EPPING The railroad station in 1905. Passengers are waiting to board the regular train on the Manchester and Portsmouth route. Note the double track, where the Worcester, Nashua and Rochester line bisected the first track.

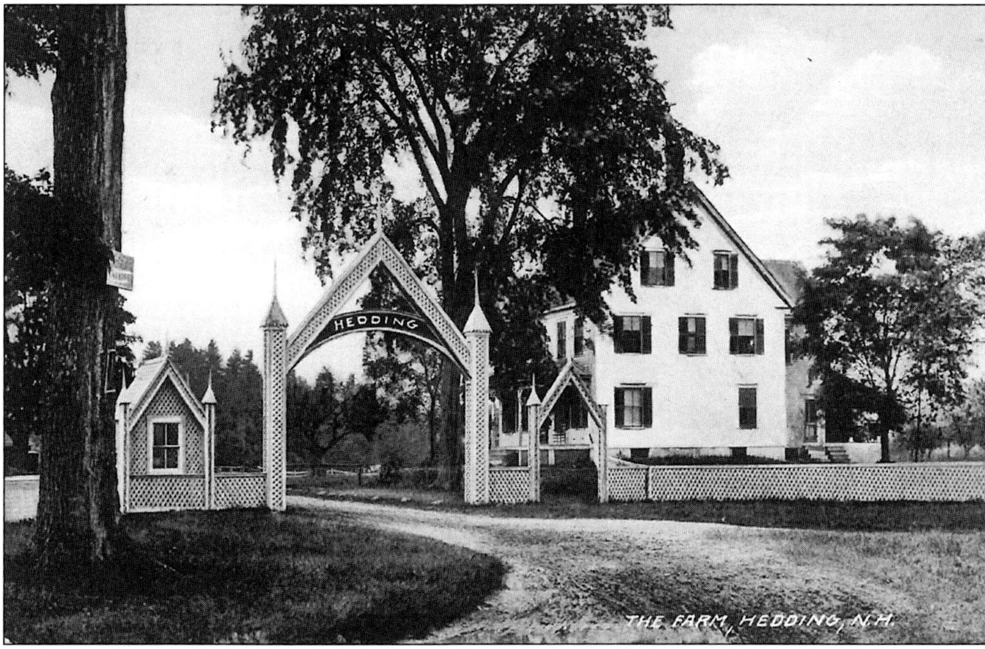

EPPING The entrance to Hedding Campground on Route 8 about 1910. The campground also had its own post office and railroad depot. Methodist camp meetings have been held here annually since 1863.

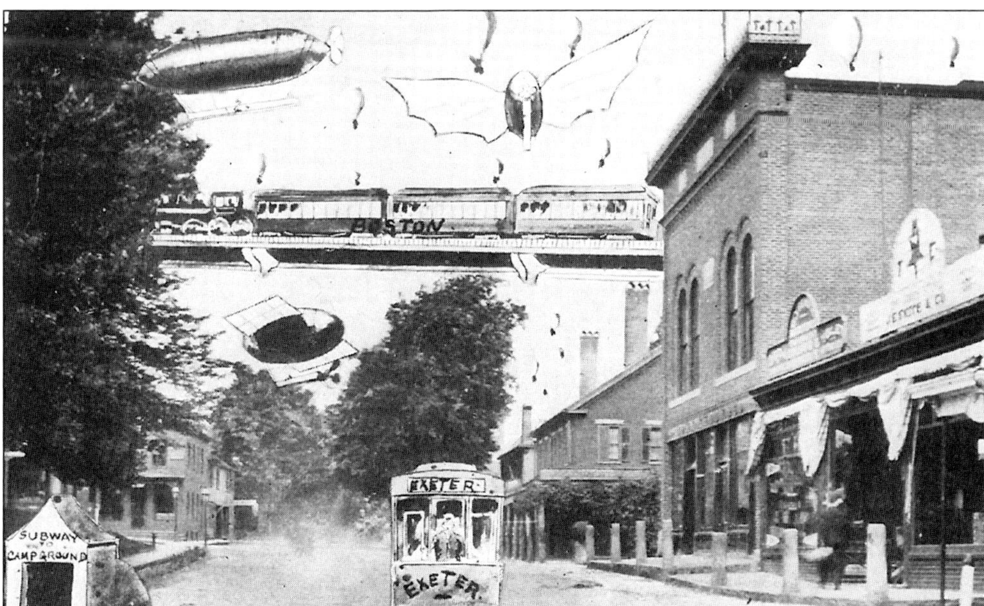

EPPING Another in the near futurel postcard, this time of Epping. It is doubtful that the elevated trolley will be constructed in the near future! The tall brick building in the photograph now serves as the Leddy Performing Arts Center.

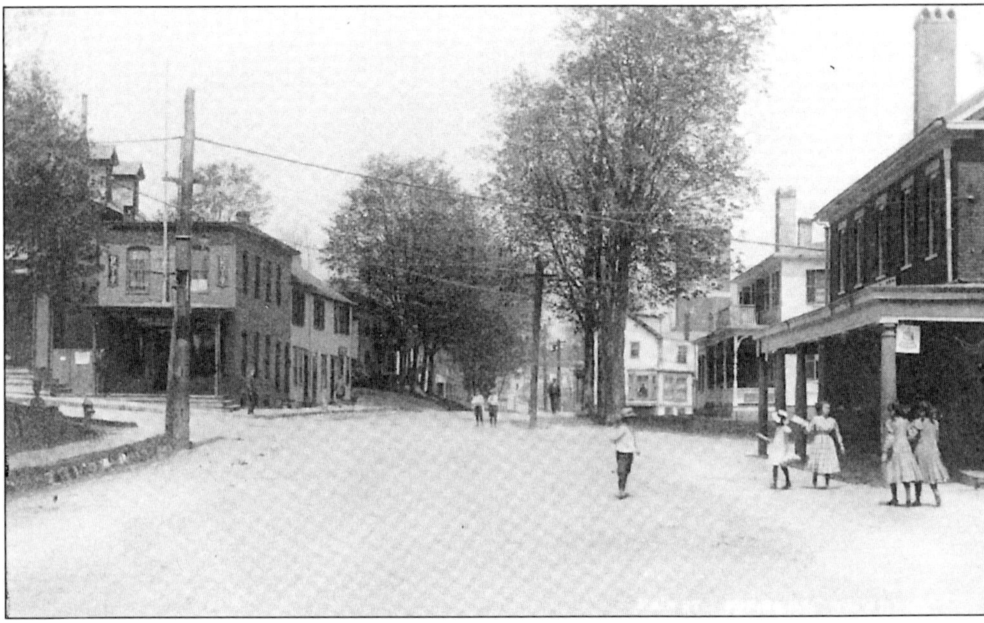

EPPING The corner of Main and Pleasant Streets at the time of the First World War.

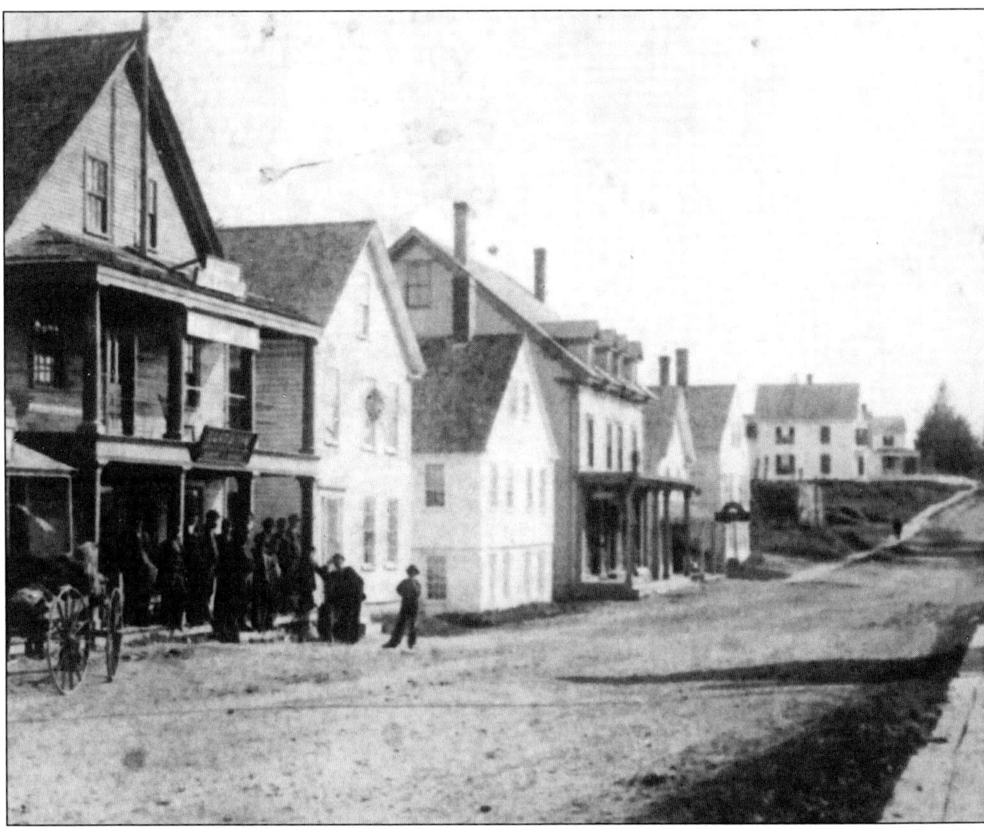

EPPING The east side of Main Street about 1890. In 1896 a large fire destroyed nearly all of these buildings in one of Epping's worst fires.

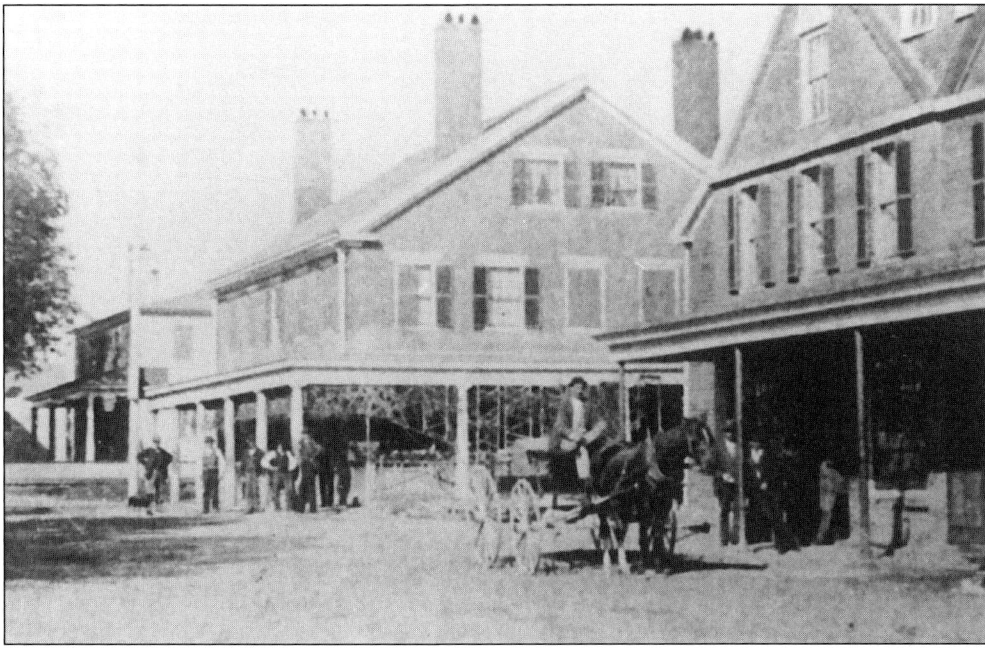

EPPING Main Street looking north about 1890. The building on the left was owned by Dr. Hosea B. Burnham and was torn down in the 1930s. The center building was Bunker's Hotel, later Perkin's Hotel, which burned in 1919. The building on the right was the original Leddy Store, torn down in 1895 to make room for the present Leddy block. (Courtesy Donald Sanborn)

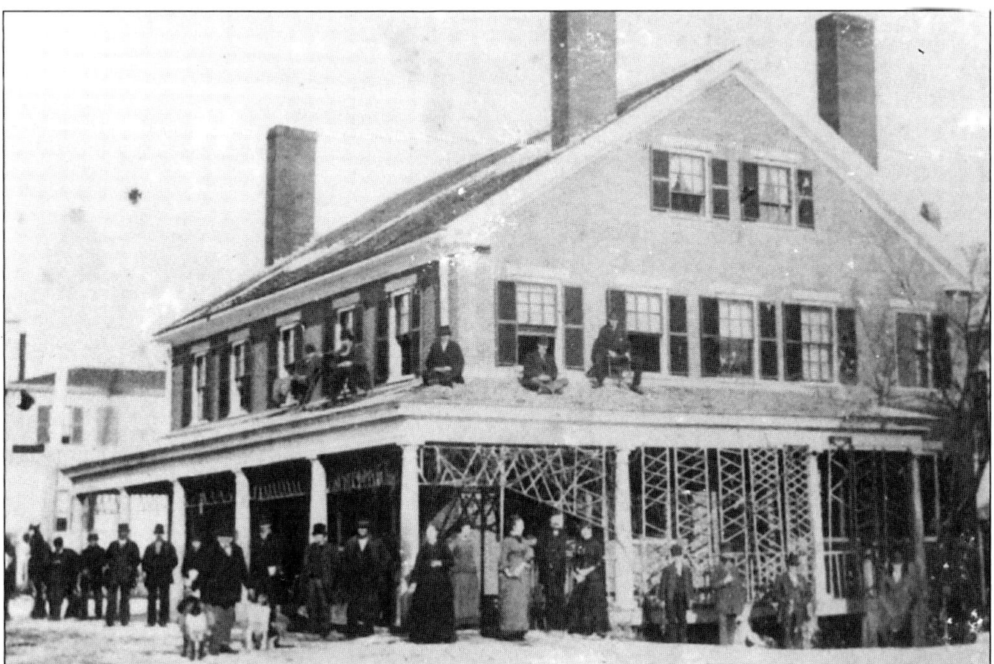

EPPING This is another shot of Bunker's Hotel. Note the huge chimneys for the cornered fire places.

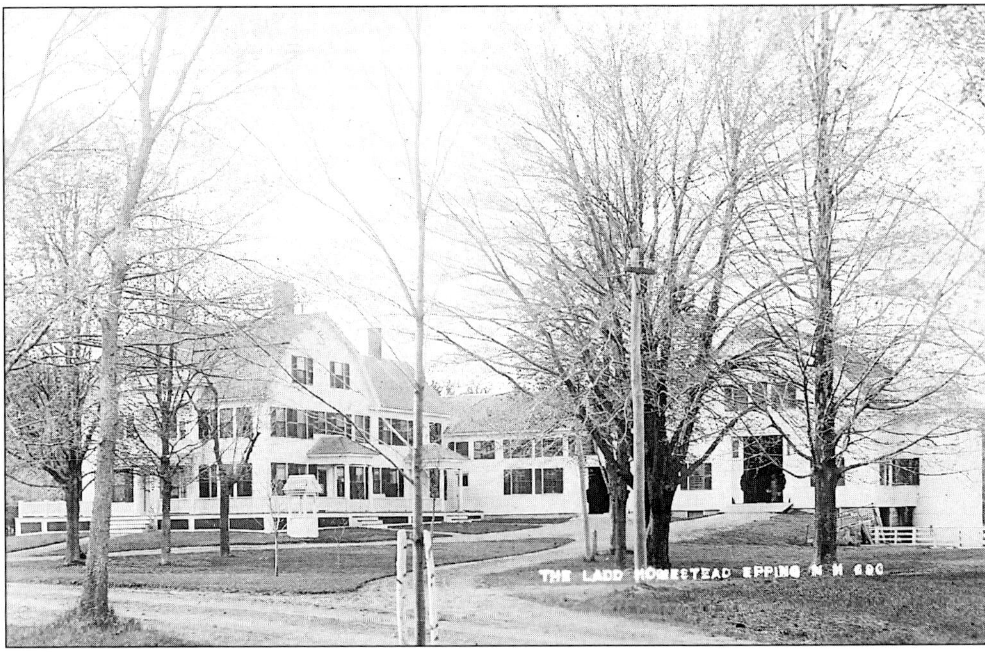

EPPING The Ladd Homestead, Ladd's Lane about 1910.

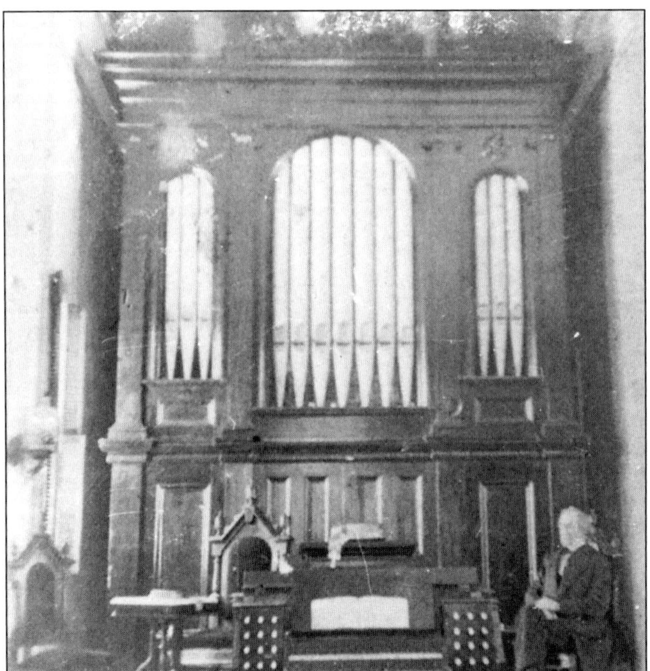

EPPING Pipe organ inside the Methodist Church which stood at the corner of Cate and Main Streets from 1866 until 1954. The photograph was taken about 1870.

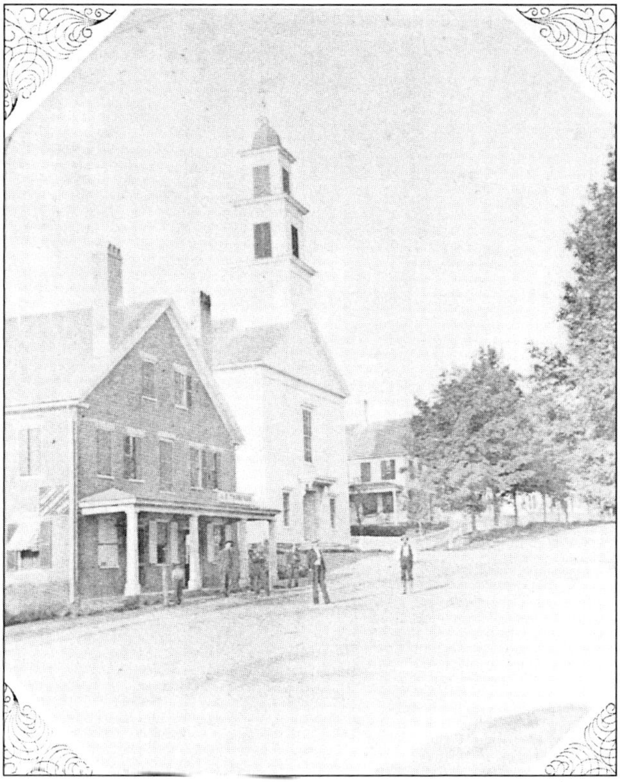

EPPING The Graves brick building which housed A. R. Thompson's Store, and the Congregational Church on Pleasant Street pictured in the late 1870s. Both burned in 1882. (Courtesy Donald Sanborn)

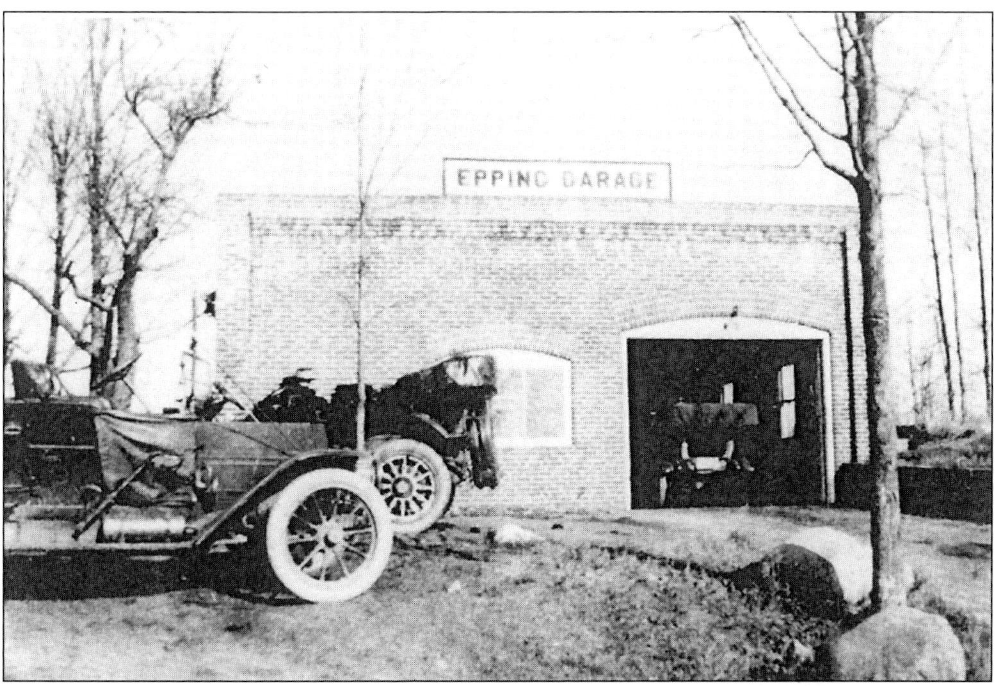

EPPING The Epping Garage on Pleasant Street about 1910. (Courtesy Donald Sanborn)

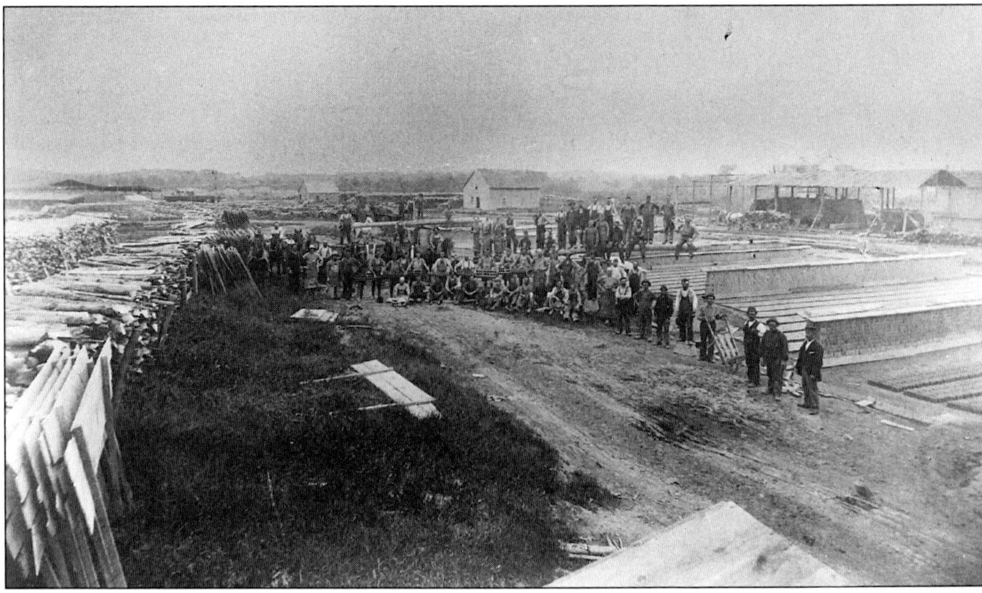

FREMONT Russell H. Fellows brickyard, Martin Road about 1885. This was the largest brickyard in New Hampshire during the late 1880s, producing over five million bricks a year. At its height it contained a store, saloon, blacksmith shop, barber shop, and several boarding houses. It ceased operation around 1912.

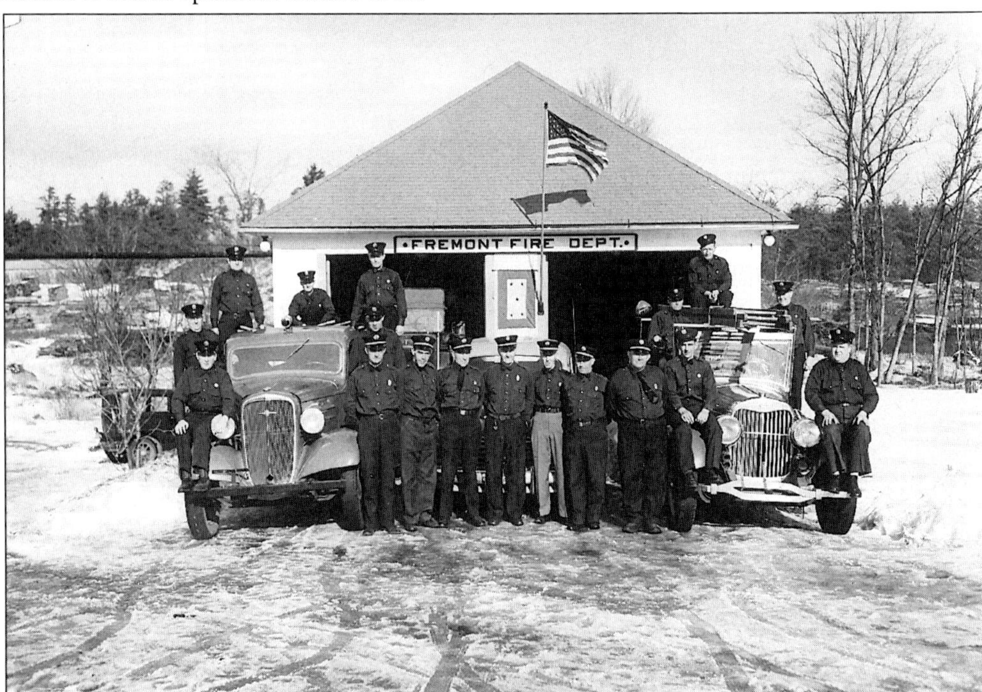

FREMONT After several disastrous village fires, Fremont established a fire department in 1925 and built a fire department in 1936. The volunteer fire department is posing in front of the station on Route 107 about 1942.

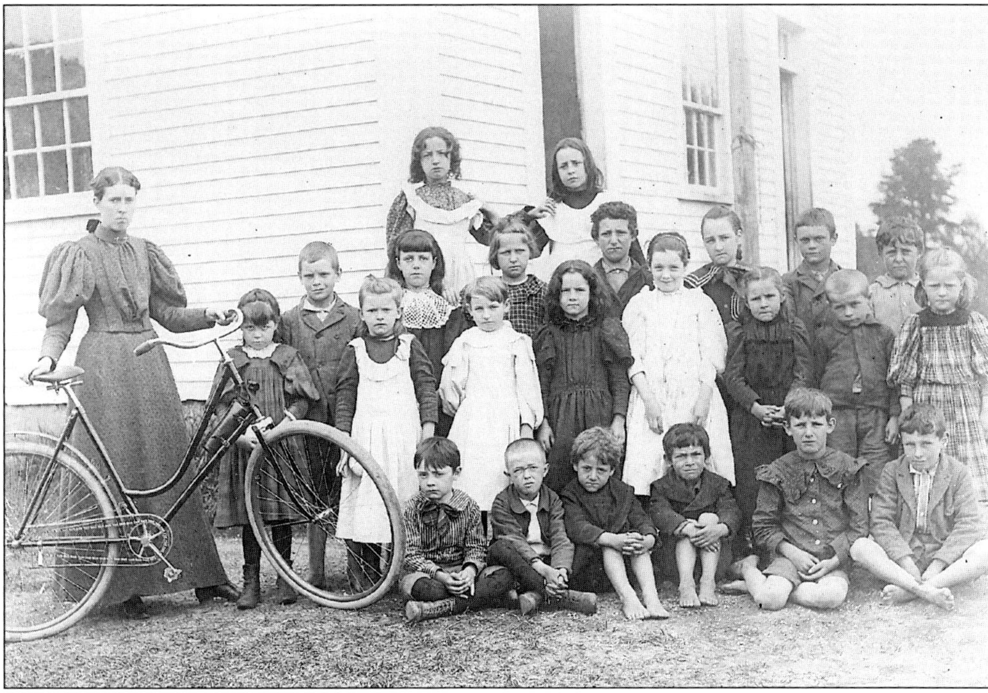

FREMONT Mary Alice Beede and class posing in front of the Primary School on Beede Road in 1896. The school was built in the early 1850s. By the late 1890s it was considered quite permissible for women to ride bicycles, in fact possession of one was a status symbol.

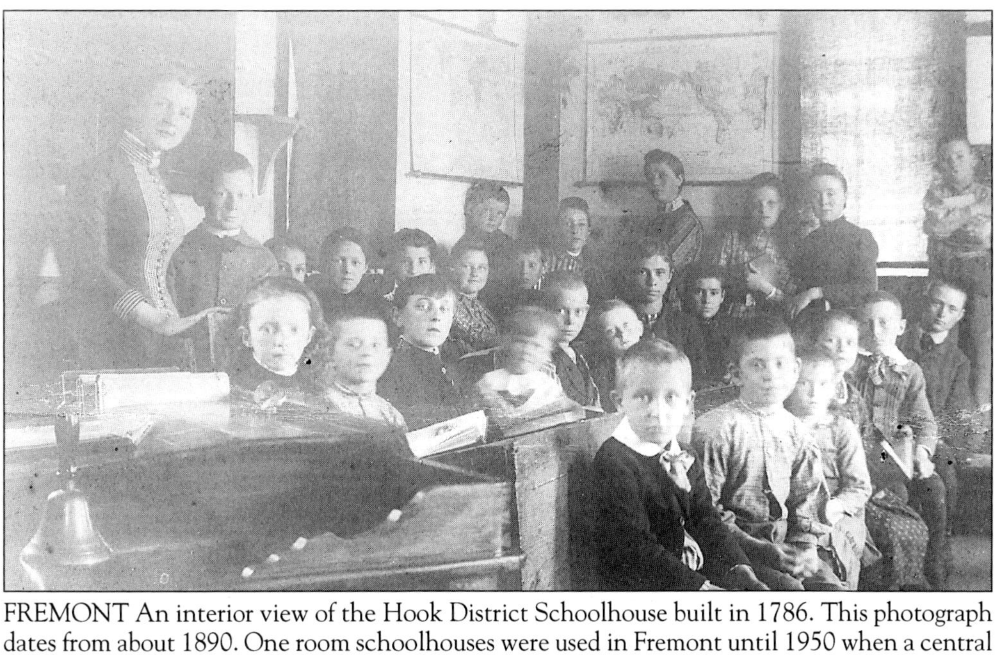

FREMONT An interior view of the Hook District Schoolhouse built in 1786. This photograph dates from about 1890. One room schoolhouses were used in Fremont until 1950 when a central school was built. This old schoolhouse was restored in the 1980s.

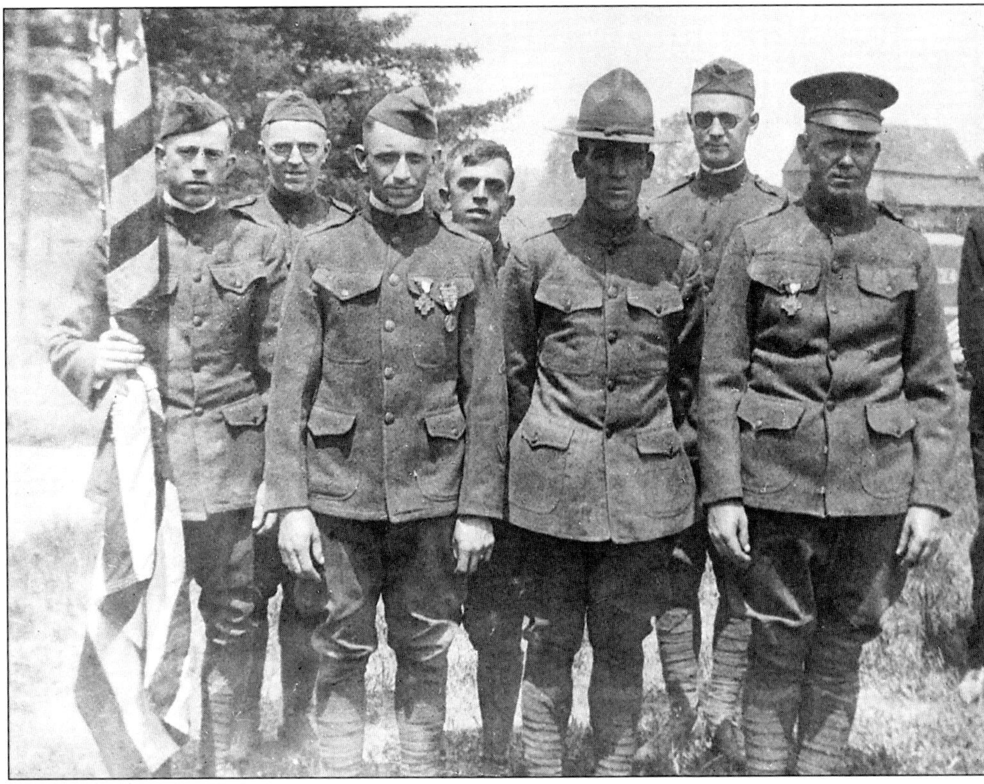

FREMONT First World War veterans posing on Memorial Day, 1920.

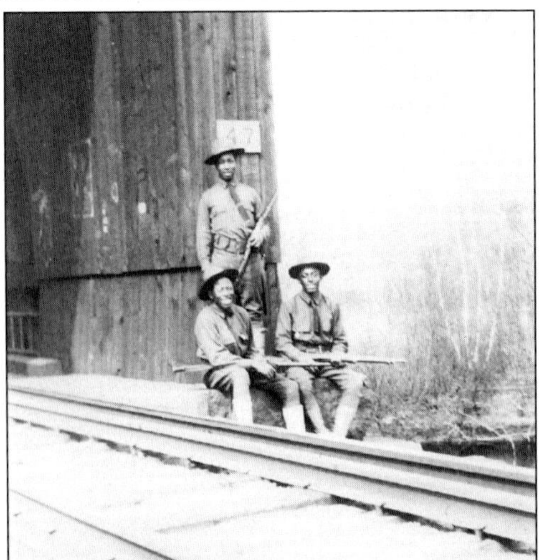

FREMONT During the First World War black soldiers, still in all black units lead by white officers, were by and large used on the home front. Here they are protecting a covered railroad bridge at Fremont from possible German sabotage in 1917.

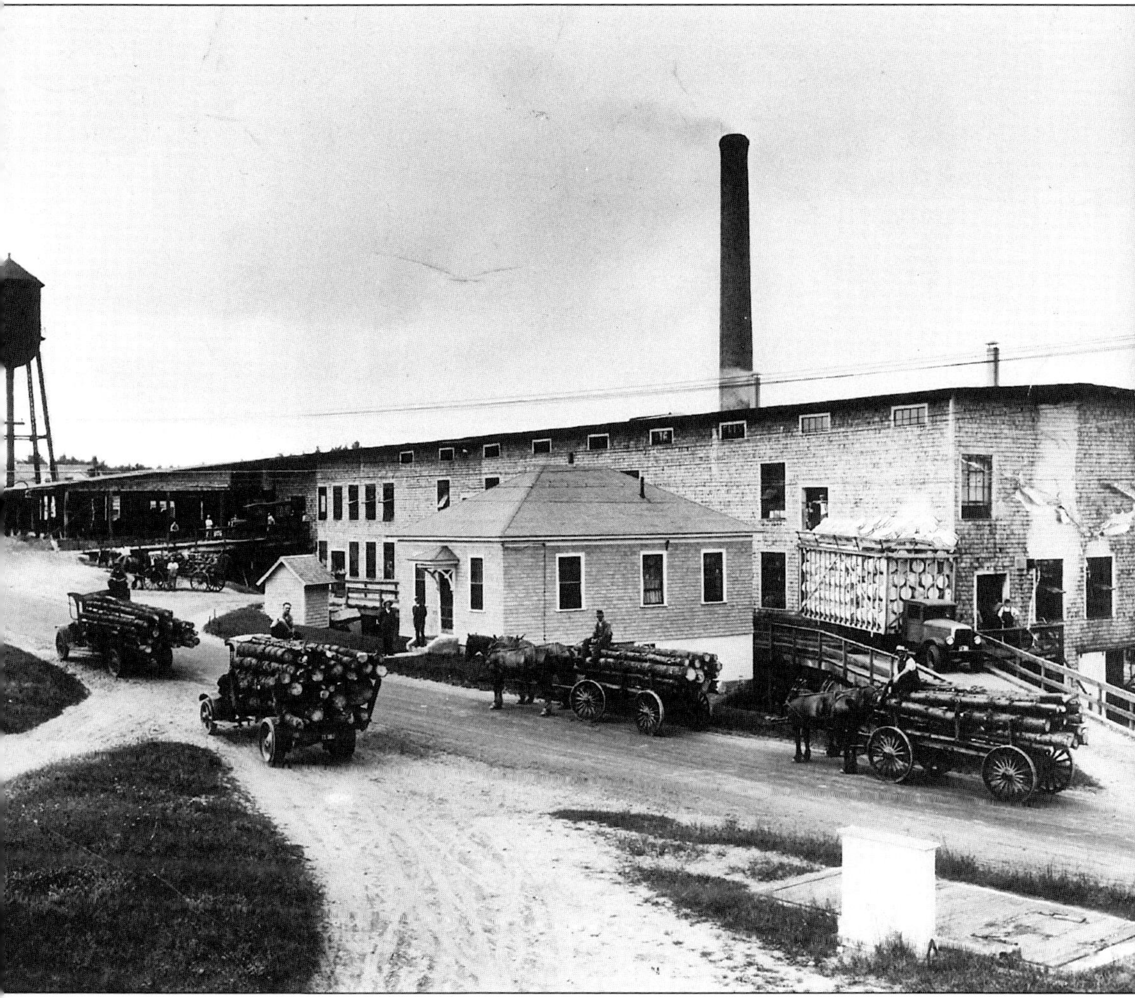

FREMONT A 1930 photograph of the Spaulding and Frost Cooperage on Route 107. This is the oldest barrel cooperage in the world and was built in 1874 by Jonas Spaulding, father of two New Hampshire governors. This structure burned in a spectacular fire in 1973.

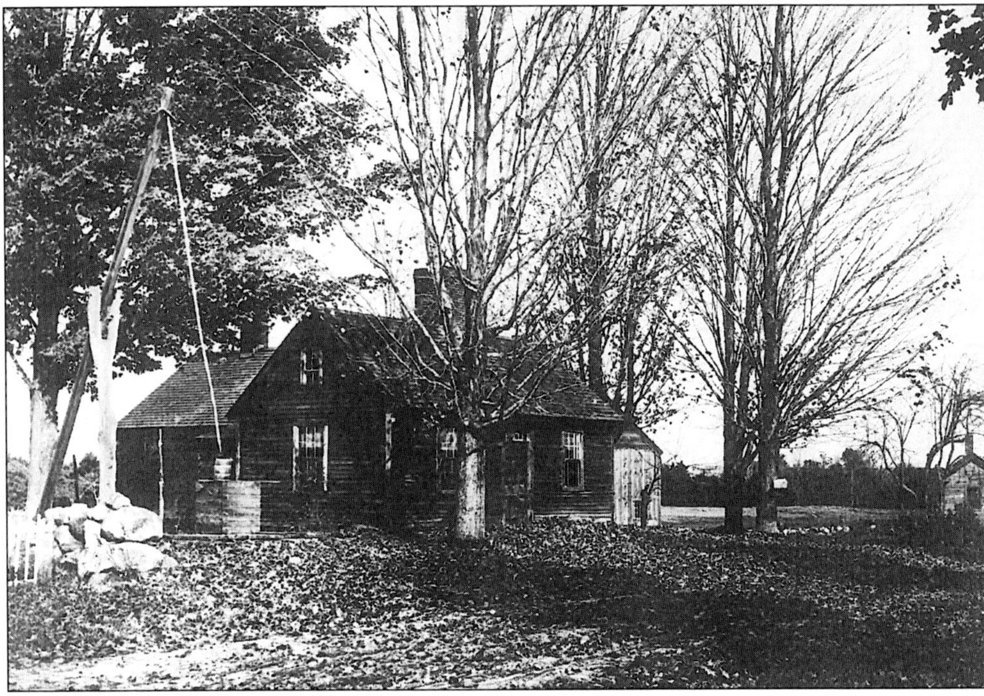

FREMONT The Tucker-Sanborn house at the corner of Scribner and South Roads in 1911. Built about 1807, this house shows a well sweep, once a familiar farmyard feature. The house burned in 1982.

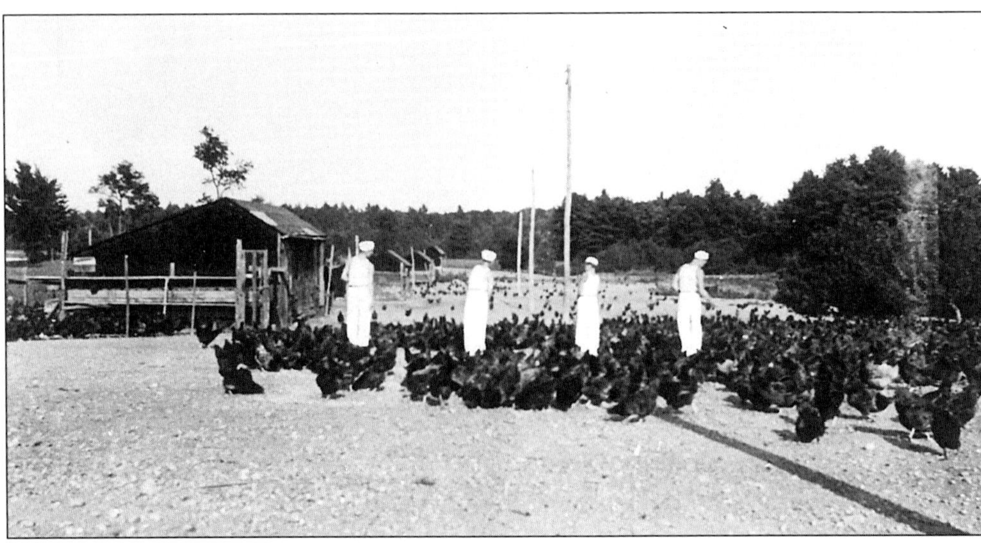

FREMONT Feeding New Hampshire reds at William Cole's poultry farm on Scribner Road about 1935. The poultry business was a major Rockingham County industry between 1920 and 1960.

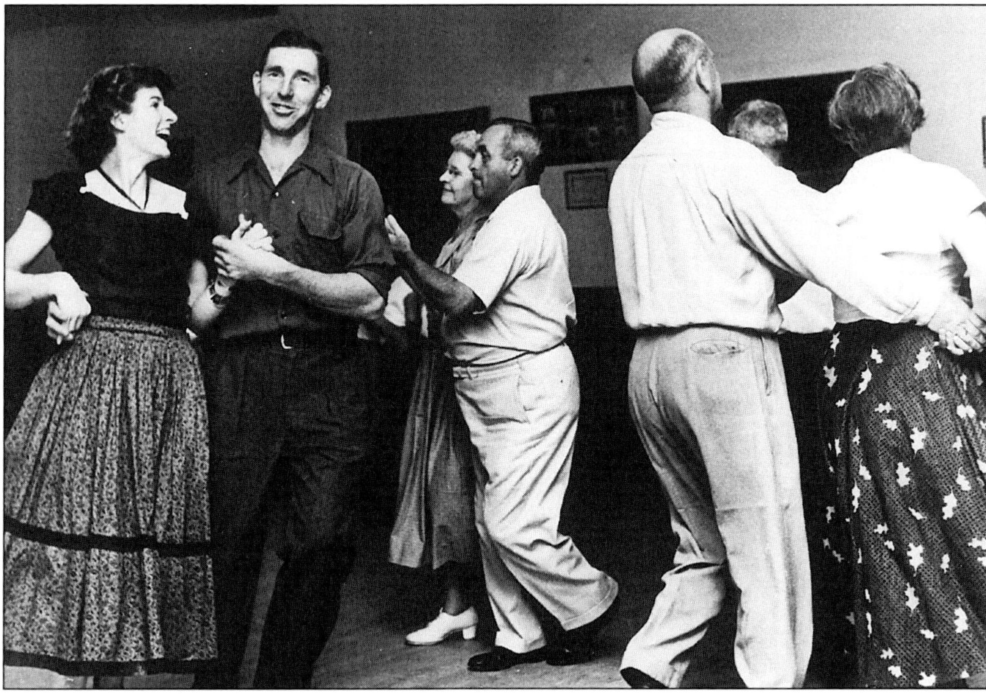

FREMONT Jonathan and Betty Quimby attending a typical Saturday night square dance at the Fremont town hall in 1953. Jonathan Quimby, a well-known square dance caller, also held many square dances at his Mistwold Farm on North Road.

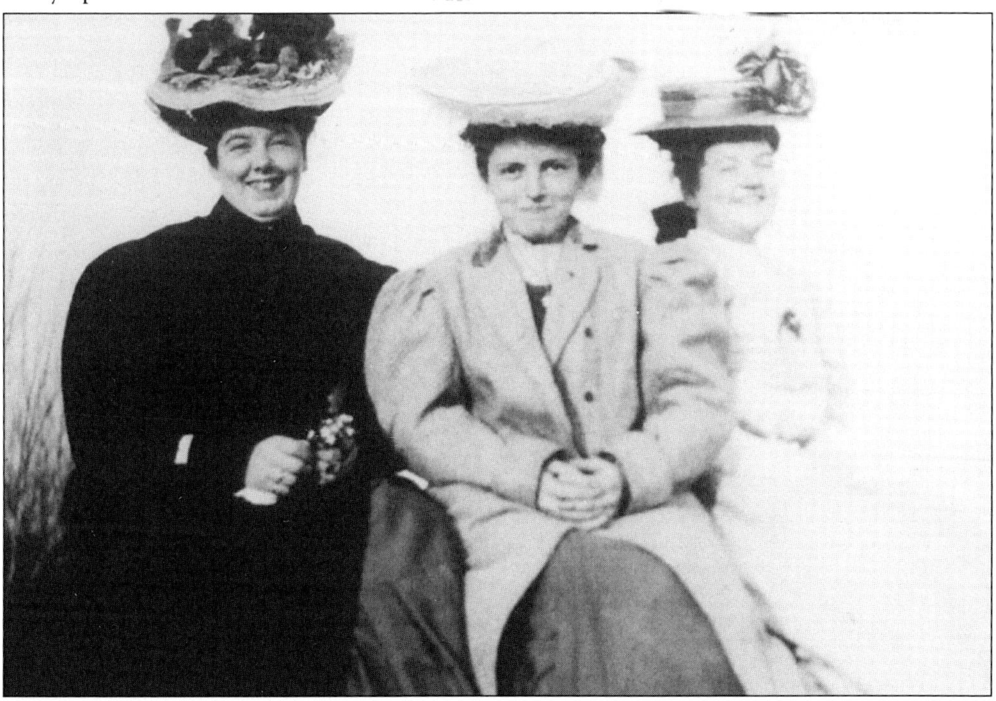

FREMONT These ladies with their fancy hats are enjoying a carefree moment at Black Rocks Mill in 1908.

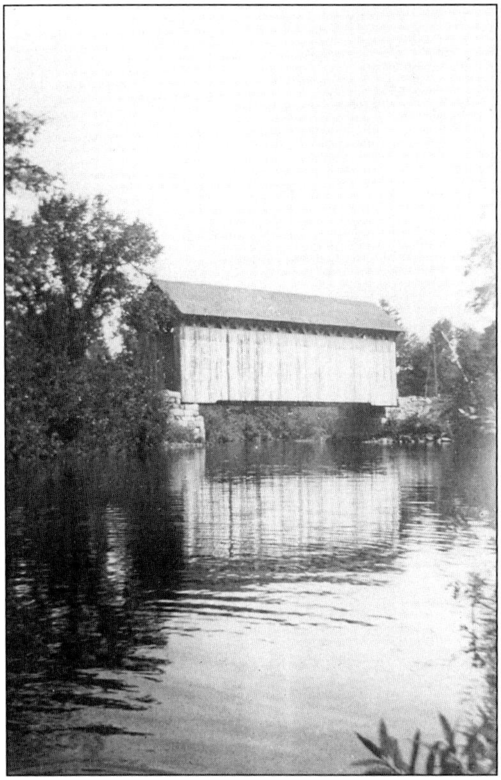

FREMONT The railroad covered bridge was built in 1903 to replace an 1874 structure that burned on the Worcester, Nashua and Rochester, Boston and Maine railroad. This bridge was replaced with an iron bridge in 1934.

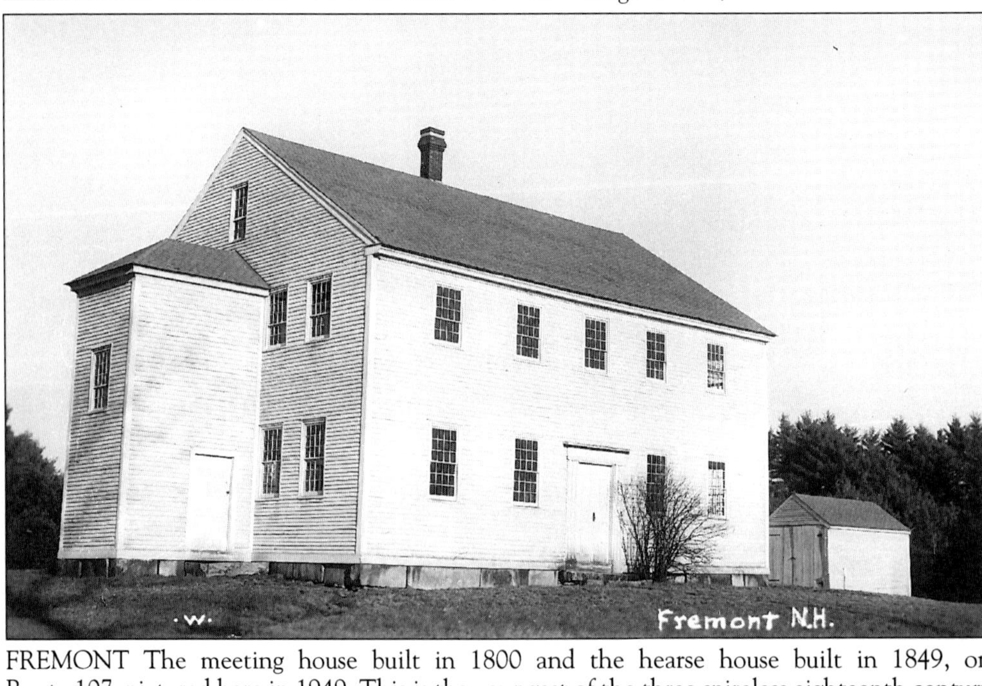

FREMONT The meeting house built in 1800 and the hearse house built in 1849, on Route 107, pictured here in 1949. This is the youngest of the three spireless eighteenth century meeting houses in Rockingham County. It is one of only two twin porch meeting houses in New England.

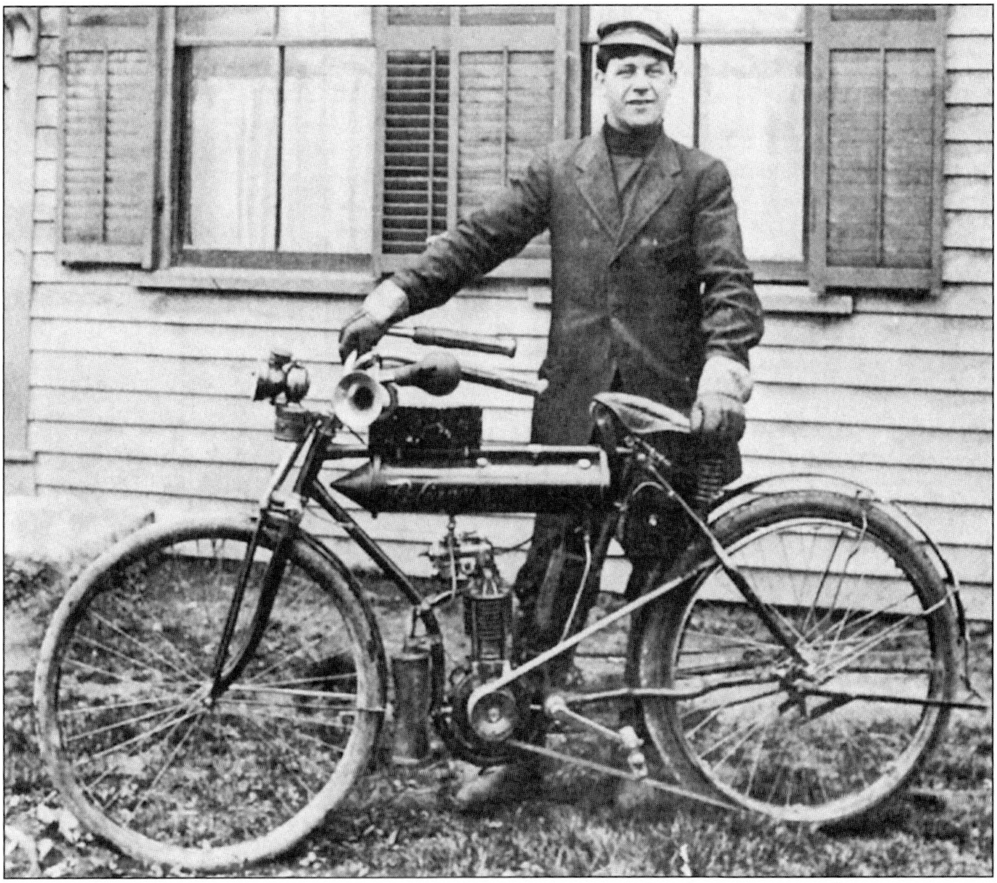

FREMONT James Clement, Sr. proudly displays one of the first motorcycles in Fremont sometime before 1920. The machine is a 1916 Reliance and was without doubt a rough riding handful on the unpaved roads of the time.

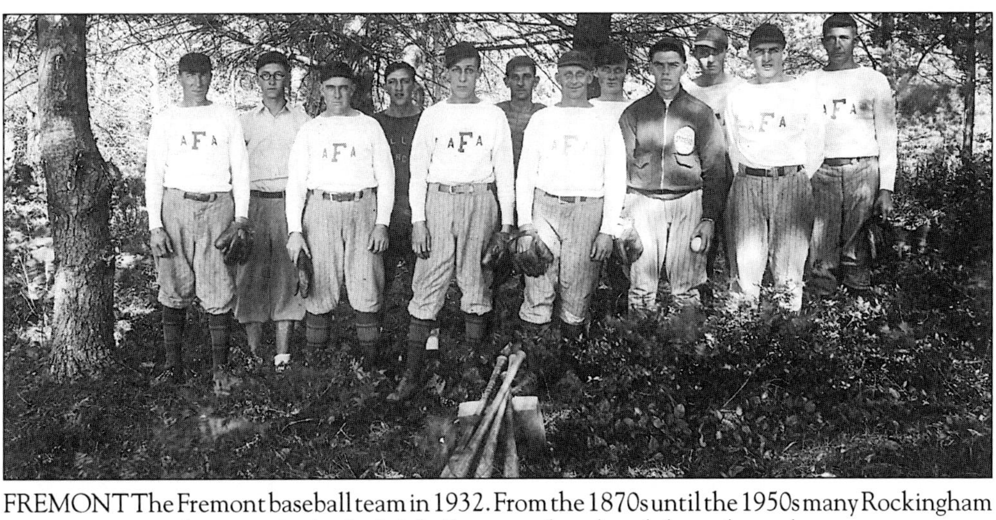

FREMONT The Fremont baseball team in 1932. From the 1870s until the 1950s many Rockingham county towns and companies had adult ball teams who played throughout the summer.

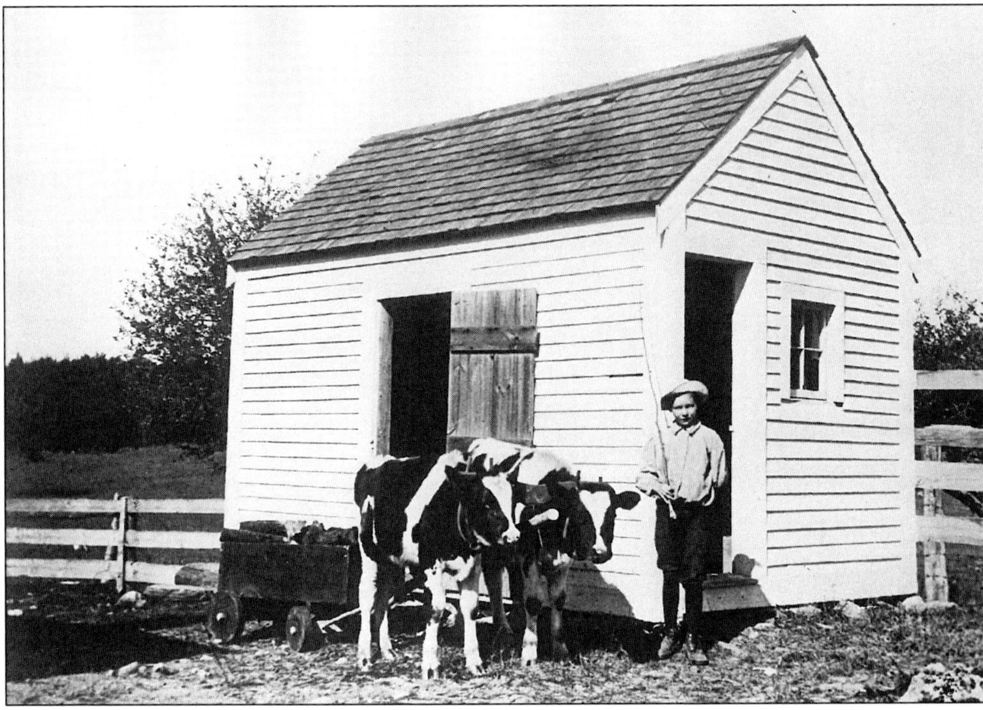

FREMONT Sidney Lyford and his wagon team posing in front of the Northside school woodshed and privy in 1914.

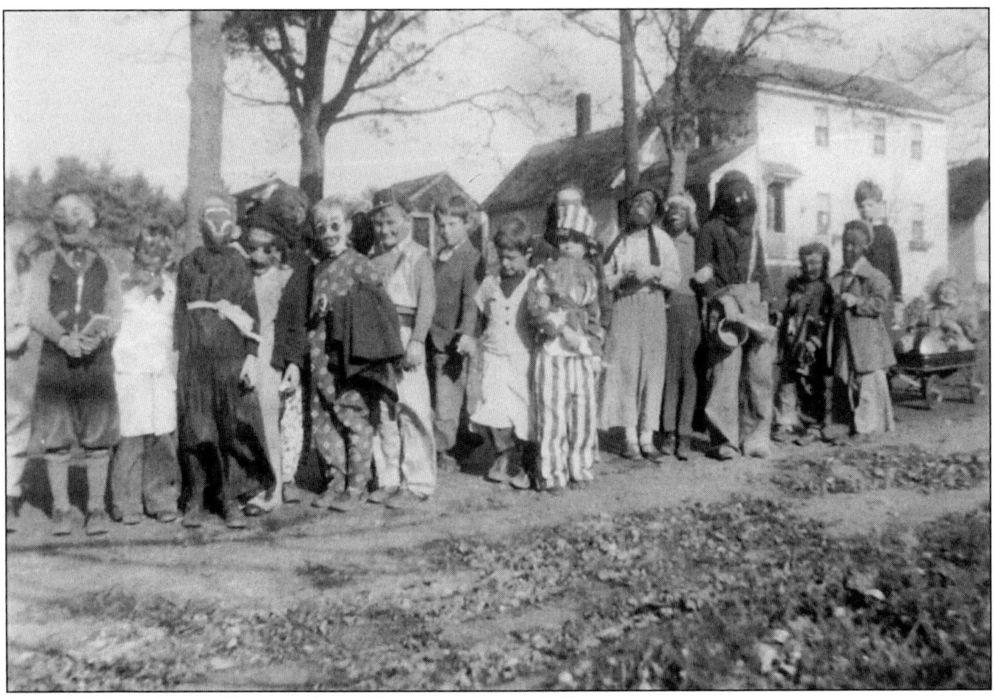

FREMONT The "Halloween horribles" parade in 1942.

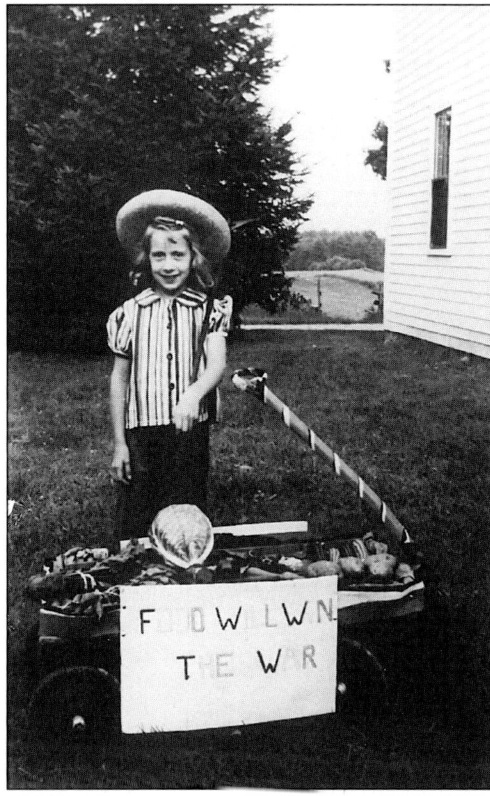

FREMONT Elizabeth Bassett is shown here helping to pool vital resources such as food, metals and newspapers in support of the war effort in 1942. The rationing effort in the United States was one of the major contributions of children.

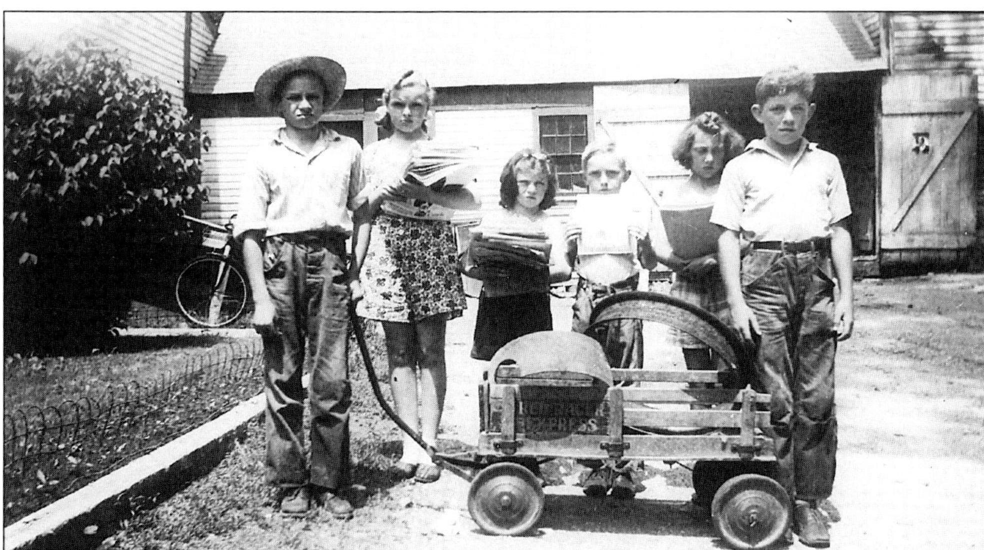

FREMONT Another picture of youngsters collecting scrap metal and newspapers to support the war effort in August 1944. Left to right: Robert Burleigh, Charlotte Seavey, Jacki Moulton, Reid Spaulding, Barbara Marcotte and Richard Moulton.

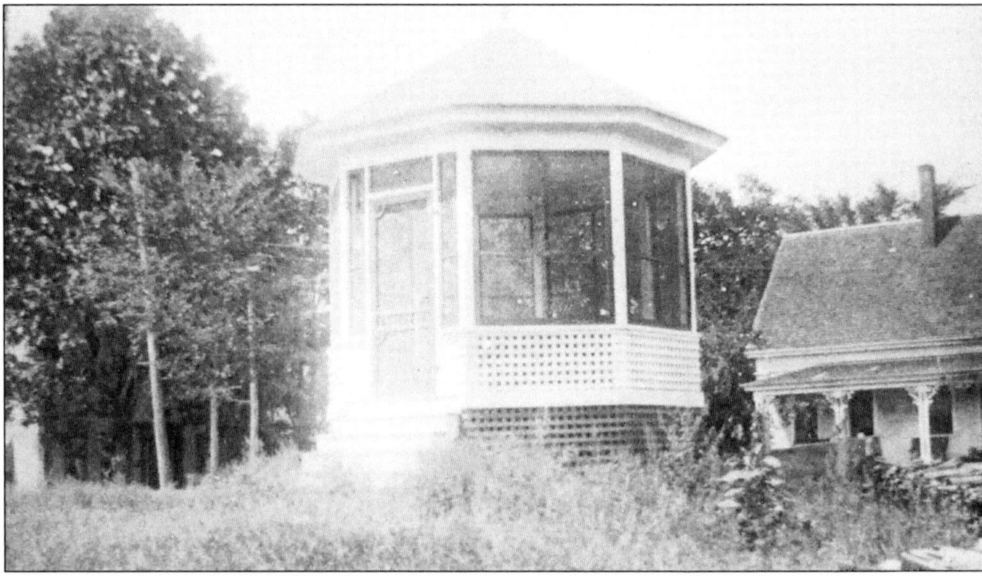

FREMONT The bandstand, built in 1909, stood opposite the town hall on Route 107 until the early 1950s.

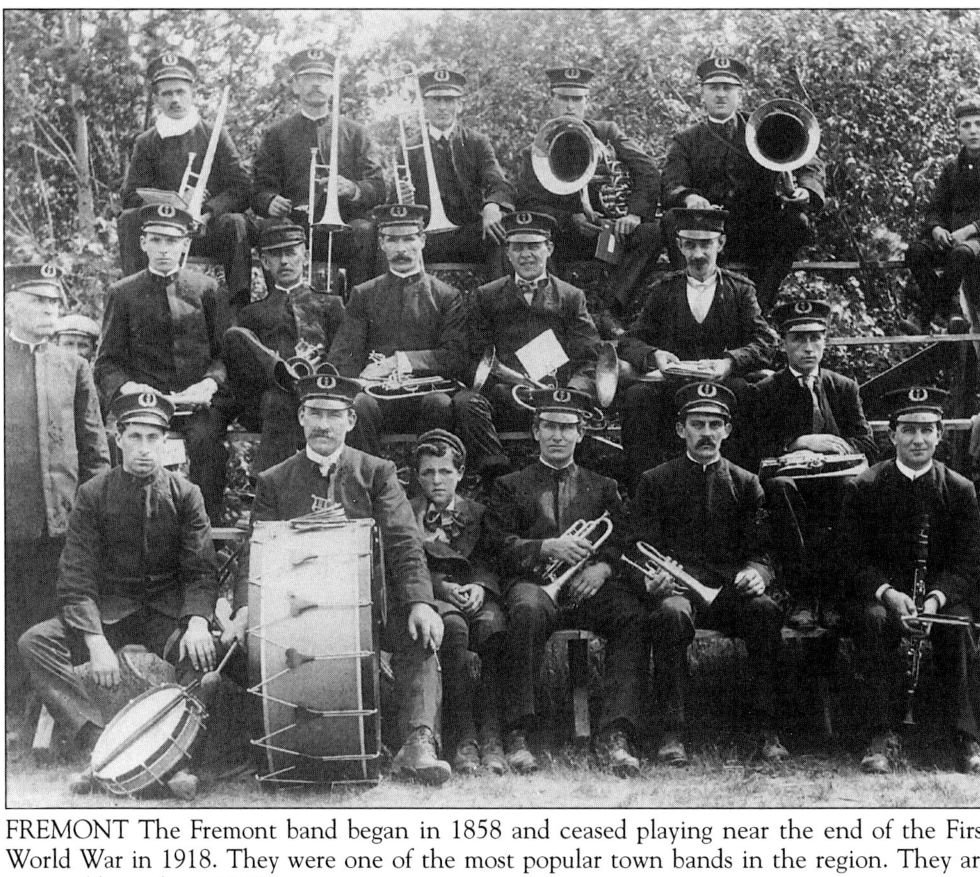

FREMONT The Fremont band began in 1858 and ceased playing near the end of the First World War in 1918. They were one of the most popular town bands in the region. They are pictured here about 1910.

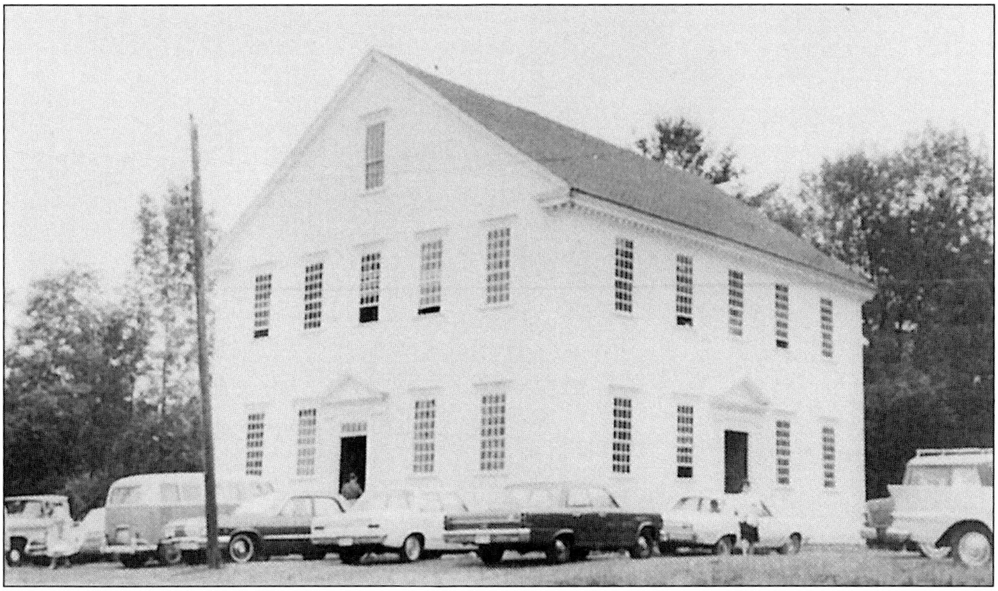

SANDOWN The old meeting house built in 1773 and 1774 on Fremont Road. This is another of the three spireless eighteenth century meeting houses in Rockingham County. It contains many detailed architectural features.

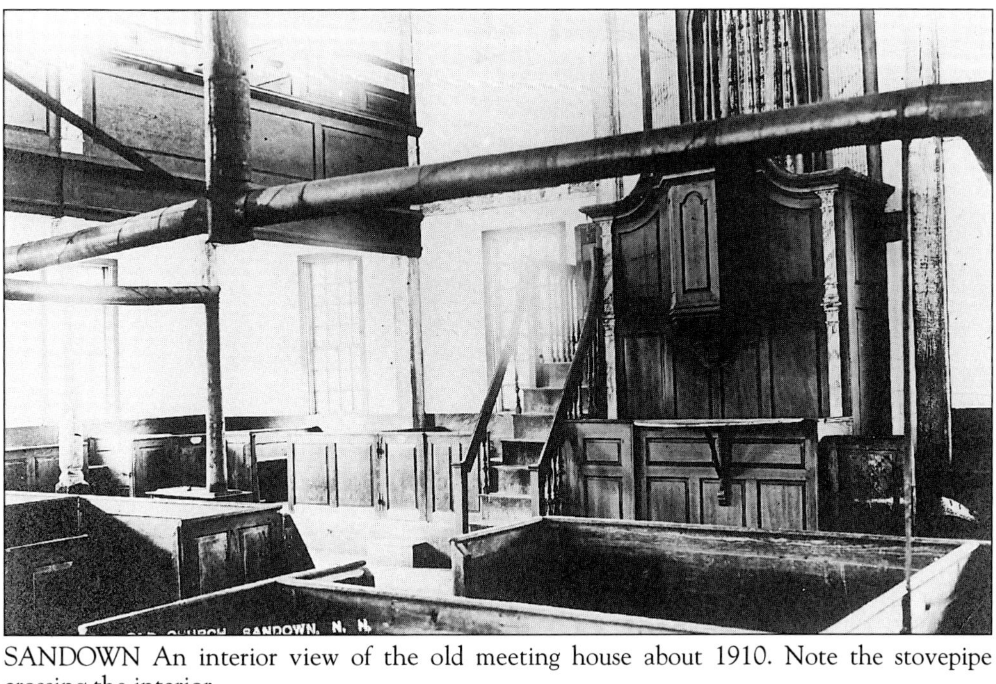

SANDOWN An interior view of the old meeting house about 1910. Note the stovepipe crossing the interior.

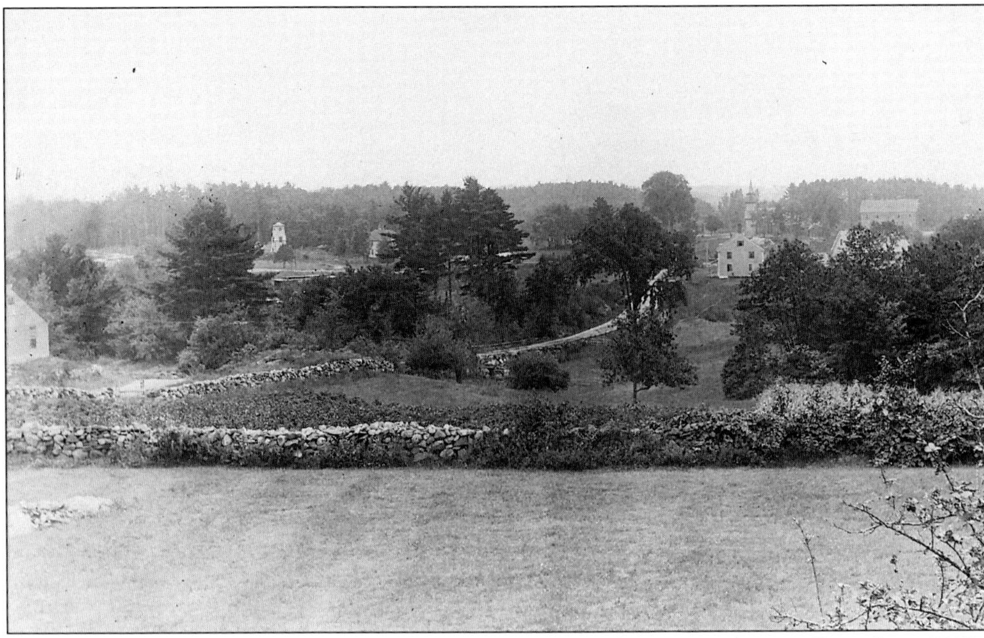

SANDOWN A view from Meeting House Hill looking south over Sandown village about 1908.

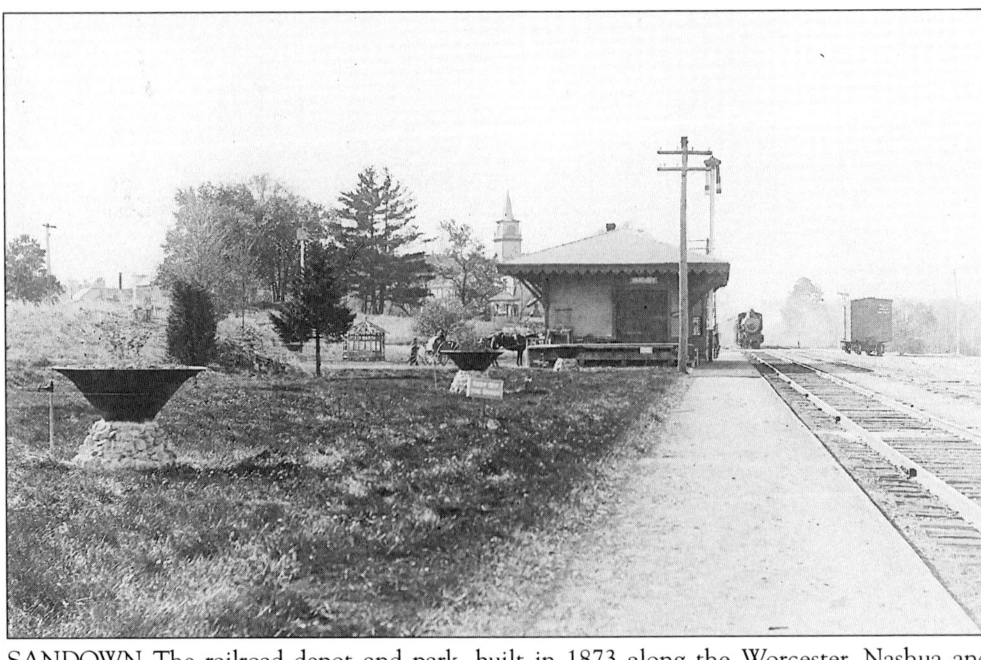

SANDOWN The railroad depot and park, built in 1873 along the Worcester, Nashua and Rochester railroad, located off Fremont Road. This photograph was taken around 1908.

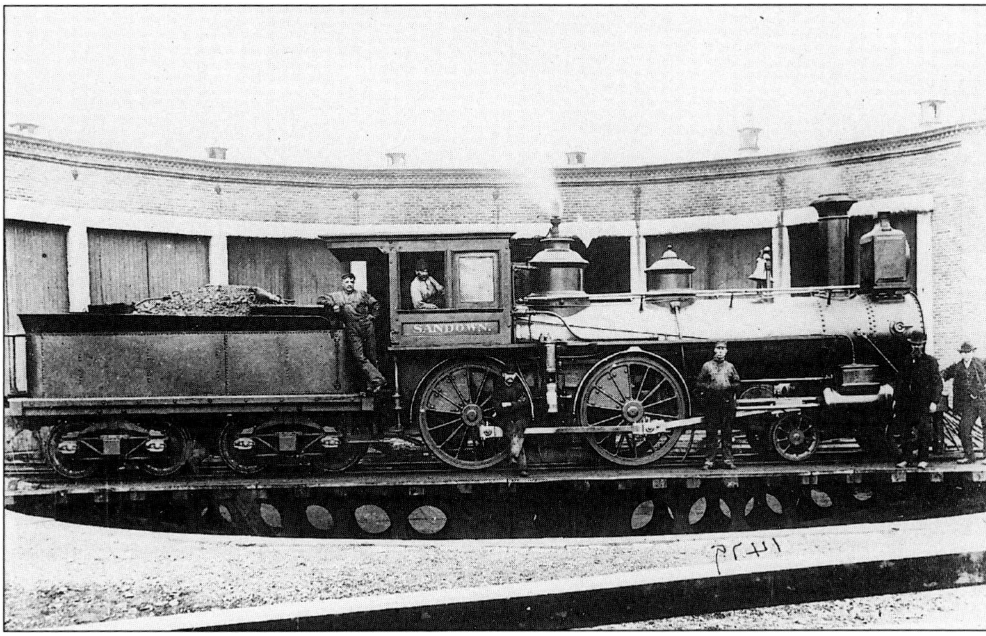

SANDOWN A view of the Sandown locomotive in 1886 which belonged to the Worcester, Nashua and Rochester railroad corporation. It was common for the corporation to name locomotives after many of the towns along its route.

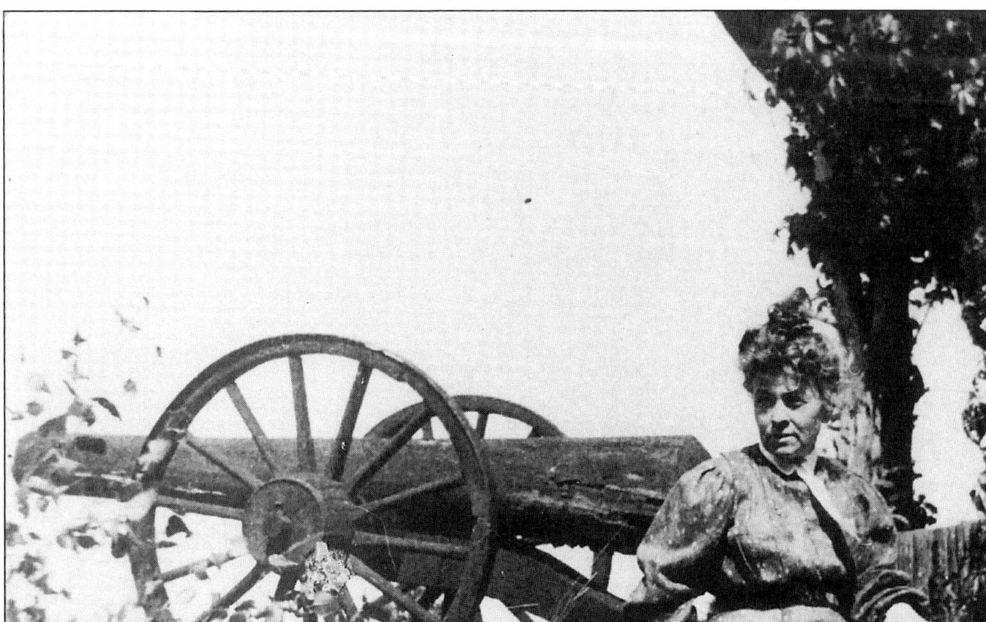

SANDOWN A photograph taken at Cannon rock near the Sandown railroad depot off Fremont Road in 1906. The cannon was made entirely of wood.

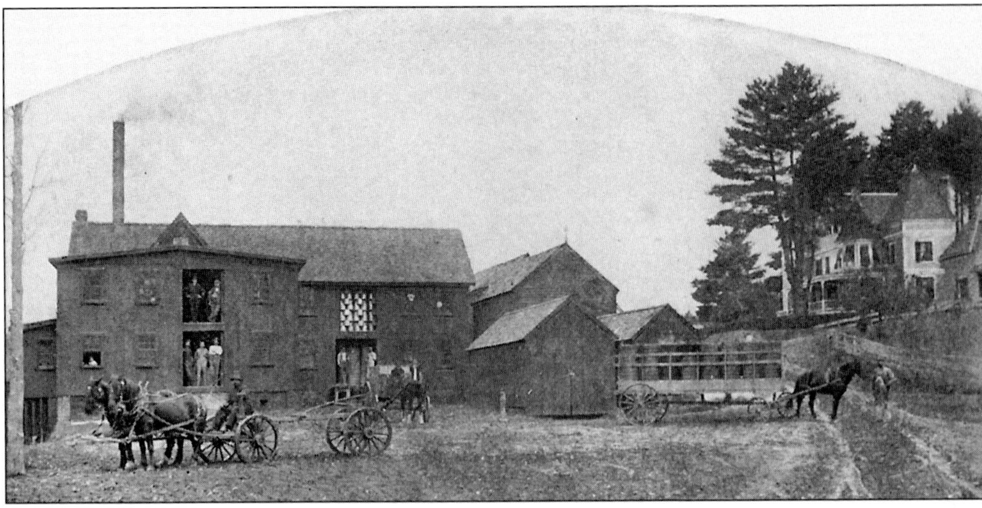

SANDOWN John W. Lovering's woodenware factory was built in 1877 and burned in 1922. The turreted Victorian style house on the right still stands off Route 121A.

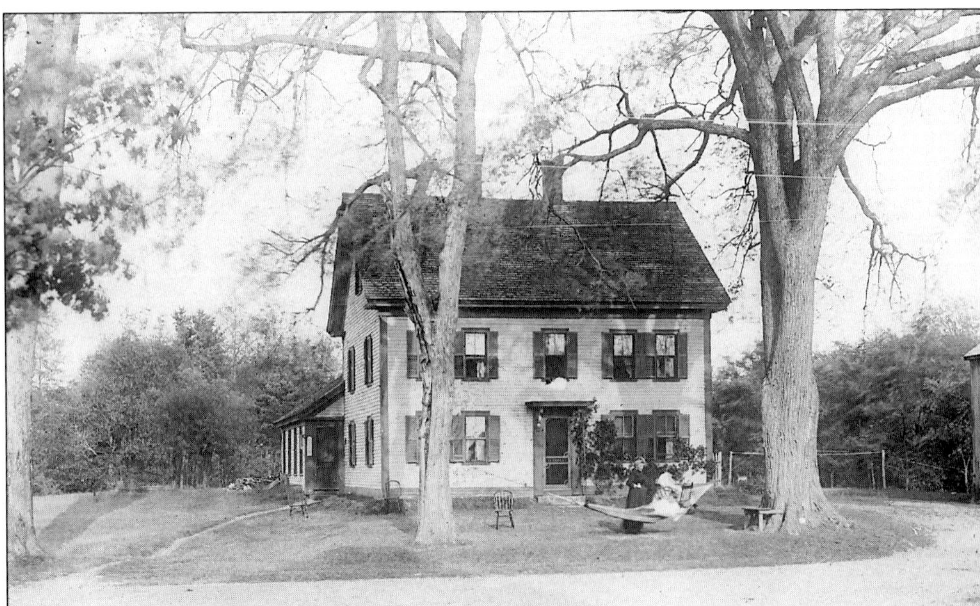

SANDOWN The Triple Elm hotel on Route 121A is pictured here about 1910-13. It operated from 1893 until about 1915. The building stands opposite Perrino's store.

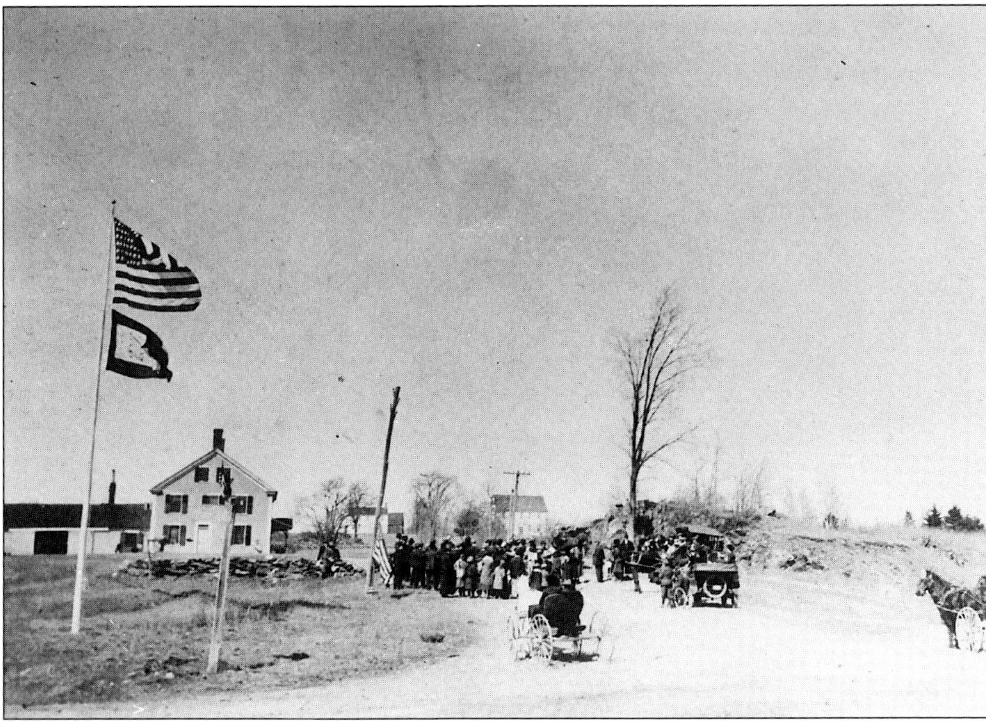

SANDOWN A First World War flag raising ceremony in front of the old parsonage on Fremont Road in April 1918.

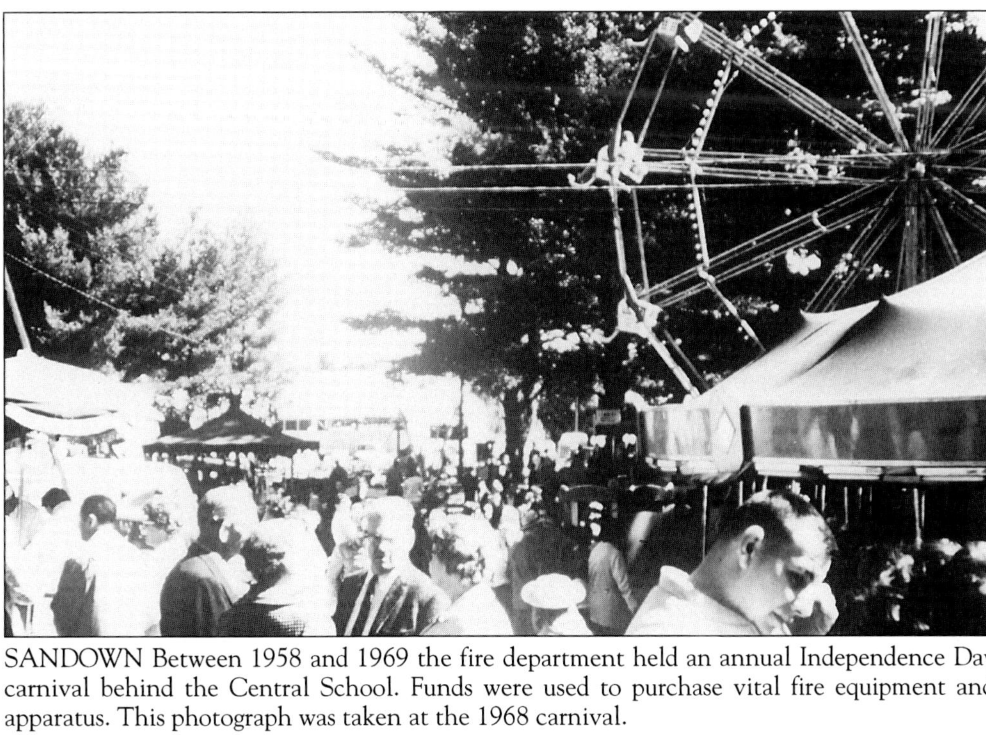

SANDOWN Between 1958 and 1969 the fire department held an annual Independence Day carnival behind the Central School. Funds were used to purchase vital fire equipment and apparatus. This photograph was taken at the 1968 carnival.

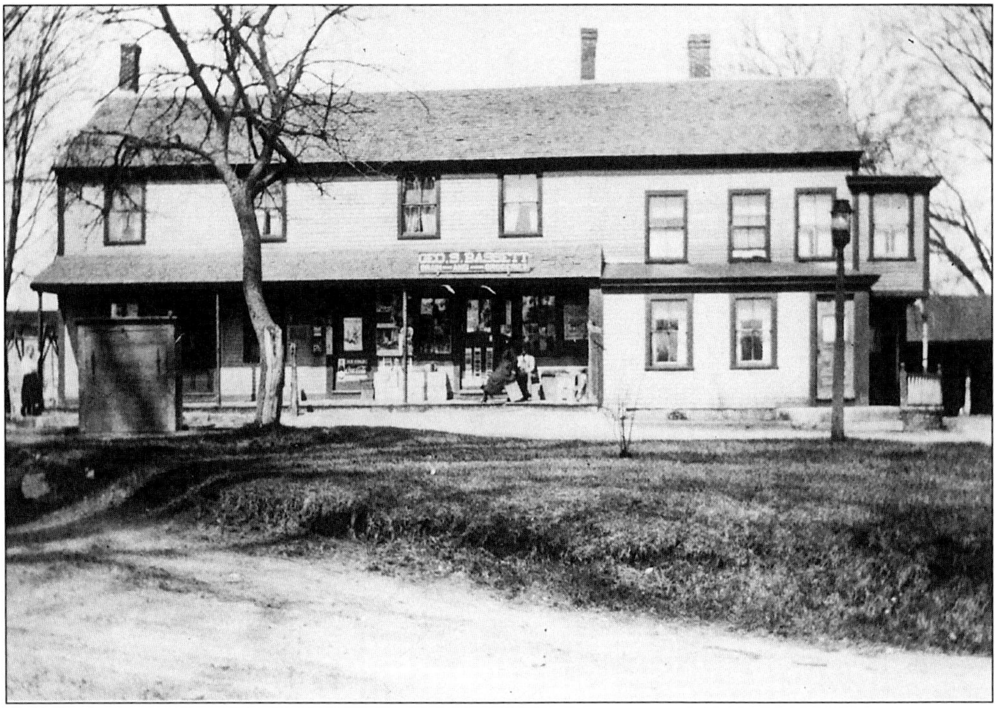

SANDOWN George S. Bassett's store, now Perrino's store, Route 121A about 1913.

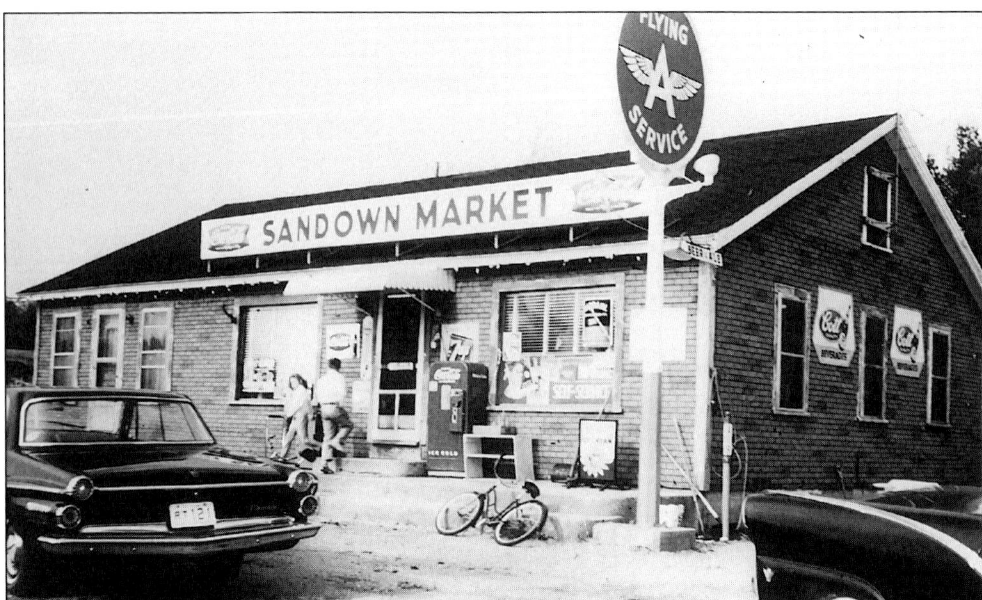

SANDOWN Dinsmore's Sandown Market on Route 121A in the village about 1955.

Five

Around Mount Pawtuckaway

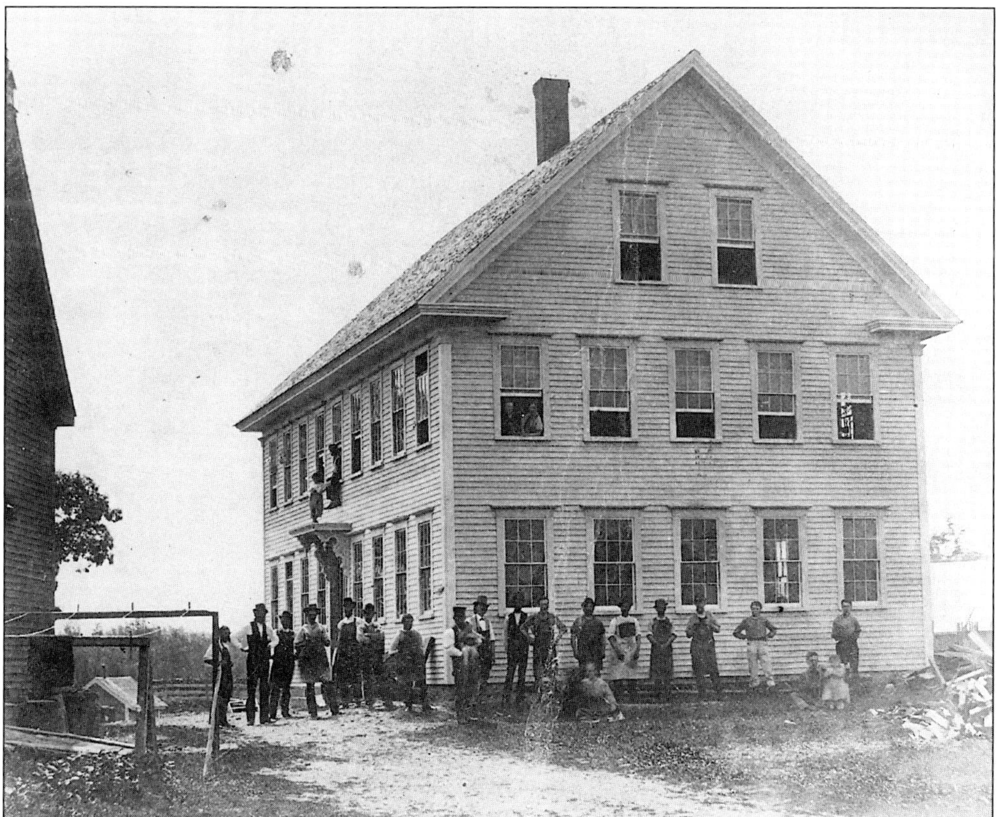

RAYMOND Ladd's shoe shop about 1874.

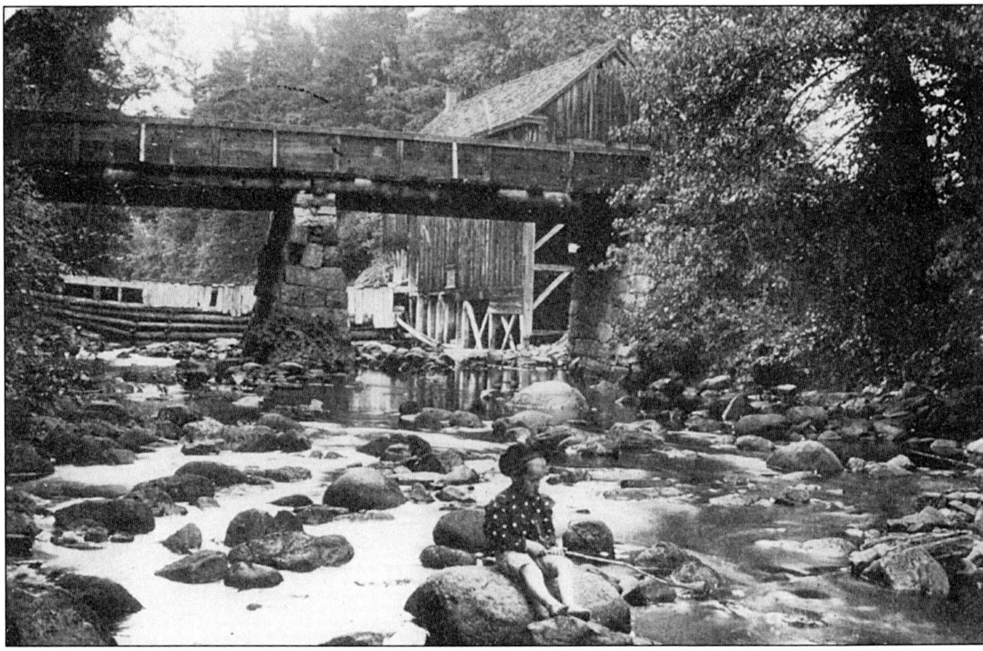

RAYMOND Brown's mill and bridge about 1907. Originally known as Freetown mill and built about 1725, this was the oldest mill in Raymond.

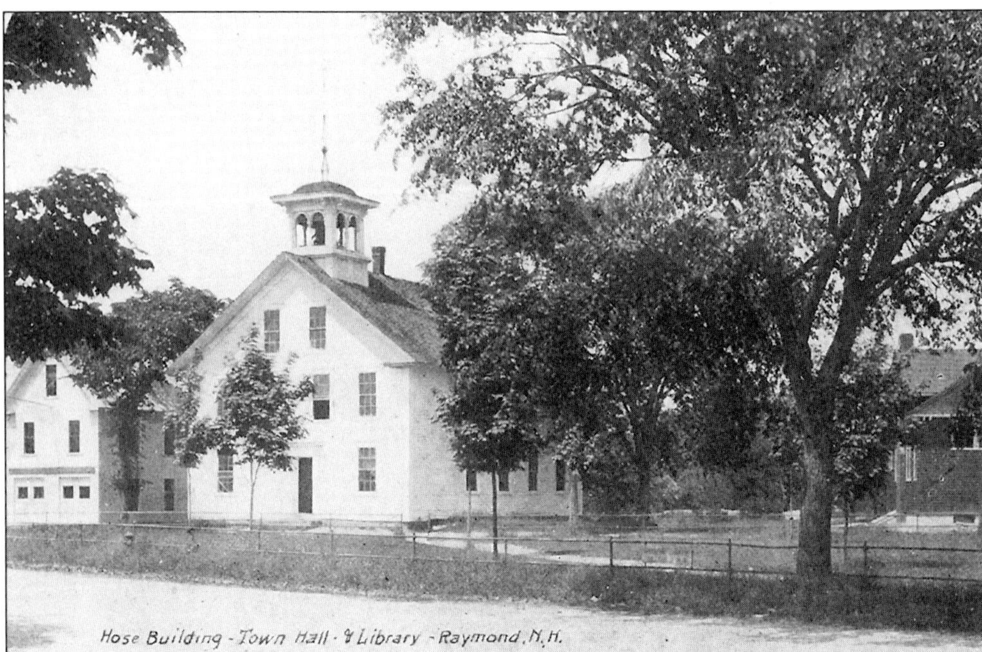

RAYMOND Epping Road about 1909. Left to right one can see the fire house, built in 1905, the town hall, built in 1786 originally as a meeting house and later moved to this site and the public library, built in 1908. The town hall burned in 1917.

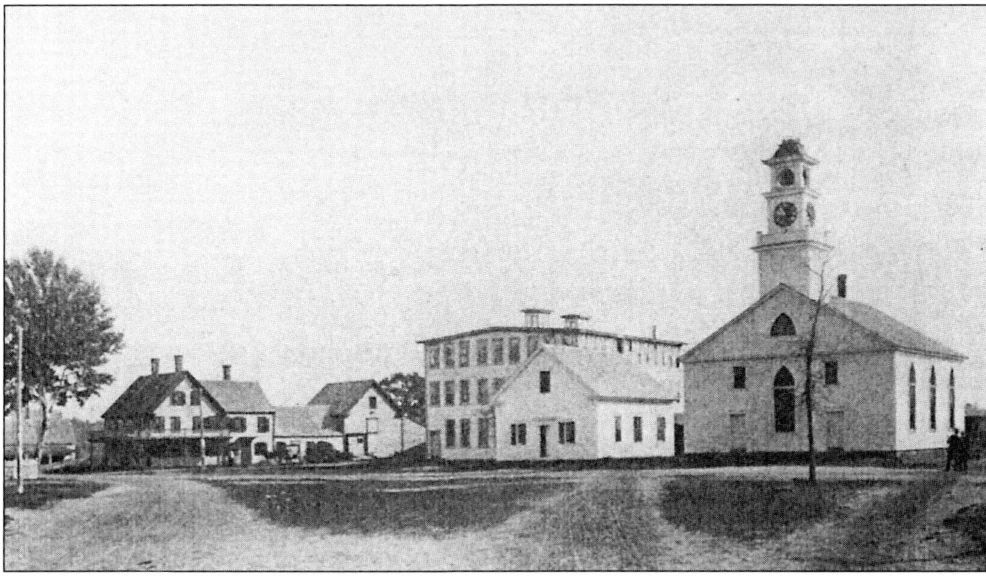

RAYMOND A view of Epping Road and portion of town common taken before the Great Fire of 1892 which destroyed the Congregational Church, built in 1834, and other nearby buildings.

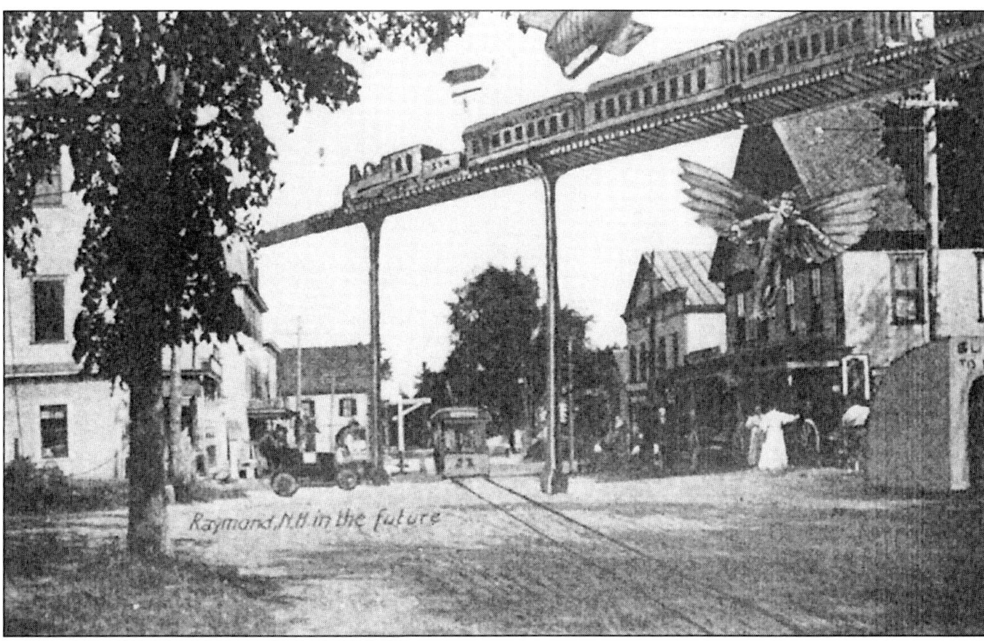

RAYMOND Another futuristic postcard, this time of Raymond center.

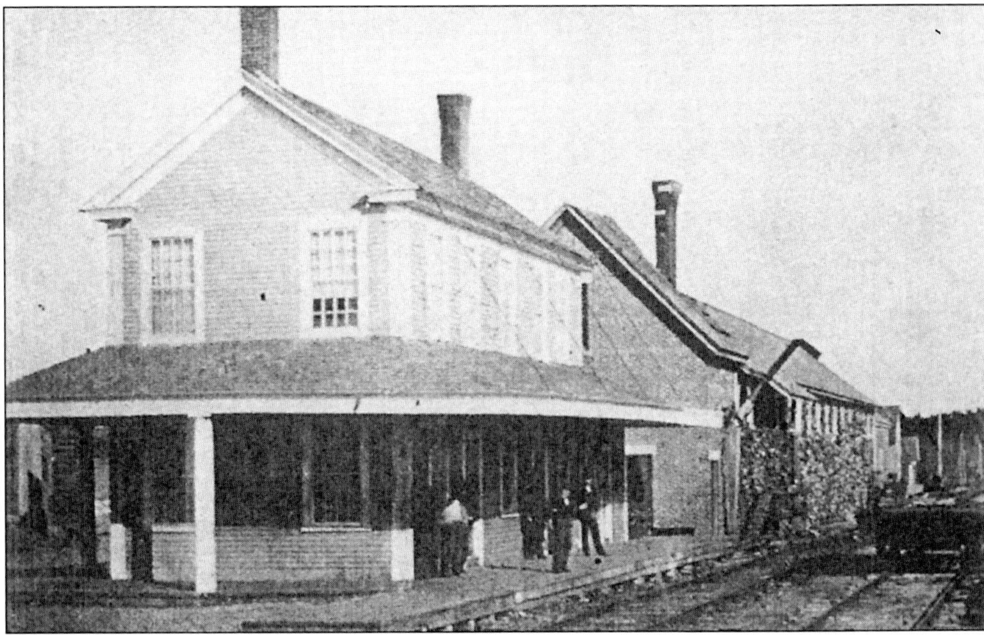

RAYMOND The first railroad depot in Raymond was built in 1850 and burned in 1878. It stood on the Portsmouth and Concord railroad line.

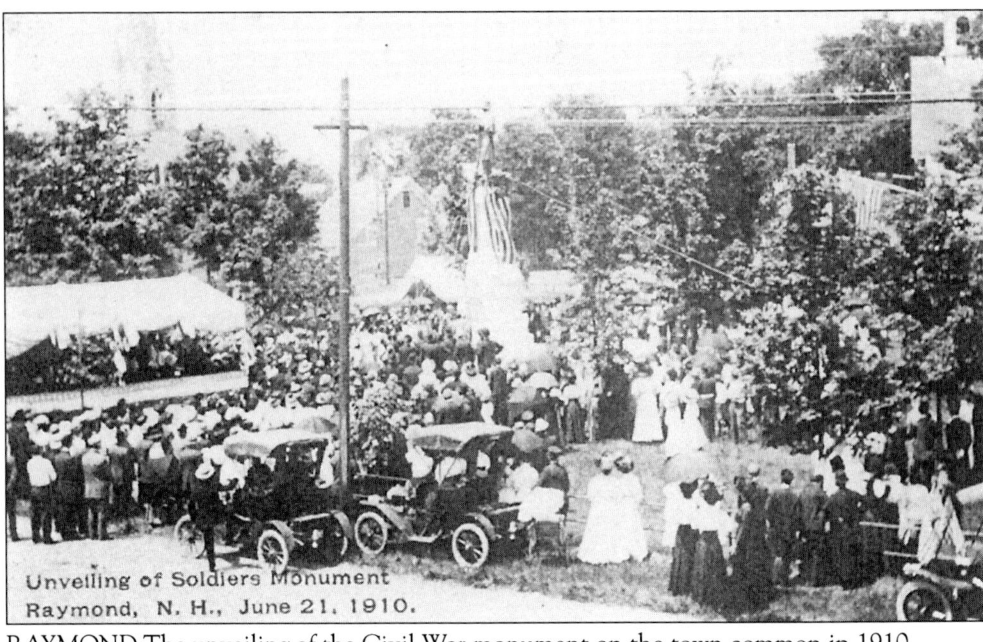

RAYMOND The unveiling of the Civil War monument on the town common in 1910.

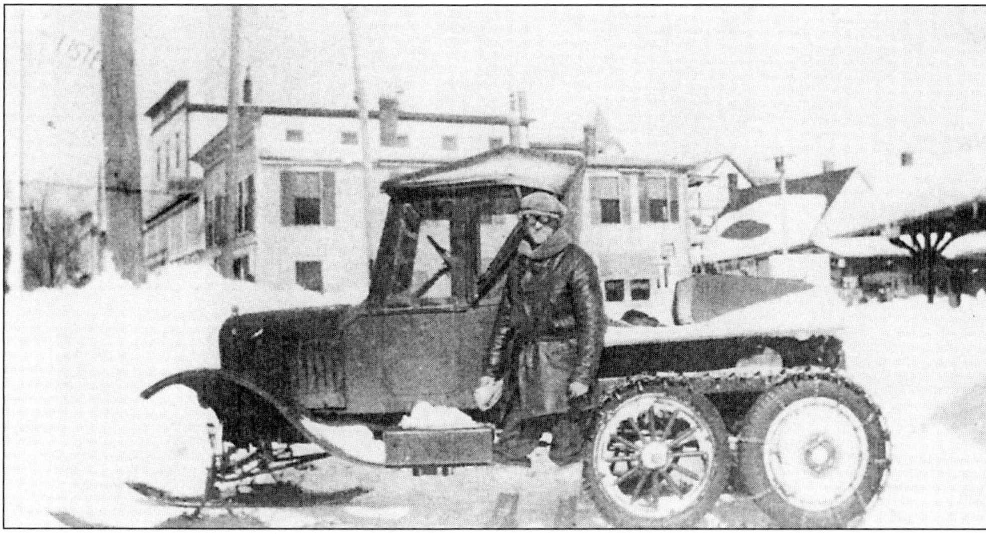

RAYMOND Emile Wason, mail carrier, with his 1933 snowmobile. Note the front mounted skis and rear traction arrangement.

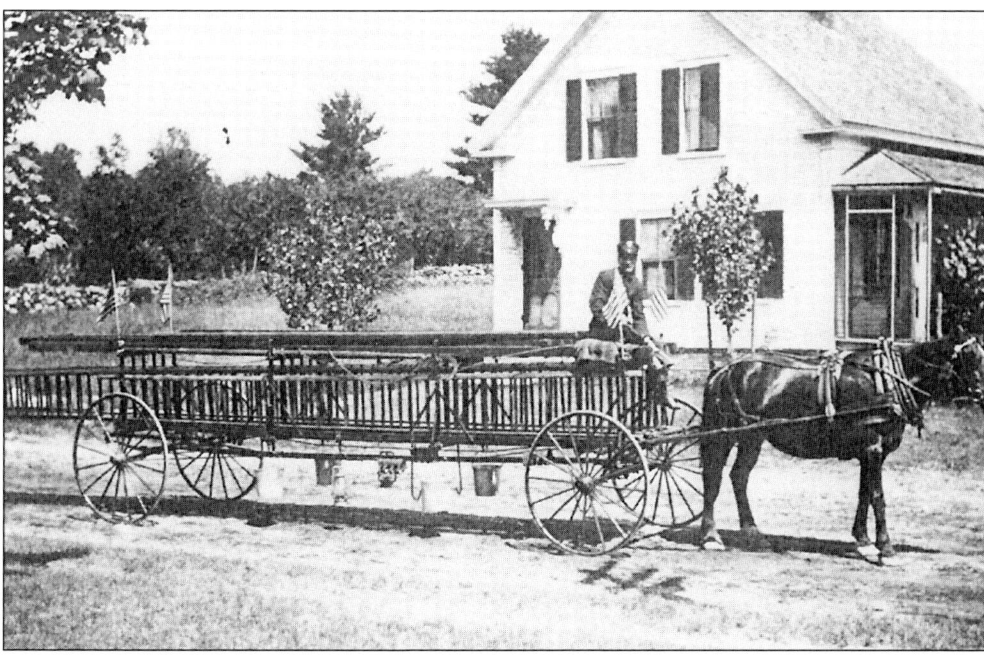

RAYMOND Ladder wagon built by Fire Chief Octavis Fellows from the remains of the old town hearse about 1905.

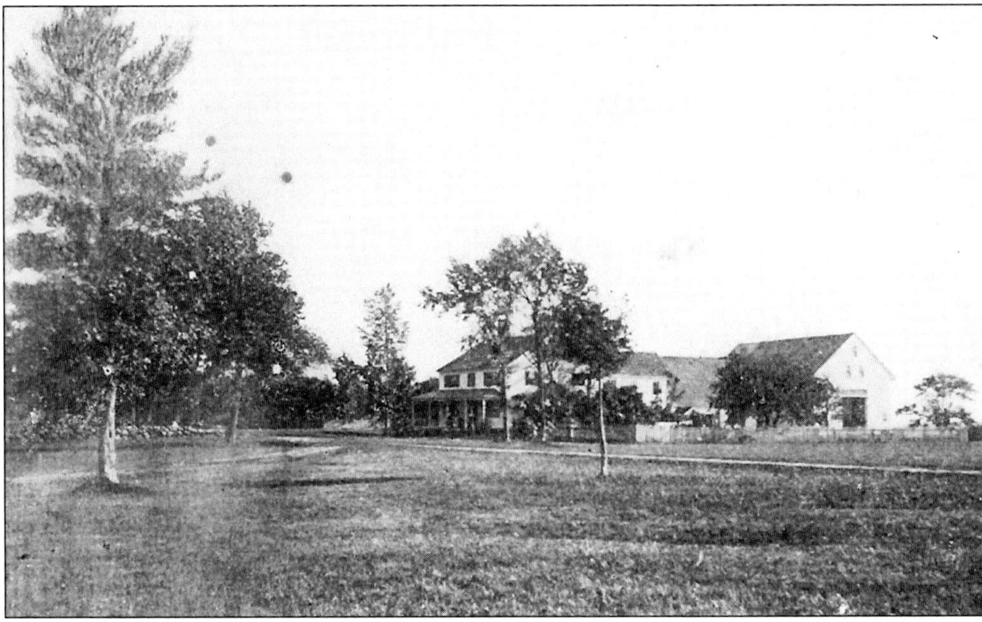

NOTTINGHAM Nottingham square around 1908. Here local militiamen trained during the American Revolution.

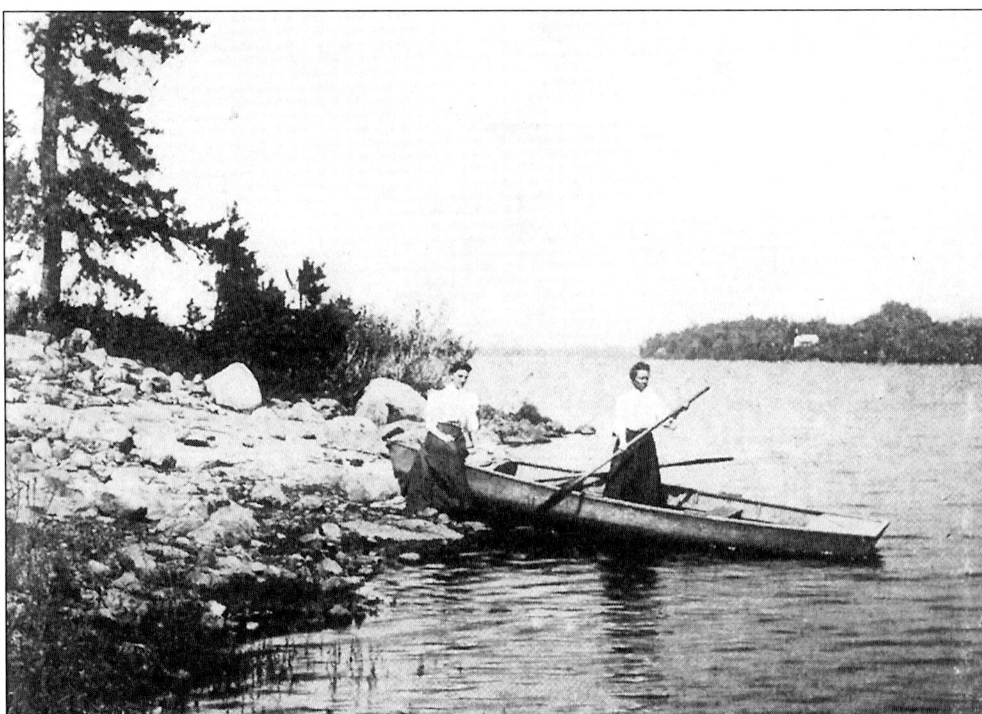

NOTTINGHAM Enjoying an afternoon boat excursion on Pawtuckaway lake about 1908.

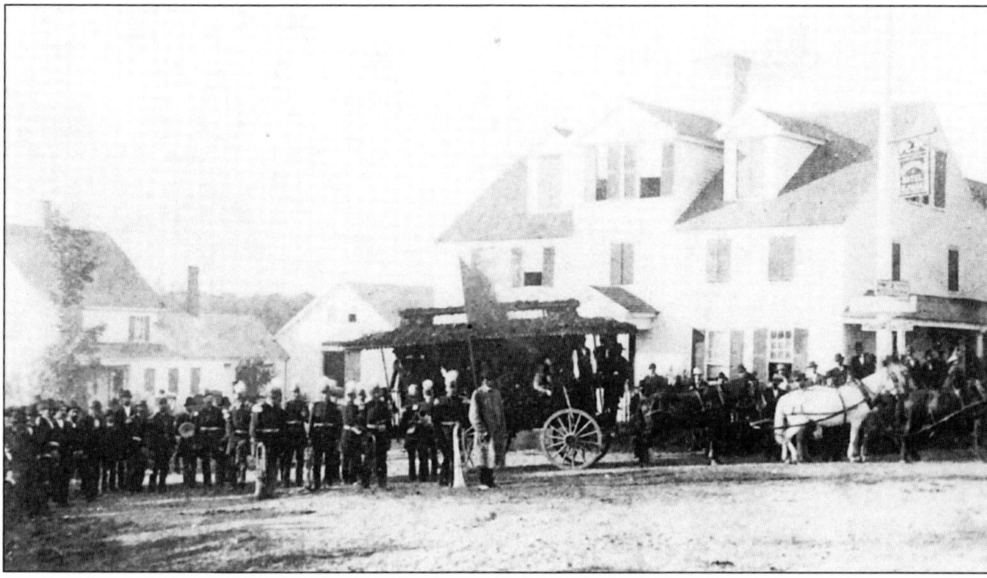

DEERFIELD The third annual Deerfield Fair in 1878 when it was still held in the village. Deerfield Fair was first held in the town hall on Old Center Road in September, 1876. In 1938 the fair was moved to its present site on Route 43. (Courtesy of Joanne Wasson)

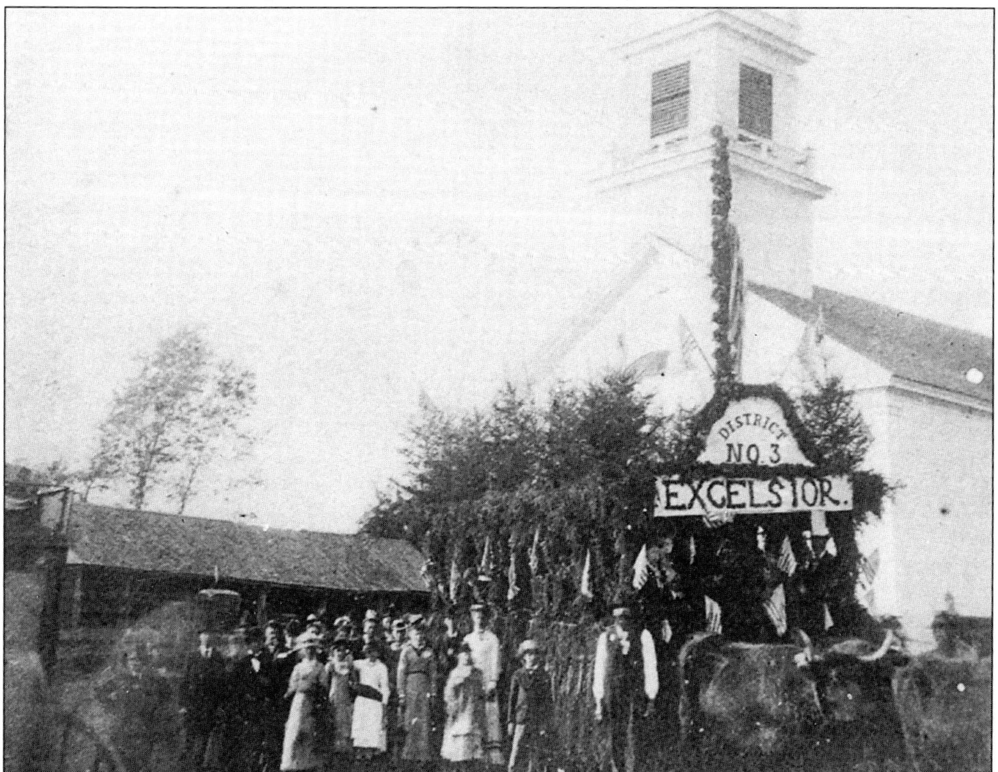

DEERFIELD District No. 3 fair float appearing in front of the Free-will Baptist Church during the Deerfield Fair parade in 1878. (Courtesy of Joanne Wasson)

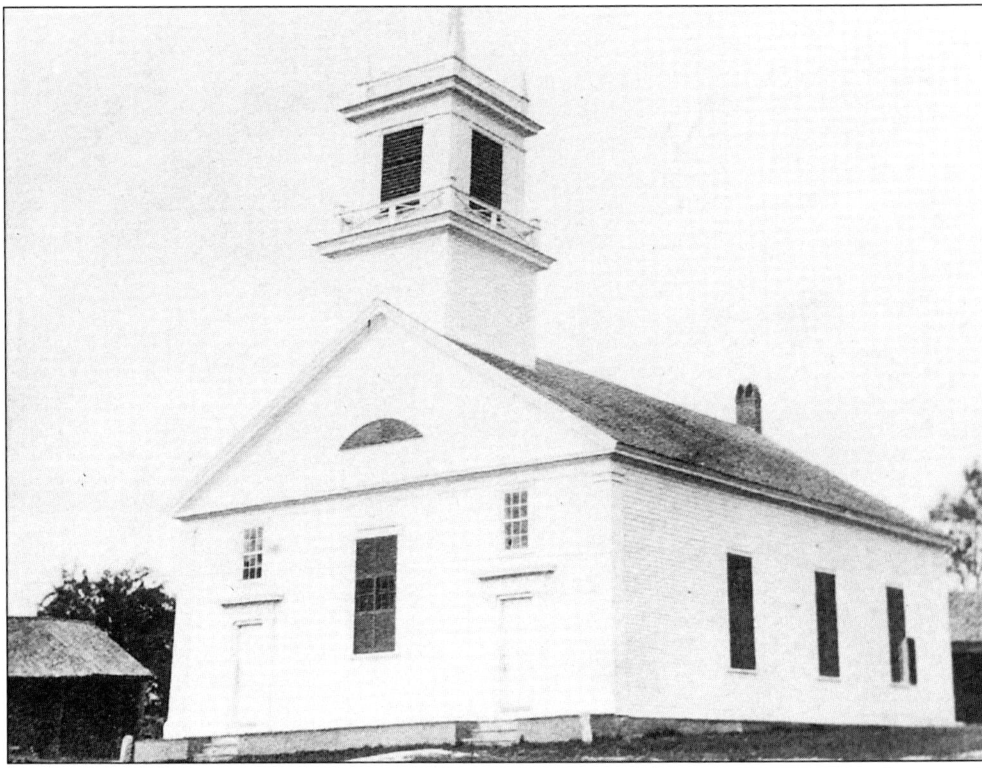

DEERFIELD The Free-will Baptist Church built in 1840 on Old Center Road. The photograph was taken about 1875.

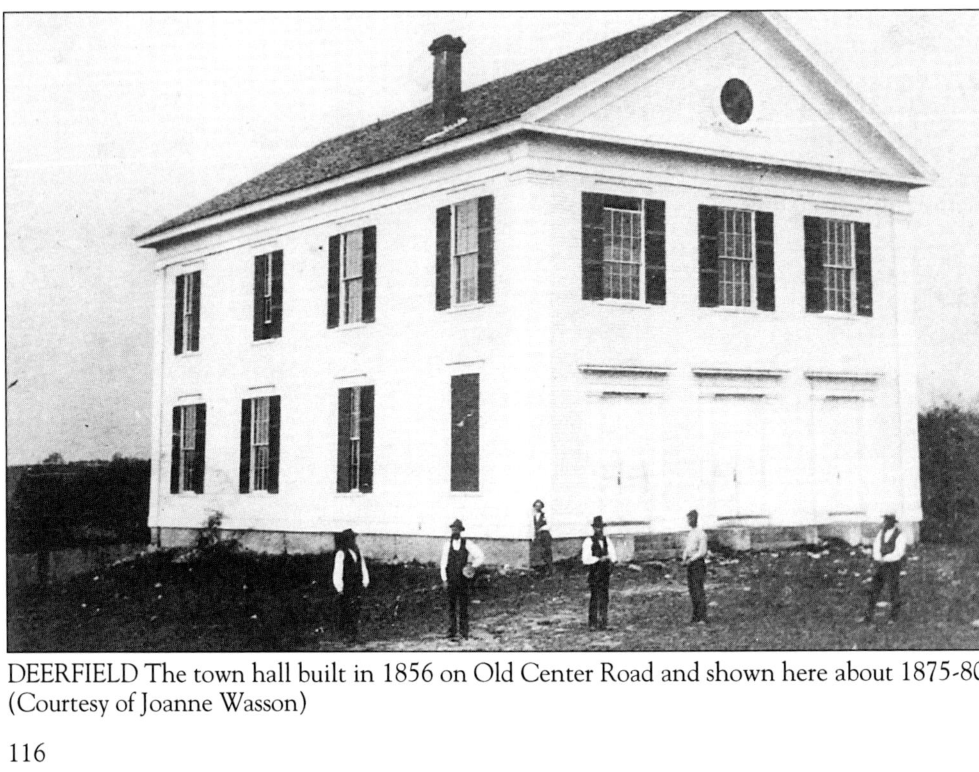

DEERFIELD The town hall built in 1856 on Old Center Road and shown here about 1875-80. (Courtesy of Joanne Wasson)

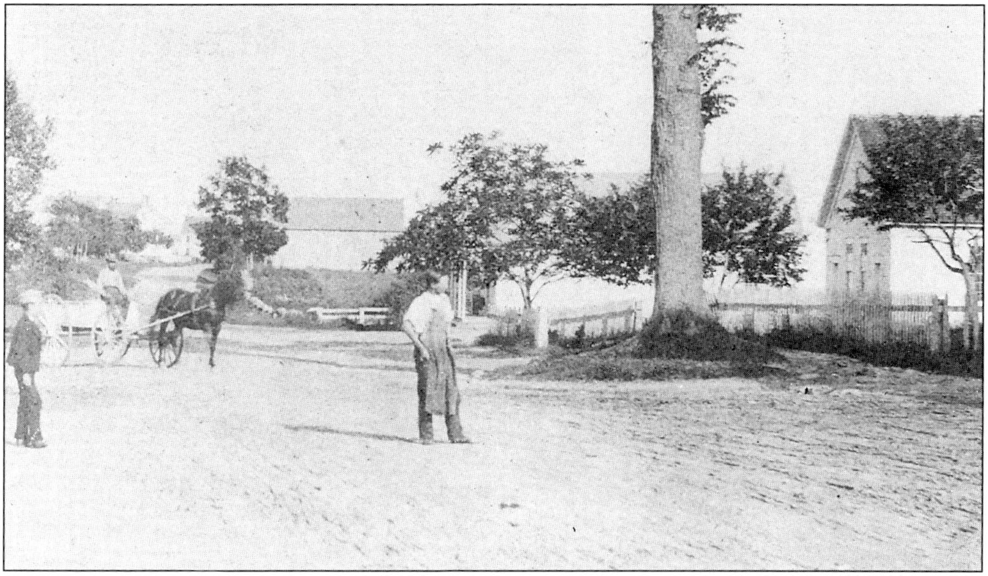

NORTHWOOD East Northwood street scene about 1880.

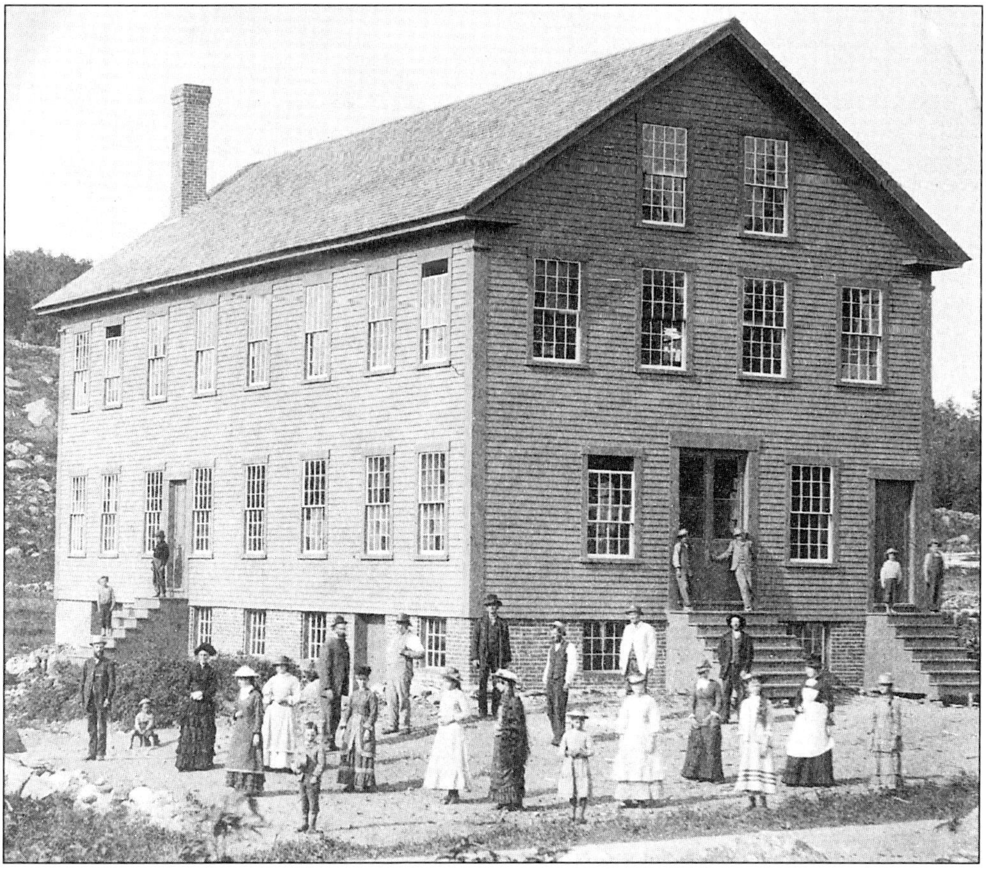

NORTHWOOD Pillsbury Brothers shoe factory during the 1870s. It went out of business in 1886 or 1887.

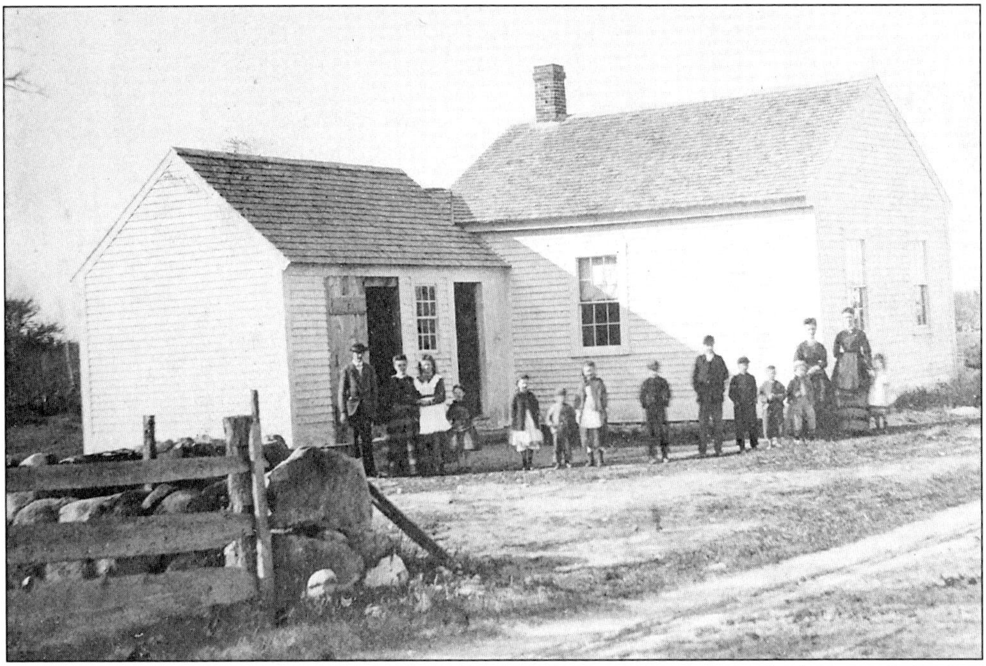

CANDIA Typical one room schoolhouse about 1880. In 1933 Candia built one of the first central schools in New Hampshire.

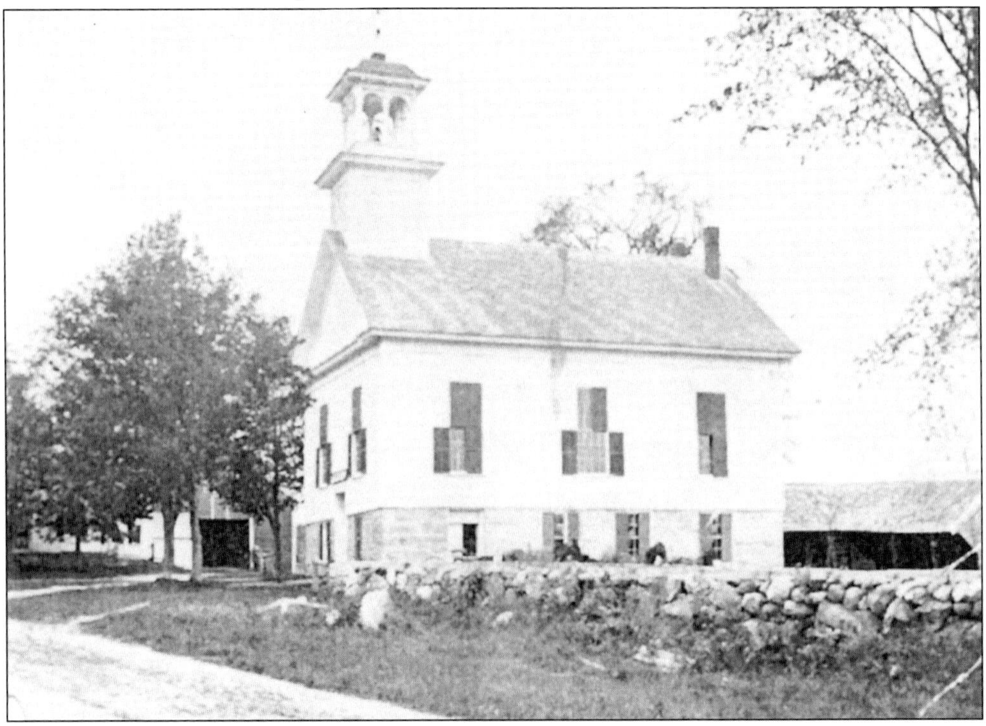

CANDIA Methodist Church built in 1859 at Candia Corners. A horse shed is in the rear. Used as a church until 1886 the building was later bought by the town and used as the town hall until it burned down on town meeting day in 1939.

Six

Western Rockingham County

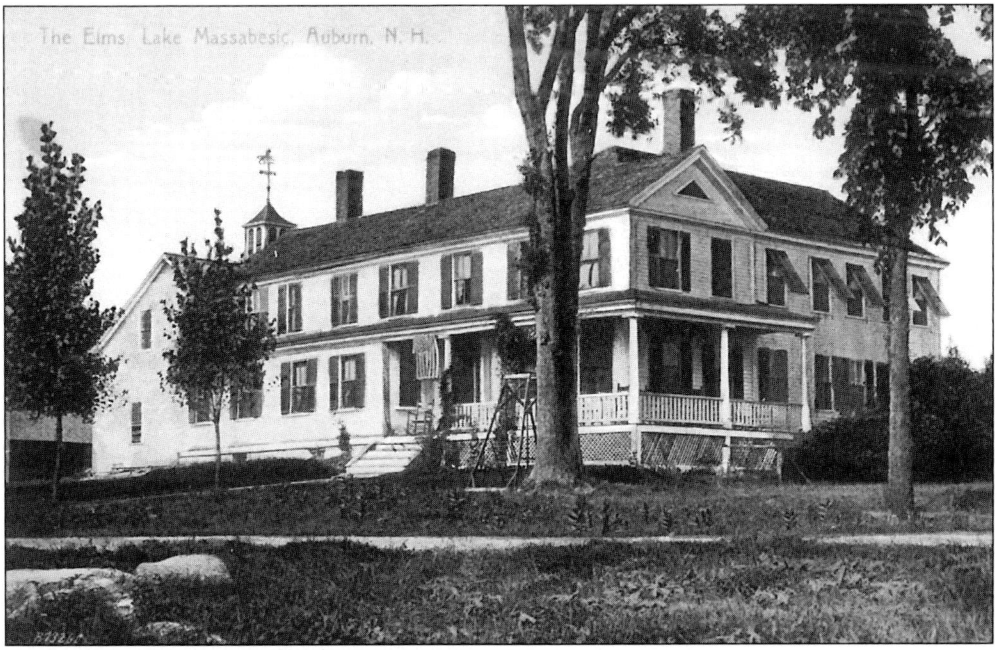

AUBURN "The Elms" about 1911, on Route 121. This was one of several resort hotels that catered to tourists coming to Lake Massabesic around the turn of the century.

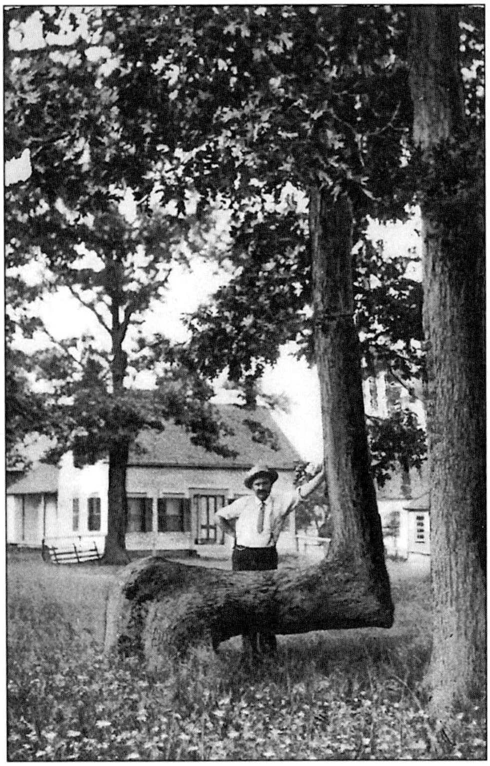

AUBURN This unusual tree was a popular tourist attraction. The photograph was taken about 1910.

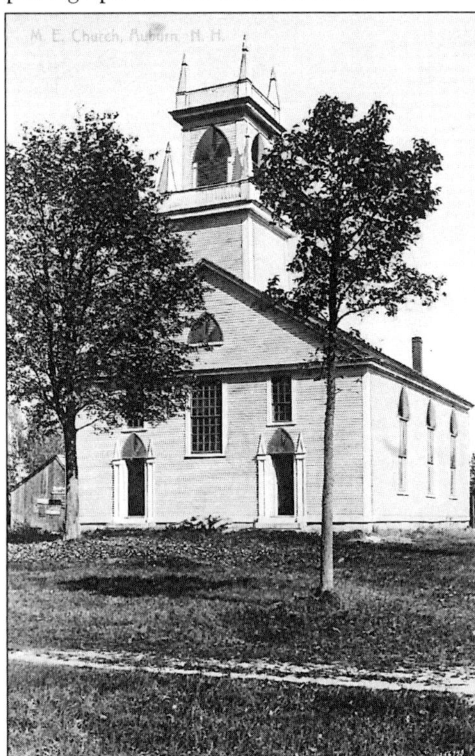

AUBURN Methodist Church, now the town hall and court house, on Route 121 about 1910. Originally a barn, it was converted into a church in 1836.

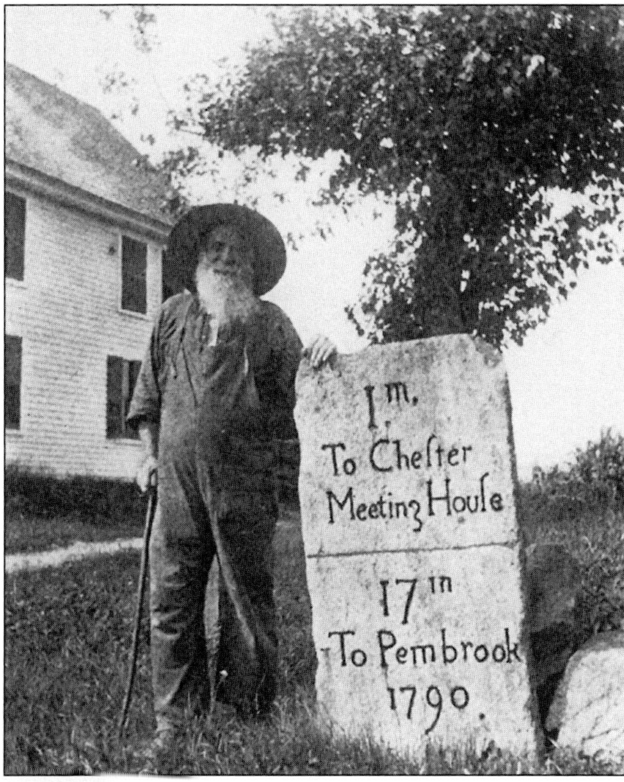

CHESTER A milestone on Chester Street or Route 121. During the 1790s Chester erected several milestones to aid travelers. Many can still be seen in Chester and Auburn. Chester has the largest collection of federal-era milestones in New Hampshire.

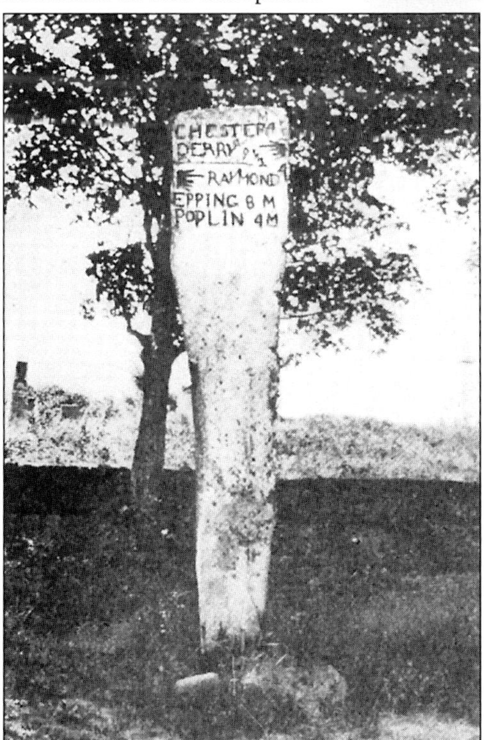

CHESTER The milestone on Route 102 at the Chester and Raymond town line. Note how the hands point the way to Chester (4 miles), Derry (8 1/2 miles), Raymond (4 miles), and Poplin (now Fremont) (4 miles).

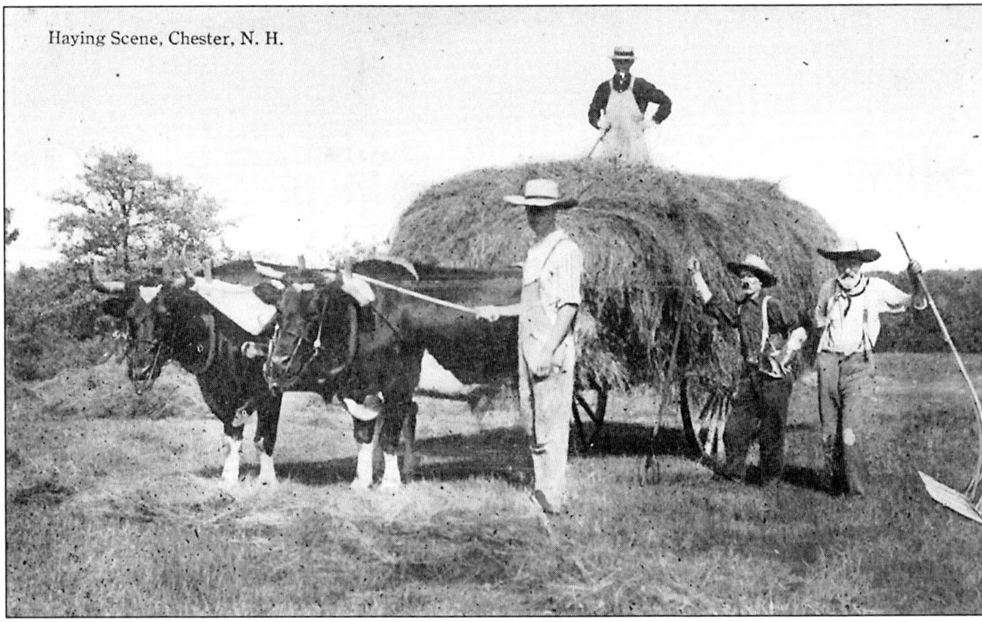

CHESTER A typical haying scene about 1912. Even today haying fields through the hot summer is an annual chore in New Hampshire.

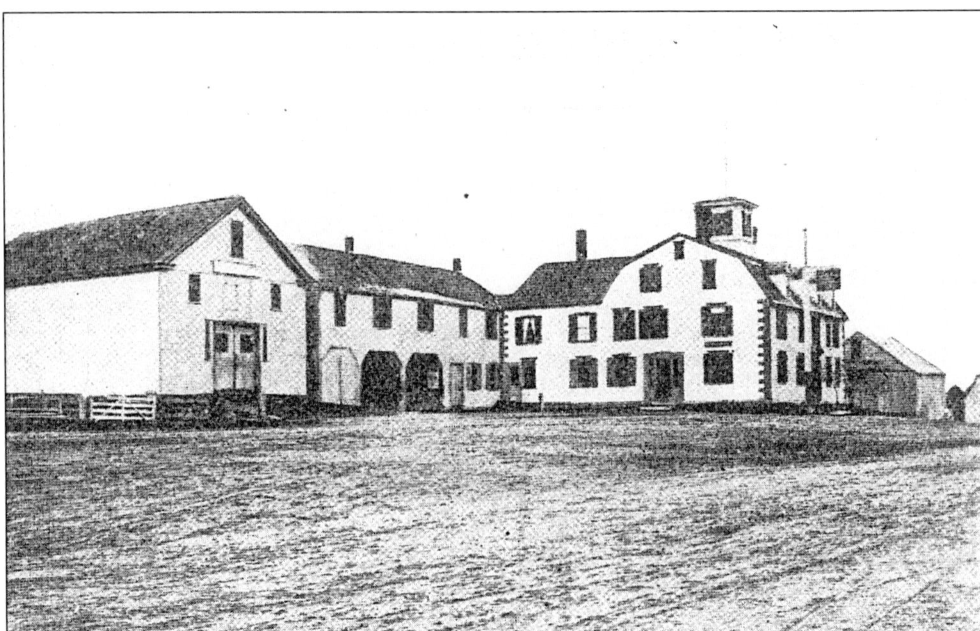

CHESTER Chester Inn was built on Chester Street by Col. John Webster in 1761 and burned in 1947. This photograph was supposedly taken in 1861. The first post office in town was located here in 1793. The inn was a popular stopping point on the Boston to Concord stage route.

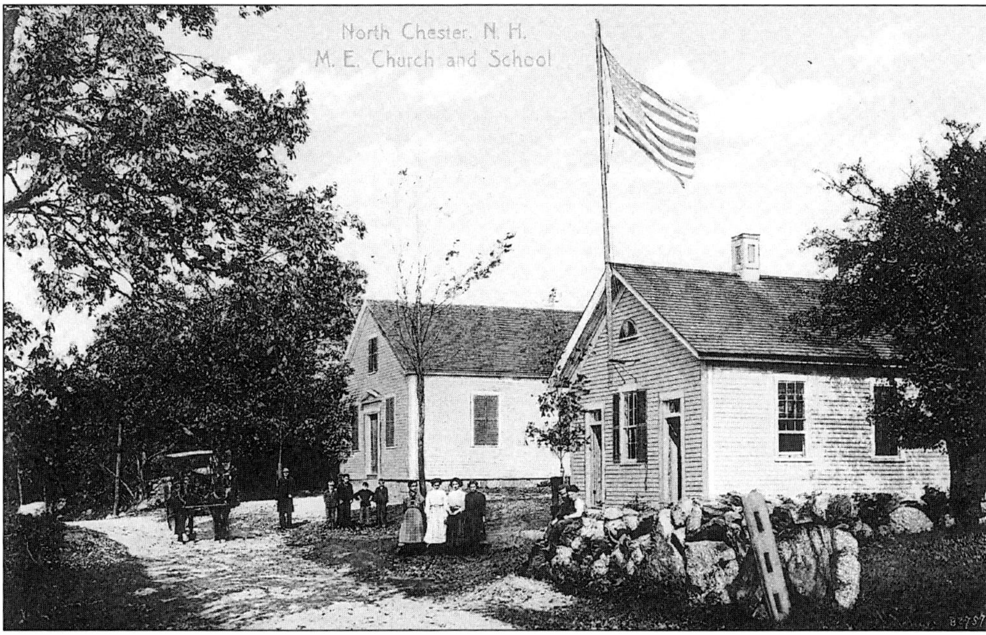

CHESTER Methodist Church and school house built in 1851 and 1853 respectively on Candia Road. The photograph was taken shortly after 1900.

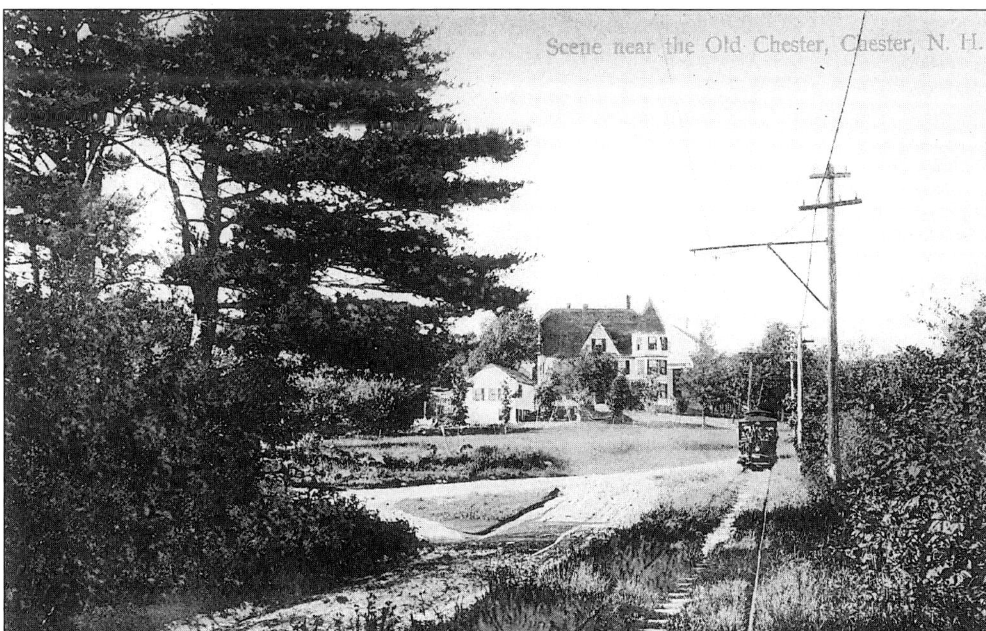

CHESTER The Old Chester was a popular boarding house along the tracks of the Chester and Derry electric trolley line. The trolley operated between the two communities from 1896 to 1928. Pictured here in 1905, the boarding house burned in 1923.

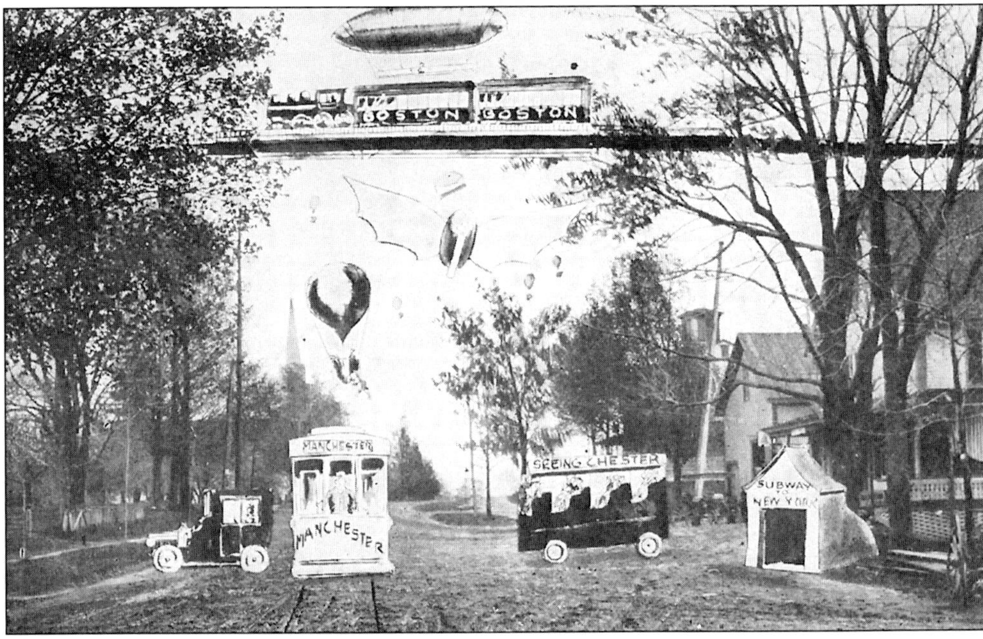

CHESTER Chester village also shown in a futuristic postcard picture.

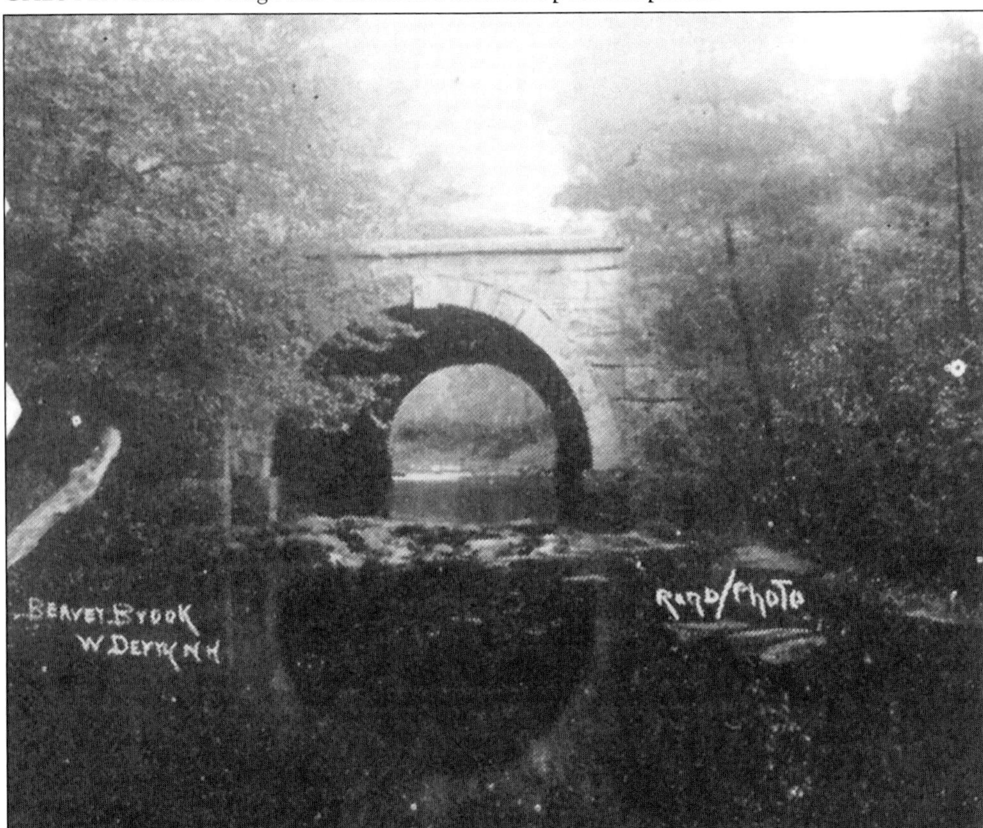

DERRY Lovers' Leap shown in a 1912 photograph.

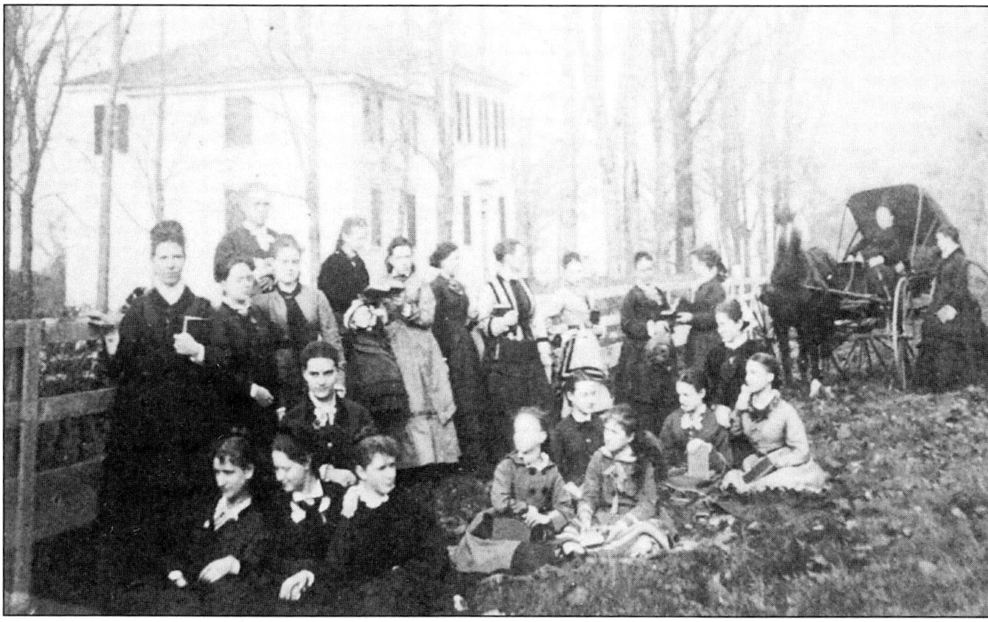

DERRY Adams Female Academy about 1865. Founded in 1824, this school for young ladies operated until 1887 when it was merged into the Derry school district. In 1825, Marquis de Lafayette enjoyed lunch here while on tour in New Hampshire.

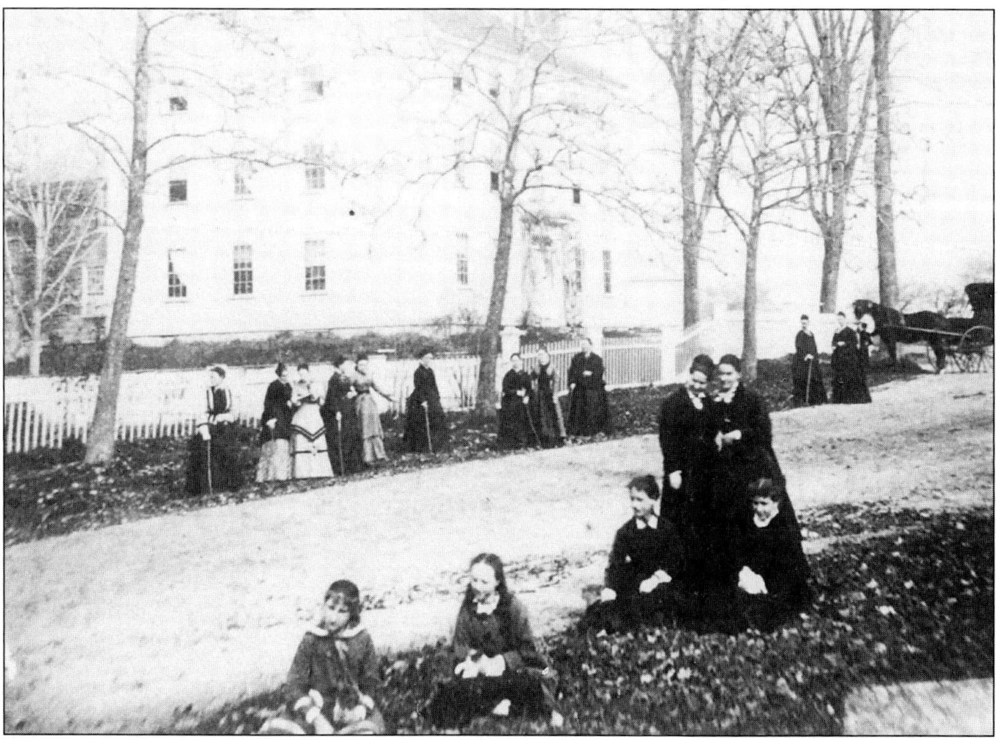

DERRY The boarding house for students attending Adams Female Academy about 1865. Later known at The Elms it became a popular hotel with the advent of the Chester and Derry electric railway in 1896.

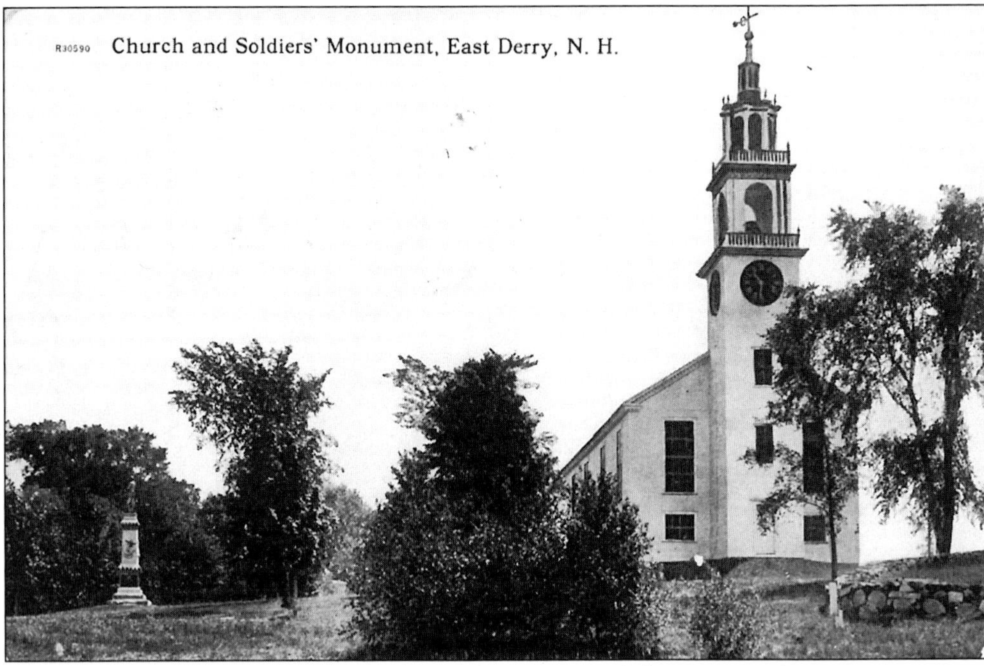

DERRY First Parish Presbyterian Church, built in 1769, and the 1889 Civil War monument on the East Derry Road about 1913. The church steeple was added in 1824. Forest Hill Cemetery behind the church contains many early gravestones.

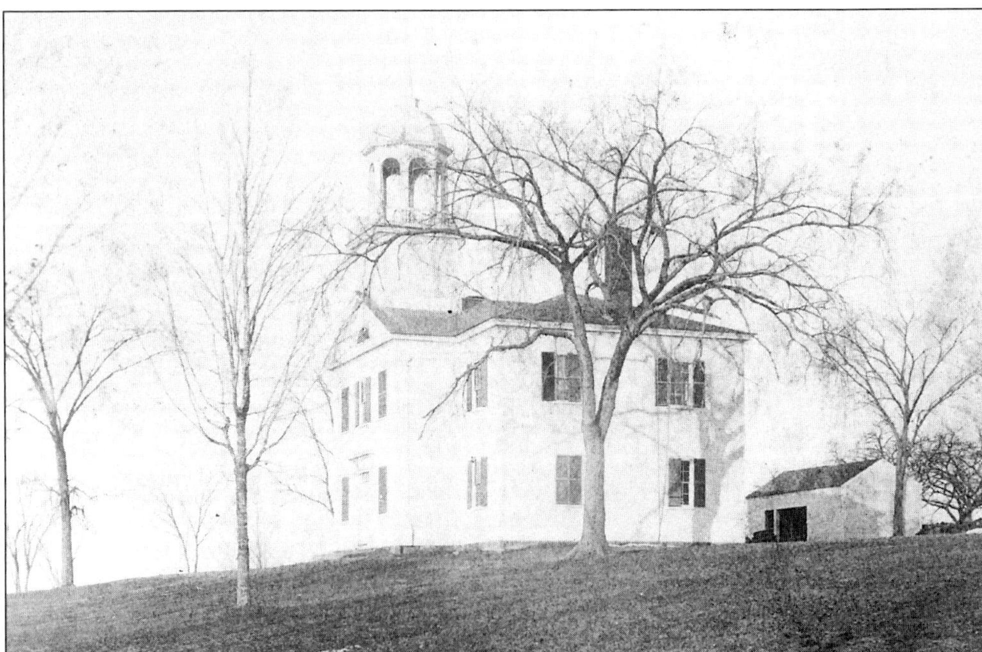

DERRY Old Pinkerton Academy Building established in 1814 with the belfry and front pavilion added in 1828. The first academy building pictured here in 1867 was moved a short distance in 1885 to make room for a second and larger brick and brownstone structure built in 1886-87.

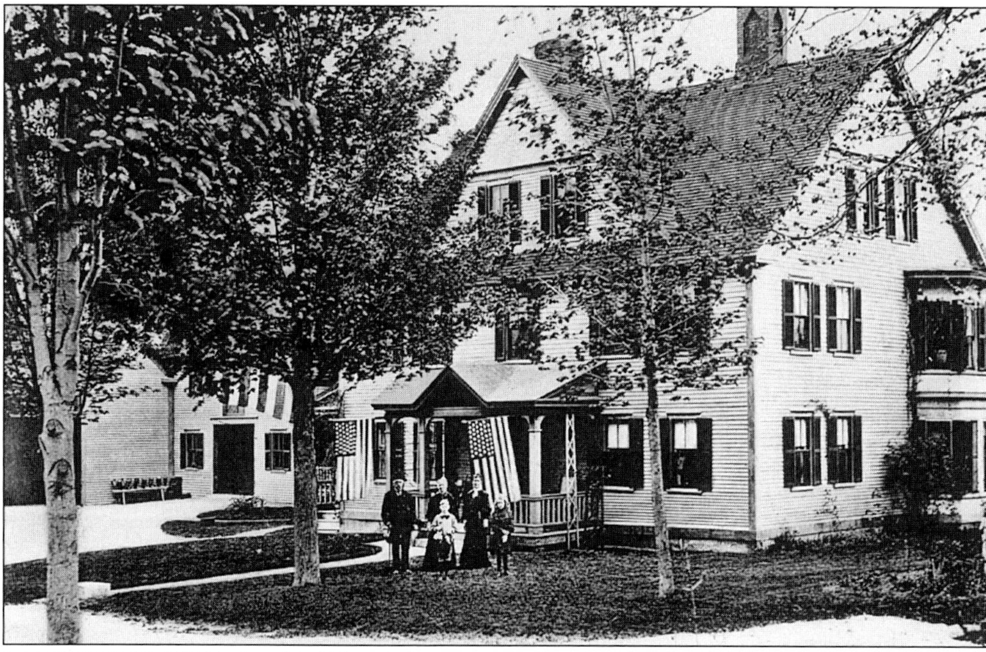

LONDONDERRY Colonel Pillsbury's homestead about 1910-15.

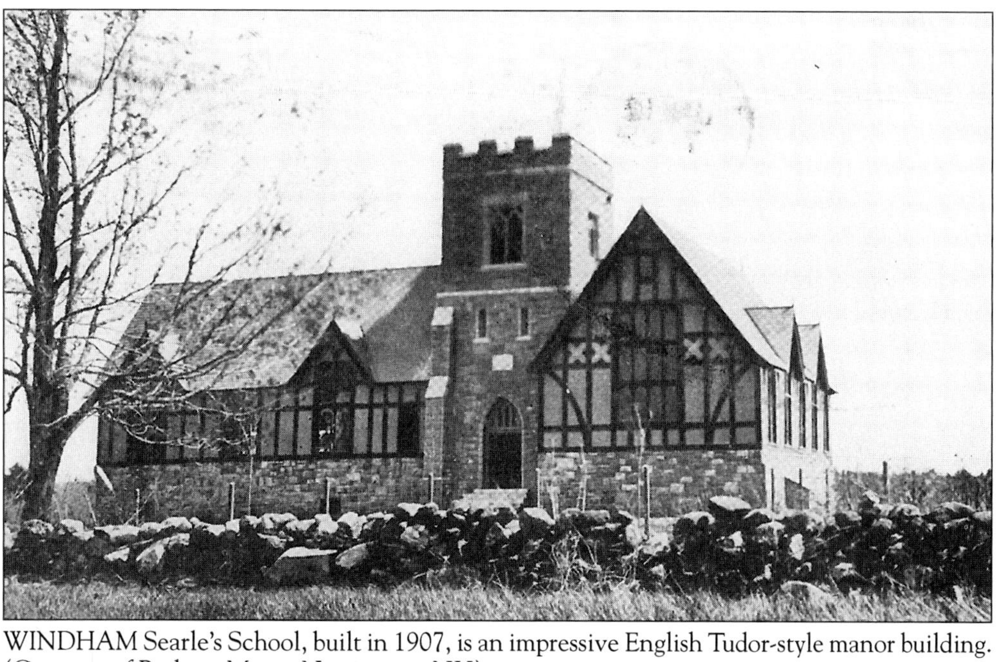

WINDHAM Searle's School, built in 1907, is an impressive English Tudor-style manor building. (Courtesy of Barbara Myers, Newington, NH)

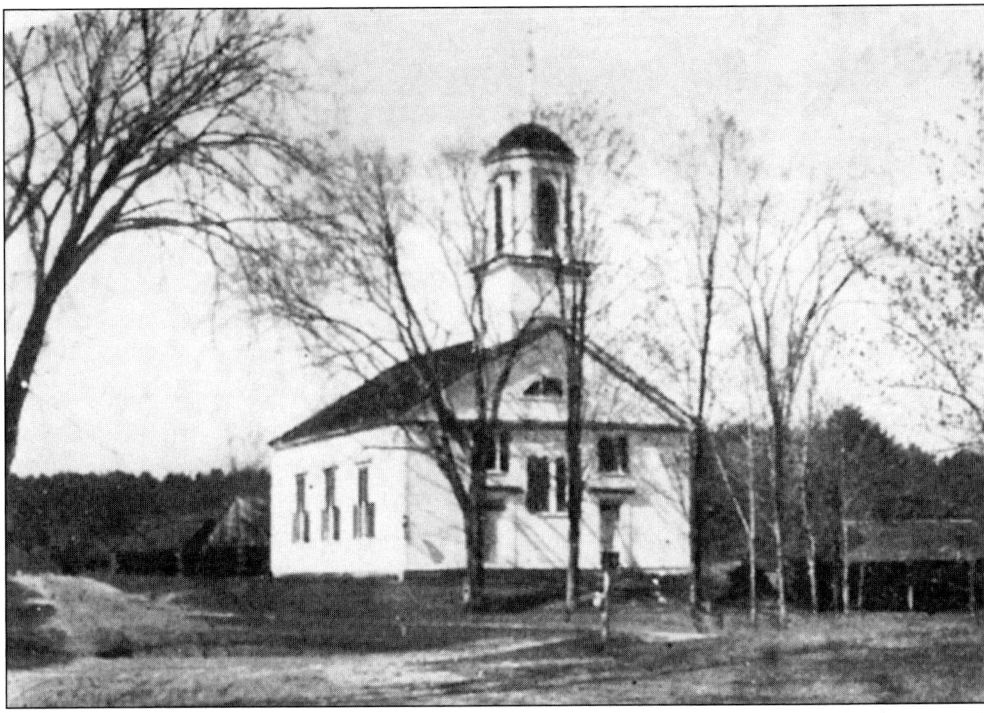

WINDHAM Presbyterian Church, built in 1834, and parsonage, Church Road, about 1911. (Courtesy of Barbara Myers, Newington, NH)

An Historical Gazetteer

ATKINSON

DATE OF FIRST SETTLEMENT: 1728
INCORPORATED: September 3, 1767

SOURCE OF TOWN NAME: In honor of Col. Theodore Atkinson, prominent New Hampshire military leader and politician.

POPULATION: 1767- 476; 1775- 575; 1790- 479; 1820- 563; 1860- 546; 1880- 502; 1900- 442; 1930- 407; 1960- 1017; 1990- 5188.

HISTORIC LANDMARKS AND EVENTS:

Atkinson Academy Building, incorporated in 1791 current building erected, 1803; second oldest co-educational academy in the United States.
Town Pound, built 1787, Route 121.

PROMINENT CITIZENS:

Dr. Nathaniel Peabody (1741-1823), delegate to the Continental Congress in 1779.
John Noyes (1764-1841), member of Congress from Vermont (1815-1817).

AUBURN

DATE OF FIRST SETTLEMENT: Approximately 1730
INCORPORATED: June 23, 1845

SOURCE OF TOWN NAME: Unknown

POPULATION: 1767- N/A; 1775- N/A; 1790- N/A; 1820- N/A; 1860- 886; 1880- 719; 1900- 682; 1930- 735; 1960- 1292; 1990- 4085.

HISTORIC LANDMARKS AND EVENTS:

Town Hall built in 1836, formerly the Methodist Church.
Devil's Den, Mine Hill, Route 121.
Once a popular resort community with several hotels on the shore of Lake Massabesic.

PROMINENT CITIZENS:

Earle Rinker, member New Hampshire Executive Council (1988-).

BRENTWOOD

DATE OF FIRST SETTLEMENT: Unknown
INCORPORATED: June 26, 1742

SOURCE OF TOWN NAME: In honor of Brentwood, England.

POPULATION: 1767- 1064; 1775- 1100; 1790- 976; 1820- 892; 1860- 887; 1880- 999; 1900- 957; 1930- 725; 1960- 1072; 1990- 2590.

HISTORIC LANDMARKS AND EVENTS:

Congregational Church built in 1815 on Route 111A.
1734, the Mast Tree Riot began in Brentwood with citizens firing upon the king's surveyor who was attempting to inspect illegally cut trees reserved for the Royal Navy.
5 August 1812, Daniel Webster delived a major speech, the "Rockingham Memorial," denouncing the War of 1812 and its adverse economic effects upon New England.

PROMINENT CITIZENS:

Francis O. J. Smith (1806-1876) member of Congress from Maine (1883-1839). He also assisted Samuel F.B. Morse in inventing the telegraph.
Wheelock Veasey (1835-1898) recipient of the Congressional Medal of Honor for valor at the Battle of Gettysburg; later became member of the Vermont Supreme Court.

CANDIA

DATE OF FIRST SETTLEMENT: Approximately 1740
INCORPORATED: December 17, 1763

SOURCE OF TOWN NAME: In honor of Candia, Crete, largest of the Greek Isles in the Mediterranean.

POPULATION: 1767- 363; 1775- 744; 1790- 1040; 1820- 1273; 1860- 1575; 1880- 1340; 1900- 1057; 1930- 812; 1960- 1490; 1990-3557.

HISTORIC LANDMARKS AND EVENTS:

Congregational Church, built in 1838, South Road.
Fitts Historical Museum, Route 27.

PROMINENT CITIZENS:

Sam Walter Foss, poet, author of "A House by the Side of the Road".
Frederick Smyth (1819-1899), governor of New Hampshire (1865-1867).

CHESTER

DATE OF FIRST SETTLEMENT: 1720
INCORPORATED: May 8, 1722

SOURCE OF TOWN NAME: Unknown

POPULATION: 1767- 1189; 1775- 1599; 1790- 1902; 1820- 2262; 1860- 1275; 1880- 1136; 1900- 861; 1930- 653; 1960- 1053; 1990- 2691.

HISTORIC LANDMARKS AND EVENTS:

Congregational/Baptist Church, built in 1773, Route 121.
Chester Village Cemetery, Routes 121 and 102.
1847, Horace Greeley, editor of the New York Tribune, spoke in Chester.

PROMINENT CITIZENS:

Benjamin Brown French (1800-1870) officer in charge of organizing President Lincoln's funeral, 1865.
Isaac Blaisdel (1738-1791), prominent New Hampshire clock maker.

DANVILLE

DATE OF FIRST SETTLEMENT: Approximately 1735
INCORPORATED: February 22, 1760

SOURCE OF TOWN NAME: In honor of three men all named Daniel who helped settle the town.

POPULATION: 1767- 488; 1775- 504; 1790- 420; 1820- 421; 1860- 620; 1880- 613; 1900- 615; 1930- 406; 1960- 605; 1990- 2534.

HISTORIC LANDMARKS AND EVENTS:

Meeting House, built in 1760, Route 111A, contains oldest Puritan pulpit in New Hampshire.
Town Pound, built 1802, Route 111A.
3 March 1847, U.S. Senator John P. Hale gave anti-slavery speech in Danville.
October 1984, two million tires burnt at Ernie Hunt's Tire Pile. The conflagration is reported on the national television news.

PROMINENT CITIZENS:

Alfred A. Collins, New Hampshire state senator (1899-1900), member of the New Hampshire Executive Council (1903-1905).
James Flanders, New Hampshire state senator (1794-1798; 1800-1803).

DEERFIELD

DATE OF FIRST SETTLEMENT: Approximately 1735
INCORPORATED: January 8, 1766

SOURCE OF TOWN NAME: Named Deerfield to commemorate ceremony in which the royal governor was presented with a gift of a deer by petitioners for incorporation.

POPULATION: 1767- N/A; 1775- 929; 1790- 1619; 1820- 2133; 1860- 2066; 1880- 1569; 1900- 1162; 1930- 635; 1960- 714; 1990- 3124.

HISTORIC LANDMARKS AND EVENTS:

Deerfield Parade, Nottingham Road, where militia trained during the American Revolution.
1876, Deerfield Fair begun, continuing today as oldest agricultural fair in New Hampshire.
1952, world horse pulling record set at Deerfield Fair.

PROMINENT CITIZENS:

John Simpson, (1749-1825) said to have fired the first shot at Battle of Bunker Hill, 1775.
Benjamin Butler (1818-1893) Union Army general, Civil War; candidate for president of the United States for the Greenback Party, 1884.

DERRY

DATE OF FIRST SETTLEMENT: 1719
INCORPORATED: July 2, 1827

SOURCE OF TOWN NAME: In honor of Isle of Derry, Ireland.

POPULATION: 1767- N/A; 1775- N/A; 1790- N/A; 1820- N/A; 1860- 1995; 1880- 2140; 1900- 3583; 1930- 5131; 1960- 6987; 1990-29603.

HISTORIC LANDMARKS AND EVENTS:

1719, first Scotch-Irish settlement in New Hampshire.
1990, sensational murder of Greg Smart; his wife and her teenage companion were accused and adjudged guilty of planning and committing the murder.

PROMINENT CITIZENS:

Matthew Thornton (1714-1803) signer of the Declaration of Independence
John Stark (1728-1822) American Revolutionary general in charge of troops at Battle of Bunker Hill and Battle of Bennington, Vermont.
Alan B Shepard (1923-) first American in space, May 5, 1961.

EAST KINGSTON

DATE OF FIRST SETTLEMENT: Approximately 1710
INCORPORATED: November 17, 1738

SOURCE OF TOWN NAME: Originally the eastern portion of Kingston named in honor of the King of England.

POPULATION: 1767- 451; 1775- 428; 1790- 358; 1820- 443; 1860- 598; 1880- 576; 1900- 496; 1930- 347; 1960- 574; 1990- 1352.

HISTORIC LANDMARKS AND EVENTS:

Boston and Maine railroad depot, built about 1840.
Mapleville Turkey Farm, one of few poultry farms left in New Hampshire.
In the 1870s three brickyards produced nearly six million bricks.

PROMINENT CITIZENS:

Ebenezer Webster, (1739-1806) father of Daniel Webster, Ebenezer commanded a company of militia at the Battle of Bennington, 1777.
Charles A.F. Currier, professor of history at Massachusetts Institute of Technology.

EPPING

DATE OF FIRST SETTLEMENT: Approximately 1730
INCORPORATED: February 23, 1741

SOURCE OF TOWN NAME: In honor of Epping Forest, England.

POPULATION: 1767- 1410; 1775- 1569; 1790- 1233; 1820- 1158; 1860- 1440; 1880- 1536; 1900- 1641; 1930- 1672; 1960- 2006; 1990- 5162.

HISTORIC LANDMARKS AND EVENTS:

Quaker Meeting House, built about 1851, on Friend Street.
Hedding Campground, site of Methodist Camp Meetings.

PROMINENT CITIZENS:

William Plummer (1759-1850), governor of New Hampshire (1812-1813); U.S. Senator (1802-1807). In 1820 Plummer as a presidential elector voted for John Quincy Adams, thus becoming the only vote not for James Monroe. Plummer did so out of a belief that only George Washington should have received a unanimous vote for President.
John Chandler (1762-1841) member of Congress from Massachusetts (1805-1809); first United States senator from Maine (1820-1829).

EXETER

DATE OF FIRST SETTLEMENT: 1638
INCORPORATED: Founded in 1638 by Rev. John Wheelwright.

SOURCE OF TOWN NAME: In honor of Exeter, England.

POPULATION: 1767- 1690; 1775- 1741; 1790- 1722; 1820- 2114; 1860- 3309; 1880- 3569; 1900- 4922; 1930- 4872; 1960- 7243; 1990-12481.

HISTORIC LANDMARKS AND EVENTS:

Congregational Church, built in 1798, Front Street.
Served as state capitol during the American Revolution (1775-1782).
Site of first recorded vote for independence from England, January 5, 1776.

PROMINENT CITIZENS:

John Taylor Gilman (1735-1828) governor of New Hampshire for fourteen terms.
Lewis Cass (1782-1866) Democratic candidate for president in 1848 losing to Zachary Taylor.
Daniel Chester French (1850-1931) sculptor of the seated Lincoln figure at the Lincoln Memorial.

FREMONT

DATE OF FIRST SETTLEMENT: Approximately 1730
INCORPORATED: June 22, 1764

SOURCE OF TOWN NAME: In honor of John Charles Fremont, western pathfinder and first Republican candidate for president in 1856.

POPULATION: 1767- 521; 1775- 552; 1790- 493; 1820- 453; 1860- 579; 1880- 624; 1900- 749; 1930- 571; 1960- 783; 1990- 2576.

HISTORIC LANDMARKS AND EVENTS:

Cavil-Turner Mills, Scribner Road, shingled sawmill built about 1745.
Spaulding and Frost Cooperage, built 1874.
4 July 1861, Southern sympathizers attempted to shoot at the United States flag in Liberty Square during a flag raising, setting off the first Civil War riot in New England.

PROMINENT CITIZENS:

Josiah H.L. Tuck (1824-1900) prominent submarine inventor.
John P. Sanborn (1844-1926) president of the Rhode Island state senate and editor of Newport Mercury, Newport, Rhode Island.

GREENLAND

DATE OF FIRST SETTLEMENT: Unknown
INCORPORATED: Set off as parish of Portsmouth in 1705, granted full municipal privileges in 1721.

SOURCE OF TOWN NAME: Unknown.

POPULATION: 1767- 805; 1775- 759; 1790- 634; 1820- 634; 1860- 762; 1880- 695; 1900- 607; 1930- 577; 1960- 1196; 1990- 2768.

HISTORIC LANDMARKS AND EVENTS:

Weeks House, built about 1710, said to be the oldest brick house in New Hampshire.
Community Church, built 1756, currently overlooking Greenland Parade.
Breakfast Hill, so named because native Americans and their captives were surprised by local militia while eating breakfast on the morning of June 26, 1696.

PROMINENT CITIZENS:

Samuel MacClintock (1732-1804), chaplain in Gen. John Stark's Regiment, American Revolution.
William P. Weeks (1803-1870), president of New Hampshre state senate (1849-1850).

HAMPSTEAD

DATE OF FIRST SETTLEMENT: Approximately 1728
INCORPORATED: January 19, 1749

SOURCE OF TOWN NAME: In honor of Hampstead, England.

POPULATION: 1767- 664; 1775- 768; 1790- 724; 1820- 751; 1860- 930; 1880- 959; 1900- 823; 1930- 775; 1960- 1261; 1990- 6732.

HISTORIC LANDMARKS AND EVENTS:

1745, Meeting House on Emerson Avenue with Paul Revere bell.
September 1786, paper money riot led by Joseph French. The riot was put down by a volunteer militia company.
Hand wrought nails were made by a number of companies during the 1790s.

PROMINENT CITIZENS:

Josiah C. Eastman, member of New Hampshire state senate (1853-1855).
Doris M. Spollett, member of New Hampshire state senate (1947-1950), second female to become a New Hampshire state senator.

HAMPTON

DATE OF FIRST SETTLEMENT: 1638
INCORPORATED: 1639
SOURCE OF TOWN NAME: In honor of Hampton, England.

POPULATION: 1767- 866; 1775- 862; 1790- 853; 1820- 1098; 1860- 1230; 1880- 1184; 1900- 1209; 1930- 1507; 1960- 5379; 1990-12278.

HISTORIC LANDMARKS AND EVENTS:

Founders Park, Park Avenue, with memorial stones in honor of town founders.
Jonathan Moulton House, Lafayette Road, home to early New Hampshire real estate baron.
1649, first tax supported school in New Hampshire started.

PROMINENT CITIZENS:

Eunice (Goody) Cole, known as the witch of Hampton, she was the only person convicted of witchcraft in New Hampshire, dying about 1673. She was restored as a citizen of the town by vote in 1938.
Jane Means Appleton Pierce (1806-1863), wife of President Franklin Pierce she remained in mourning over the death of her young son throughout Pierce's term of office, never entertaining at the White House.
Stephen Merrill, former Attorney General and Governor of New Hampshire (1992-).

HAMPTON FALLS

DATE OF FIRST SETTLEMENT: Approximately 1650
INCORPORATED: November 23, 1726

SOURCE OF TOWN NAME: Area of falls on the Hampton Falls River.

POPULATION: 1767- 1381; 1775- 645; 1790- 541; 1820- 572; 1860- 621; 1880- 678; 1900- 560; 1930- 481; 1960- 885; 1990- 1503.

HISTORIC LANDMARKS AND EVENTS:

Unitarian Church, built in 1838 on Route 88, considered the finest example of Doric Greek revival architecture in New Hampshire.
1892, John Greenleaf Whittier died at his summer residence.

PROMINENT CITIZENS:

Ralph Adams Cram, prominent architect, designer of the Chapel at West Point.
Wesley Powell, governor of New Hampshire (1959-1963).

KENSINGTON

DATE OF FIRST SETTLEMENT: Approximately 1663
INCORPORATED: April 1, 1737

SOURCE OF TOWN NAME: In honor of Kensington, England

POPULATION: 1767- 755; 1775- 797; 1790- 800; 1820- 709; 1860- 672; 1880- 614; 1900- 524; 1930- 438; 1960- 708; 1990- 1631.

HISTORIC LANDMARKS AND EVENTS:

Christian Church/Grange Hall, built 1838, Route 150.
During the Revolutionary War some twenty New York Tories were held prisoner.
September 1965, a UFO was allegedly seen off Route 150 by a hitch-hiker who reported it to the Exeter police. This incident led to the best seller, 'Incident at Exeter' by John G. Fuller.
PROMINENT CITIZENS:

Ezekiel Worthen, major in charge of troops at the siege of Louisburg in Nova Scotia, 1745
Ebenezer Clifford, architect, inventor, and clock-case maker.

KINGSTON

DATE OF FIRST SETTLEMENT: Approximately 1690
INCORPORATED: August 6, 1694

SOURCE OF TOWN NAME: In honor of the King of England.

POPULATION: 1767- 999; 1775- 961; 1790- 906; 1820- 847; 1860- 1216; 1880- 1080; 1900- 1132; 1930- 1017; 1960- 1672; 1990- 5591.

HISTORIC LANDMARKS AND EVENTS:

Josiah Bartlett House, built 1774.
September 1786, two hundred rioters assemble at Kingston to march on the legislature at Exeter to demand the issuance of additional paper money. Many of the rioters were arrested.
One of the largest poultry breeding communities in the world during the 1950s.

PROMINENT CITIZENS:

Josiah Bartlett (1721-1795) one of three New Hampshire signers of the Declaration of Independence.
Josiah Bartlett, Jr. (1768-1838) member of Congress (1811-1813).
George B. Prescott, inventor of pneumatic tube.

LONDONDERRY

DATE OF FIRST SETTLEMENT: 1719
INCORPORATED: June 21, 1722

SOURCE OF TOWN NAME: In honor of Londonderry, Ireland.

POPULATION: 1767- 2389; 1775- 2590; 1790- 2622; 1820- 3127; 1860- 1717; 1880- 1363; 1900- 1408; 1930- 1373; 1960- 2457; 1990-19781.

HISTORIC LANDMARKS AND EVENTS:
Presbyterian Church, Pillsbury Road, built in 1837.
World famous Londonderry linen was worn by George Washington and Thomas Jefferson.
Flora Stewart, believed to have been a former slave, lived in Londonderry until 1868 dying at the age of 118.

PROMINENT CITIZENS:

George Reid (1733-1815) American Revolution general, served at Bunker Hill, Saratoga, and Valley Forge.
James Wilson, designer and constructor of the first terrestrial globes in America.

NEW CASTLE

DATE OF FIRST SETTLEMENT: Approximately 1625
INCORPORATED: May 30, 1693

SOURCE OF TOWN NAME: In honor of Newcastle on Tyne, England

POPULATION: 1767- 606; 1775- 449; 1790- 534; 1820- 932; 1860- 692; 1880- 610; 1900- 581; 1930- 378; 1960- 823; 1990- 840.

HISTORIC LANDMARKS AND EVENTS:

Fort Constitution, built 1808 (formerly Fort William & Mary).
Wentworth Hotel, one of the grand hotels of the Victorian era.
December 1774, first overt act of the American Revolution when colonists attacked the fort and captured arms and ammunition which in turn was moved to Lexington and Concord.
Provincial capital of New Hampshire from 1682-1697.

PROMINENT CITIZENS:

Theodore Atkinson (1697-1779), secretary and president of the New Hampshire Provincial Council.
Benjamin Randall (1749-1808) founder Free-will Baptist Church in 1780.

NEWFIELDS

DATE OF FIRST SETTLEMENT: 1631
INCORPORATED: June 27, 1849

SOURCE OF TOWN NAME: From its designation as the new fields during the 1600s.

POPULATION: 1767- N/A; 1775- N/A; 1790- N/A; 1820- N/A; 1860- 786; 1880- 829; 1900- 647; 1930- 376; 1960- 737; 1990- 888.

HISTORIC LANDMARKS AND EVENTS:

Squamscott Bottling Works, Route 85, soda bottling business dating back to 1863.
First toll bridge in New Hampshire, built about 1775, made a toll bridge in 1792.

PROMINENT CITIZENS:

Rev. John Brodhead (1770-1838) member of Congress (1829-1833).
James Pike (1818-1895) member of Congress (1855-1859).

NEWINGTON

DATE OF FIRST SETTLEMENT: 1600s
INCORPORATED: Set off as parish from Dover in 1713. Granted full town privileges approximately 1714.

SOURCE OF TOWN NAME: In honor of Newington, England.

POPULATION: 1767- 514; 1775- 532; 1790- 542; 1820- 541; 1860- 475; 1880- 433; 1900- 390; 1930- 381; 1960- 1045; 1990- 990.

HISTORIC LANDMARKS AND EVENTS:

Congregational meeting house, built 1712, Nimble Hill Road.
Old Parsonage, built about 1725, Nimble Hill Road.
Parson Joseph Adams ordained in 1715. He served as minister for 68 years.
One of New Hampshire's largest retail districts built over the last thirty years.

PROMINENT CITIZENS:

John Pickering (1738-1805) judge, US District Court (1795-1804).

NEWMARKET

DATE OF FIRST SETTLEMENT: Approximately 1650
INCORPORATED: Set off as parish from Exeter on December 15, 1727. Granted full town privileges on August 18, 1737.

SOURCE OF TOWN NAME: In honor of Newmarket, England.

POPULATION: 1767- 1286; 1775- 1289; 1790- 1137; 1820- 1083; 1860- 2034; 1880- 2368; 1900- 2892; 1930- 2511; 1960- 3153; 1990- 7157.

HISTORIC LANDMARKS AND EVENTS:

Stone Textile Mill buildings, built 1823-1827, Route 108.
Stone Church, built 1833, and Stone School, built 1841, on Zion's Hill.
1916, site of largest weaving room in the world.
Prominent shipbuilding community in the 1700s and 1800s.

PROMINENT CITIZENS:

George W. Kittredge (1805-1881) member of Congress (1853-1855).
William B. Small (1817-1878) member of Congress (1873-1875).

NEWTON

DATE OF FIRST SETTLEMENT: 1720
INCORPORATED: December 6, 1749

SOURCE OF TOWN NAME: Unknown

POPULATION: 1767- 529; 1775- 540; 1790- 530; 1820- 477; 1860- 850; 1880- 1006; 1900- 924; 1930- 848; 1960- 1419; 1990- 3473.

HISTORIC LANDMARKS AND EVENTS:

First Christian Church, built 1835, Bear Hill Road.
1755, first Baptist Church in New Hampshire organized.
Hayford's Carriage Factory produced thousands of carriages between 1870 and 1900.

PROMINENT CITIZENS:

Edmund Peaslee, author of medical books, professor at Darmouth College from 1841-1871.
Elijah R. Currier, member of New Hampshire Executive Council (1843-1845).

NORTH HAMPTON

DATE OF FIRST SETTLEMENT: 1639
INCORPORATED: November 26, 1742

SOURCE OF TOWN NAME: Northern section of Hampton before incorporation.

POPULATION: 1767- 583; 1775- 652; 1790- 657; 1820- 764; 1860- 771; 1880- 774; 1900- 812; 1930- 695; 1960- 1910; 1990-3637.

HISTORIC LANDMARKS AND EVENTS:

Centennial Hall, built 1876, as a primary and grammar school, Post Road.
Congregational Church, built 1838, Post Road, bell built by Paul Revere and Sons.
Breakfast Hill, so named because native Americans and their captives were surprised by local militia while eating breakfast on the morning of June 26, 1696.
Milestone post on Post Road, erected 1774, Portsmouth 10 miles, Newburyport 12 miles.

PROMINENT CITIZENS:

Henry Dearborn (1751-1829) American Revolution general, U.S. Secretary of War under Jefferson (1801-1809).

NORTHWOOD

DATE OF FIRST SETTLEMENT: 1763
INCORPORATED: February 6, 1773

SOURCE OF TOWN NAME: Unknown.

POPULATION: 1767- N/A; 1775- 313; 1790- 744; 1820- 1260; 1860- 1502; 1880- 1345; 1900- 1304; 1930- 872; 1960- 1034; 1990- 3124.

HISTORIC LANDMARKS AND EVENTS:

Congregational Church, built 1840, Route 4.
Coe-Brown Academy, founded 1867, Route 4.
Marquis de Lafayette stopped at Northwood on June 23, 1825 while on a tour of the U.S.
President James Monroe visited in 1817.

PROMINENT CITIZENS:

William Burleigh (1785-1827), member of Congress from Maine (1823-1827).
Ella F. Knowles assistant attorney general of Montana.

NOTTINGHAM

DATE OF FIRST SETTLEMENT: Approximately 1720
INCORPORATED: May 10, 1722

SOURCE OF TOWN NAME: In honor of Daniel Finch, Second Earl of Nottingham.

POPULATION: 1767- 708; 1775- 994; 1790- 1068; 1820- 1126; 1860- 1297; 1880- 1095; 1900- 638; 1930- 451; 1960- 623; 1990- 2939.

HISTORIC LANDMARKS AND EVENTS:

Nottingham Square, site of training ground for militia during American Revolution.
Pawtuckaway State Park, Mountain Road, with erratic boulders and cemetery on trail to mountain summit.

PROMINENT CITIZENS:

Joseph Cilley (1735-1790) major in American Revolution.
Jonathan Cilley (1802-1838) member of Congress from Maine (1837-1838) killed in last legal duel in U.S. history.

PLAISTOW

DATE OF FIRST SETTLEMENT: Unknown
INCORPORATED: February 28,1749

SOURCE OF TOWN NAME: From plaistowe, meaning an "open space or greenwood".

POPULATION: 1767- 576; 1775- 575; 1790- 521; 1820- 492; 1860- 861; 1880- 1002; 1900- 1027; 1930- 1366; 1960- 2915; 1990- 7316.

HISTORIC LANDMARKS AND EVENTS:

Pollard Park, Main Street with town common, bandstand, and town hall built in 1895.
President George Washington passed through Plaistow in 1789.
Site of large brickmaking industry in the mid-19th century.

PROMINENT CITIZENS:

Asa Eaton, founder of first Sunday School in Boston, Massachusetts.
Nathaniel H. Clark, member of New Hampshire state senate (1885-1886), member of New Hampshire Executive Council (1887-1889).

PORTSMOUTH

DATE OF FIRST SETTLEMENT: 1623
INCORPORATED: May 28, 1653, incorporated as a city in 1849.

SOURCE OF TOWN NAME: In honor of Portsmouth, England.

POPULATION: 1767- 4466; 1775- 4590; 1790- 4720; 1820- 7327; 1860- 9335; 1880- 9690; 1900- 10637; 1930- 14495; 1960- 26900; 1990- 25925.

HISTORIC LANDMARKS AND EVENTS:

Richard Jackson House, built 1664, Northwest Street, oldest house in New Hampshire.
Wentworth-Coolidge House, Little Harbor Road, built 1650, 1700, 1750, home of Royal Governor Benning Wentworth, last colonial governor of New Hampshire.
1777, American flag raised on Ranger, first ship to fly American flag.
1905, Japanese-Russian peace treaty was signed at Portsmouth.

PROMINENT CITIZENS:

William Whipple (1730-1785) signer of Declaration of Independence.
Levi Woodbury, (1789-1851) Secretary of the Navy & Treasury under Jackson and Van Buren, governor and United States senator, member of the U.S. Supreme Court.

RAYMOND

DATE OF FIRST SETTLEMENT: Approximately 1725
INCORPORATED: May 6, 1764

SOURCE OF TOWN NAME: Unknown.

POPULATION: 1767- 455; 1775- 683; 1790- 727; 1820- 961; 1860- 1269; 1880- 1053; 1900- 1100; 1930- 1165; 1960- 1867; 1990- 8713.

HISTORIC LANDMARKS AND EVENTS:

Benjamin Bean Tavern, built about 1750, Old Fremont Road.
Boston and Maine Railroad Station, Fremont Road, built about 1893.

PROMINENT CITIZENS:

William B Green (1844-1879) wrote extensive letters detailing his Civil War experiences. It is considered one of the finest existing collections of Civil War letters.
John Dudley (1725-1805) New Hampshire Superior Court Judge, prominent Revolutionary War political leader.
Carlton Fisk, all star baseball catcher for Boston Red Sox and Chicago White Sox.

RYE

DATE OF FIRST SETTLEMENT: 1623
INCORPORATED: April 30, 1726

SOURCE OF TOWN NAME: Rye, England.

POPULATION: 1767- 1020; 1775- 870; 1790- 958; 1820- 1193; 1860- 1326; 1880- 1111; 1900- 1142; 1930- 1081; 1960- 3244; 1990- 4612.

HISTORIC LANDMARKS AND EVENTS:

Odiorne Point State Park, site of first settlement in New Hampshire, 1623.
Drowned forest off Jenness Beach on Atlantic coast. Last exposed in 1889 and 1958.
Isles of Shoals, nine miles of the New Hampshire coast, formerly the town of Gosport.
1814, Battle of Rye Harbor, only naval battle on New Hampshire coast during War of 1812.
First transatlantic cable laid from Rye in 1874.

PROMINENT CITIZENS:

John W. Parsons, member of state senate (1826-1829).
Robert E. Whalen, member of New Hampshire Executive Council (1973-1975).

SALEM

DATE OF FIRST SETTLEMENT: Approximately 1725
INCORPORATED: May 11, 1750

SOURCE OF TOWN NAME: In honor of Salem, Massachusetts.

POPULATION: 1767- 847; 1775- 1084; 1790- 1218; 1820- 1311; 1860- 1670; 1880- 1809; 1900- 2041; 1930- 2751; 1960- 9210; 1990- 25746.

HISTORIC LANDMARKS AND EVENTS:

Meeting House, now Town Hall, built in 1756.
America's Stonehenge, Mystery Hill, Haverhill Road, pre-historic rock formations.
Canobie Lake Park, popular amusement park.

PROMINENT CITIZENS:

Silas Benton (1768-1822) member of Congress (1803-1807).
Vesta M. Roy, acting governor of New Hampshire from December 1982 to January 1983. Only woman to serve as governor.
John Sununu, governor (1983-1988), chief of staff to President George Bush.

SANDOWN

DATE OF FIRST SETTLEMENT: 1736
INCORPORATED: April 6, 1756

SOURCE OF TOWN NAME: Sandown, Isle of Wright, England.

POPULATION: 1767- 509; 1775- 635; 1790- 561; 1820- 527; 1860- 553; 1880- 500; 1900- 400; 1930- 229; 1960- 366; 1990- 4060.

HISTORIC LANDMARKS AND EVENTS:

Meeting House, built 1773-1774, Fremont Road.
Railroad Depot, built 1873, now containing a railroad museum, Fremont Road.
Family legend says David Clark of Sandown crossed the Delaware with George Washington, 1776.

PROMINENT CITIZENS:

Stark Fellows (1840-1864) Led first parade of black troops to parade down Pennsylvania Avenue in Washington D.C. before President Lincoln.
Jethro Sanborn, wealthy ships' captain who donated large amount of gold for blankets and shoes of soldiers at Valley Forge, 1777-1778.

SEABROOK

DATE OF FIRST SETTLEMENT: 1638
INCORPORATED: June 3, 1768

SOURCE OF TOWN NAME: From Seabrook river which flows into the Atlantic.

POPULATION: 1767- N/A; 1775- 607; 1790- 715; 1820- 885; 1860- 1549; 1880- 1745; 1900- 1497; 1930- 1666; 1960- 2209; 1990- 6503.

HISTORIC LANDMARKS AND EVENTS:

Dearborn Academy, built 1853-1854, Route 1.
Old South Meeting House, built 1764, Route 1.
1683, Gove's Rebellion begins with Edward Gove leading men to Hampton to overthrow the provincial government of New Hampshire. The rebellion was unsuccessful.
Large settlement of Quakers during the late 1700s and 1800s.

PROMINENT CITIZENS:

Meshech Weare (1713-1786) president (governor) of New Hampshire (1776-1785).
Edward Gove, leader of failed 1683 rebellion. Gove died in 1691 having been imprisoned in the Tower of London from 1683-1686.

SOUTH HAMPTON

DATE OF FIRST SETTLEMENT: Prior to 1729
INCORPORATED: May 25, 1742

SOURCE OF TOWN NAME: It was a border community on the southern boundary of Hampton, though never a part of Hampton.

POPULATION: 1767- 491; 1775- 498; 1790- 448; 1820- 416; 1860- 549; 1880- 383; 1900- 297; 1930- 261; 1960- 443; 1990- 740.

HISTORIC LANDMARKS AND EVENTS:

Town Hall, Route 107A, built in 1832 as a Universalist Church.
Baptist Church, built in 1833, Jewell Street.
1768, Ruth Blay, a town schoolteacher was hanged for murder of her newborn child. She was later determined to be innocent.
1856-1901, territory of Delaware, disputed and unclaimed land between New Hampshire and Massachusetts.
As a result of its position on the New Hampshire, Massachusetts boundary, South Hampton had the largest number of religious denominations of any community in New Hampshire.

PROMINENT CITIZENS:

Phillips White (1729-1811) member of Continental Congress (1782-1783), Speaker of the New Hampshire House of Representatives (1776-1782), (1786-1787).
William Graves, secretary of state, Michigan.

STRATHAM

DATE OF FIRST SETTLEMENT: 1659
INCORPORATED: March 14, 1716

SOURCE OF TOWN NAME: In honor of Streatham, England.

POPULATION: 1767- 916; 1775- 1137; 1790- 882; 1820- 892; 1860- 859; 1880- 720; 1900- 718; 1930- 552; 1960- 1033; 1990- 4955.

HISTORIC LANDMARKS AND EVENTS:

Congregational Community Church, built 1837, Emery's Lane.
July 4, 1860, Robert Todd Lincoln, son of President Lincoln, read the Declaration of Independence to a

crowd at Stratham Hill Park.
November 1789, President George Washington stopped briefly at Paine Wingate's house in Stratham while on a tour of New England.

PROMINENT CITIZENS:

Paine Wingate (1739-1838) member of Continental Congress (1787-1788), U. S. Senator (1789-1793).
Josiah Bartlett, Jr. (1788-1853), member of Congress (1811-1813).

WINDHAM

DATE OF FIRST SETTLEMENT: 1720
INCORPORATED: February 12, 1742

SOURCE OF TOWN NAME: In honor of Sir Charles Wyndham of England.

POPULATION: 1767- 402; 1775- 529; 1790- 663; 1820- 889; 1860- 846; 1880- 695; 1900- 641; 1930- 538; 1960- 1317; 1990- 9000.

HISTORIC LANDMARKS AND EVENTS:

Presbyterian Church, built 1834, Church Street.
Searle's Castle, built between 1907 and 1915, impressive English Tudor style manor buildings, Route 111A.
1825, Marquis de Lafayette passed through Windham.

PROMINENT CITIZENS:

Samuel Dinsmoor (1766-1835) governor of New Hampshire (1831-1834).
Robert Dinsmoor, noted poet.

Acknowledgements

This book contains the largest collection of photographic views of Rockingham County ever assembled. Many of the photographs have never been published and some are extremely rare. The background information on each community is up to date with special emphasis on the people, places, and events that give each community its own unique character. The information has been meticulously researched for accuracy. Dates have been provided when known.

An historical research project of this nature is never the effort of a single person. It requires the thoughtful and willing cooperation of many knowledgeable individuals. All those who have generously contributed material for this book share a common devotion to researching, assembling, and preserving history. In doing so, they educate all those interested in learning more about the diverse and colorful heritage of their communities. For this, we should all be grateful for their perseverance and hard work.

I would especially like to acknowledge and thank the following individuals and organizations for their unselfish assistance: Ruth R. Albert, Kingston; Una Collins, Atkinson; Paul Hughes, Jr., Greenland; Nancy Merrill, Exeter; Barbara Myers, Newington; Donald Sanborn, Epping; Duane Schaffer, Epping; Eric Small, Seabrook; Joanne Wasson, Deerfield; Dennis Waters, Exeter; Atkinson Historical Society; Exeter Historical Society; Fremont Historical Society; Newington Historical Society.